Here's what folks are saying about Cowboys, Gambler's & Hustlers...

Cowboy Wolford is one of the all-time characters I've ever met. He and I have been friends for thirty-five years, and he was a good friend of my father Benny in the old days when the World Series of Poker was just starting and the big gambling action was Downtown Las Vegas. He was quite a cowboy in his rodeo days and is still a top poker player. This book is more than just a biography of his life, it is a memorial to the players who rescued poker from smoky backrooms and brought it to the heights of public popularity that it enjoys today.

—Jack Binion
Horseshoe Casino
Tunica, Mississippi

Cowboy and I had just come off a loss in a big poker game and decided to stop for a hamburger at a roadside joint on our way back to Dallas and figure out how we could parlay our last fifty bucks into a win. We shouldn't have wasted our time—Wolford tipped off every cent of it to the waitress! He didn't exactly have a "super system" for money management. This is just one of Cowboy's true stories about the old days when a lot of us were fading the white line from town to town playing poker. I've been friends with him for years and I've probably heard Cowboy tell this tale a hundred times. Every time I hear it, I could get mad all over again—if I wasn't laughing so hard. I think you'll laugh, too, and get some insights into how far poker has come in the last few decades.

—Doyle "Texas Dolly" Brunson
World Poker Champion
Author of *Super/System* & *Super/System 2*

He's quite a player, Cowboy is, and he's probably the best gambling story teller in the world. I saw him put the biggest bluff in World Series of Poker history on one of the best poker players in the world and get away with it. But then, what else would you expect from an old-time cowboy gambler who used to shoot dice on bales of hay in the barns behind the rodeo.

—*Bobby Baldwin*
CEO, Mirage Resorts
World Poker Champion

Only a cowboy, gambler and hustler could have lived through the situations that Byron Wolford got himself into and out of. I was rodeoing at about the same time that he was winning all those calf roping titles and I can tell you that he's the real thing—and funny as all get out. Get this book and if you don't enjoy it, there's something wrong with you.

—*Montie Montana Jr.,*
Buffalo Bill's Wild West

All the big names in poker played at Cowboy's joint in Dallas in the old days because that's where the best games were. If you want an inside look at how things were back then—when there were no center dealers, when you had no protection against hijackers and card sharps except your own wits, and when you might get hauled off to jail for playing poker—read this book. It's the fastest-paced and most colorful "history course" you'll ever take.

—*Pat Callihan*
Las Vegas Poker Host

Being an ole cowboy and a poker player too, I couldn't put Cowboy Wolford's book down until I had read it all. It is very entertaining and brought back a lot of good memories.

—*Tex Morgan*
Father of "Tex's TEARS"

COWBOYS, GAMBLERS AND HUSTLERS

COWBOYS, GAMBLERS AND HUSTLERS

The True Adventures of a Poker Legend and Rodeo Champion

Cardoza Publishing

BYRON "COWBOY" WOLFORD
with Dana Smith

Cardoza Publishing is the foremost gaming publisher in the world, with a library of over 175 up-to-date and easy-to-read books and strategies. These authoritative works are written by the top experts in their fields and with more than 8,500,000 books in print, represent the best-selling and most popular gaming books anywhere.

FIRST CARDOZA EDITION

Copyright © 2002, 2005 by Byron Wolford and Dana Smith
- All Rights Reserved -

Library of Congress Catalog Card No: 2004101417
ISBN: 1-58042-083-4

Visit our web site—www.cardozapub.com—or write for a full list of books and computer strategies.

CARDOZA PUBLISHING
P.O. Box 1500, Cooper Station, New York, NY 10276
Phone (800) 577-WINS
email: cardozapub@aol.com
www.cardozapub.com

ACKNOWLEDGMENTS

I want to acknowledge some people who have been important to me in my life. My dad, Wiley Raymond Wolford, who threw me on the back of a Shetland pony when I was six years old, taught me how to be a gentleman and treat women with respect.

My granddaddy, Charlie Cannady, traveled all over the country with me rodeoing when I was young and taught me to always try to be a good person and take good care of my horse. He also tried to teach me how to take care of my money, but I never did learn that lesson very well. My father's daddy, Pappy Wolford, was a frontiersman and Texas Ranger who entertained me with his cowboy and Indian stories and left me with a lot of fond memories.

Family has always been important to me. I admire and respect my brother Ray, my brother Bernie, my sister Patsy Ruth, and my mother Betty Mae. My wife Evelyn, who sews all my clothes, has made life a whole lot easier for me and I thank her for that.

The fine folks who helped me with this book are my patient editor and co-writer Dana Smith; her husband Don Vines;

Montie Montana Jr., who proofread and helped promote the book to the cowboy crowd; and Tex Morgan, who gave me valuable suggestions on editing the rodeo chapters.

I am very grateful to my longtime friends Benny Binion, Jack Binion, Doyle Brunson, and Pat Callihan. And to Mike Pancer and Jim Shapiro. These men helped me when I needed it the most and never asked for anything in return.

I miss the great players that I started playing poker with fifty years ago—men that I sure wish were still around today— Robert A. Brooks, Ken Smith, Jack Straus, Sailor Roberts, Freddy Ferris, Johnny Moss, Mac McCorquodale, Blondie Forbes, Bill Boyd, George Barnes, and Harlan Dean. That was a tough crew to beat!

And I especially thank the good Lord for the guardian angel that He sent me to help see me through all the stuff in my life. I believe that everyone has a guardian angel, but I got lucky and was dealt a really good one.

TABLE OF CONTENTS

Prologue by Dana Smith

★ CHAPTER SIX ★
Cowboy Celebrities & Other Famous Folks

Willie 'n' the Boys
The Women in My Life
Hanging Up My Rope and Saddle

★ CHAPTER SEVEN ★
Road Gamblers

The Red Men's Club in Dallas
Fadin' the White Line
The Road Gamblers

★ PHOTOS ★

★ CHAPTER EIGHT ★
A Titanic Proposition

Titanic Bowls 'Em Over
Titanic's Poker Psychic
Titanic Plays a Satellite
Titanic Moves a Mountain

★ CHAPTER NINE ★
Texas Gamblers

Mr. Robert A. Brooks
Everett Goulsby
Bobby Chapman
Harlan Dean
Lawrence "Broomcorn" Herring
Hugh Briscoe and Some Others
Blondie Forbes
Bobby "The Owl" Baldwin
The Gamblers Named Smith

Byron Wolford and Good Eye in 1951 when the 21-year old cowboy and his all-time favorite horse won the roping title at the Houston Fat Stock Show and set the record at the rodeo in San Antonio. With Good Eye's talent and Byron's speed, they won $20,000 for the year, a good win in those days, especially on a horse that cost only $600.

PROLOGUE

by Dana Smith

Money was scarce as hens' teeth in the 1930s. Poor people who had chased the American dream only to find that it ended in a nightmare called the Great Depression were living in shanty towns called "Hoovervilles." In dusty East Texas, adventurous wildcatters and their families lived hand-to-mouth in "shotgun" houses and tents hastily erected in boomtowns like Kilgore and Longview while they tried in vain to coax liquid gold out of dry oil wells. That is, until seventy-year-old "Dad" Joiner struck it rich when he brought in the gusher on the Daisy Bradford farm that stimulated the East Texas oil boom.

Byron "Cowboy" Wolford was born in one of those boomtown tents about fifty miles from Houston in 1930. When Byron was two years old his father, a roughneck, was injured in the oil fields and bought a small farm near Tyler with the money that he received from an insurance settlement with the oil company. It took him only a few months to find a ray of sunshine at the end of the tunnel—he struck oil on the land that he had intended to farm. Oil was selling for a dollar a barrel with over a million barrels a day flowing from the East Texas oil fields—so much oil, in fact, that it glutted the market and eventually fell to fifteen cents a barrel.

While the young cowboy was enjoying a life of comparative ease in Tyler, a 40-year-old gambler named Titanic Thompson was plying his wizardry across Texas, laying suckers incredible odds on propositions that they couldn't refuse. "Between Tyler and the little towns of Longview, Gladewater and Kilgore, the derricks stretched across the open prairies as far as the eye could see," Jon Bradshaw wrote in Fast Company. "There was a lot of money—Texas money—and Tyler had attracted the usual assortment of prospectors, speculators, oilmen and gamblers. It was the kind of town that Titanic knew well and felt most at home in. Where there was oil there was loose money and loose money meant action." About the same time, a 30-something road gambler was crisscrossing the state in the hope of making a score at a strange new poker game called Texas hold'em. His name was Johnny Moss.

In later years the two legendary gamblers would sit across the same poker table with the then elementary-school student playing heads-up, no-limit poker for all the marbles. In fact Cowboy would become business partners with Titanic about thirty years later in Tyler and he would defeat Johnny in a heads-up duel for the deuce-to-seven championship at the $10,000 buy-in Super Bowl of Poker in Las Vegas. And Cowboy and Johnny would be playing cash games together in a little joint called the Horseshoe that was owned by Benny Binion, a former Texas bootlegger who was to become a lifelong friend of the cowboy from Tyler. But destiny had to wait until the cowboy retired from his first career as a calf roper on the professional rodeo circuit.

Byron "Cowboy" Wolford's story begins with a lifelong passion for the rodeo and the open road, living by the seat of his pants and loving it all the way from Texas to Canada to New York and Oregon. In 1947, he graduated from high school and traveled with his grandfather-chaperone and a buddy in a pickup truck with a horse trailer, camping by the side of the road, cooking sumptuous repasts of bacon and beans on a Coleman stove, dreaming of roping calves a tenth of a second faster than the best of the 200 other cowboys he would be competing against in the arena. During the 1950s when he started making real money at rodeoing—as much as $20,000 a year—Byron's concept of luxury became "slow room service and unpressed sheets" in the hundreds of $5-a-night hotel rooms he rented on his million-mile quest for silver belt buckles and bronze trophies.

During his fifteen years on the pro rodeo circuit, Cowboy roped calves alongside and became buddies with rodeo legends Dean Oliver, Casey Tibbs and Jim Shoulders. And he became a legend of sorts himself when he set the all-time record for roping a calf at the old Madison Square Garden, a feat that was never matched until the ancient Garden fell prey to the trend of tearing down those nostalgic relics of yesteryear and building modern, sterile, edifices on top of their skeletons, just as today's megacasinos in Las Vegas have risen like flocks of phoenix from the ashes of imploded history.

Things have changed since the teenaged cowboy from Tyler first hit the open road with his horse and dreams in tow—cowboys fly from rodeo to rodeo these days, and the stars at the top of the heap have corporate sponsors and television endorsements that augment their six-figure income. But the heart of the true cowboy never changes as Fred Schnell captured so well in Rodeo! The Suicide Circuit: "The hotly competitive rodeo cowboy is still as much a rugged, sometimes cussed, often brawling—above all, independent—gambler as were his range-riding ancestors."

Drawing a comparison between the three lives that Cowboy Wolford has lived—rodeo rider, road gambler, professional poker player—is easy. Read Schnell's 1971 description of a cowboy, substituting "gambler" for "cowboy," and you'll see what I mean: "The cowboy still sets his own schedule, pays his own fees and expenses, provides for his own future (if any), arranges his own travel, and competes with his own skills. He resists both conformity and manipulation with a fierce, if sometimes irresponsible, sense of independence and self-reliance." Titanic and Johnny and Amarillo Slim and Puggy and Cowboy—and Dean and Casey and Jim—would defend their right, indeed their good fortune, to lead their lives unfettered by the bonds of conventionality. And therein lies the essence of their mystique.

Cowboy's multifaceted life produced a bottomless reservoir of the damnedest stories you'll ever hear about cowboys, gamblers and hustlers. The old road gamblers are a dying breed, you see, and the world of poker and its players are becoming homogenized, milk-fed by corporate casino cardrooms that offer neither the flexibility nor the opportunities for exploitation that the vintage gamblers enjoyed fading the white line across endless dusty backroads to gamble in smoky backrooms. "Gamblin' for a livin' just ain't that excitin' no more," an old-timer told me, though I don't think today's new generation of young, moneyed, aggressive poker players would believe him.

They arrive in droves, all decked out in tattered jeans and rumpled tee shirts, to play in the Big One these days. Television, the Internet, and the satellite system have teamed up to swell the field at the World Series of Poker to numbers that even Benny Binion couldn't have dreamed. From one make-shift poker table set up in an alcove at the Horseshoe Club in 1970, the world's biggest poker extravaganza has mushroomed to a ten-acre convention hall at Harrah's Rio casino.

The explosion of international interest in poker has spawned overnight millionaires and super stars, who arrive at televised poker events in limousines with an entourage of paparazzi and fans. Yet I say thank the poker gods for leaving some living legends standing in the arena. Thank you for Doyle "Texas Dolly" Brunson, who won the championship in '76-'77 and took home his tenth WSOP bracelet almost thirty years later. And thanks for Chip Reese, Crandell Addington, Bobby Baldwin and T.J. Cloutier. I'd rather watch these dudes play poker any day for any stakes than most of the milktoast chip pushers you see at so many tournament final tables these days.

I wish the colorful cowboy were still standing among his peers, the pioneers of poker. Byron Wolford cashed in his chips in 2003. "Cowboy Wolford stood for a special generation of self-taught, street-smart players who lived an exciting, energetic life spanning many generations. He will be sorely missed," Howard Schwartz of the Gamblers Book Shop in Las Vegas commented in memorium. The hard-working cowboy played his last hand of poker back home in Dallas. Texas was where he belonged "I'll always be a cowboy at heart," he told me. And if I know Cowboy, he's looking to meet up with Glass Eye, his champion horse, for one more trip out of the chutes in that big rodeo in the sky. And maybe shoot some dice on the hay bales in the rodeo barns. And for sure, play some poker with his ol' buddies Benny Binion, Jack Straus, Bill Smith, Bob Brooks, Sailor Roberts and Titanic Thompson.

"I've lost one of my oldest and dearest friends," Doyle Brunson said of Cowboy Wolford. So has the world of poker—and so have I. And I miss him—Cowboy always brought a smile to my face with his inimitable country wit and was forever honorable in all our dealings. He worked hard to make his book a best-seller, seeing it as his legacy to his beloved wife Evelyn. I immensely enjoyed working with Cowboy on this biography of his life as a cowboy, road hustler and poker player. You might not find his grammar to be perfect, but you had to watch your step when he put in the perfect raise against you at the poker table, the exact amount that you were willing to call to find out whether he had the nuts. Chances are you found out the hard way.

Now tie your horse to the nearest hitching rail, saunter through the swinging doors, hang your hat on the carved oak halltree and grab a stool at the mahogany-paneled bar while you're waiting, and read a few of Cowboy's stories while you down a beer or two. Chances are you'll find some of the rip-roaringest tallest tales this side of Texas about how it was in the old days when cowboyin' and gamblin' were still wild and wooly.

GETTIN' STARTED
ON BIG INDIAN

"A rope was in my hand all the time.
At home, at school, everywhere. I roped anything
that moved—chickens, dogs, cats, and kids."
—Montie Montana, "Not Without My Horse"

I was born in a tent on the edge of the oil fields in a
boomtown called Barbers Hill, Texas about fifty miles south
of Houston. In the boomtowns they'd move those rigs in, drill
down just so deep, and there would come that oil shooting up
through the top of the rig. Overnight poor people became rich
and rich people got broke drilling other spots looking for more
oil.

It was 1930 during the Great Depression and my daddy
worked as a roughneck and a truck driver in the oil fields
around Barbers Hill, Goose Creek, Pelley, and Baytown
(today the whole area is called Baytown). Daddy's name was

Wiley Raymond Wolford and my mother's maiden name was Betty May Cannady. Mother was mighty proud that we had a wooden floor in our tent because having a wooden floor back in the boomtown days proved that you were doing pretty good.

One day Daddy's truck broke down out on one of the dirt roads that connected all the oil fields. He got out to find out what the trouble was and discovered that something was wrong with one of the tires, so he started taking it off the truck. Just before he got it off, the tire blew out and the rim shot up and hit him in the head. Might near knocked his eye out. Daddy had to have a silver plate put in his head, but at least he lived. I was just a baby when it happened—so was my mother, bless her heart.

Daddy got a little bit of insurance money out of the accident. Not a lot, about $1,700, but it seemed like a lot back then when he was making only three or four dollars a day. (It would be more like a million dollars now.) As soon as he got well, he and my mother got in the car, threw me in with them, and took a trip to Wright City in East Texas near Tyler. Momma's daddy, Papaw, lived nearby in Arp. "Instead of throwing all this money off," Daddy thought, "I'll buy me a little farm." Took the money and bought a forty-five-acre spread for about $800, went by to visit Papaw and then drove back to the oil patch in Barbers Hill where all the poor folks lived.

★ Big Indian Number One ★

What do you think happened next? The East Texas oil boom, one of the biggest oil booms in the history of the United States, hit about three months later! Almost overnight Daddy had forty oil wells on that little farm of his, every one of them a gusher. The first well they brought in on his land was called "Big Indian Number One." Suddenly he went from poor man to rich man and if anyone ever deserved it, he did. Not because he was my daddy, but because he was a kindhearted man. Never heard him say anything bad about anybody. He's the only man I've ever known who could honestly say, "If I've got an enemy in the world, I don't know who it is." Maybe he was too good, but what a sweet man he was.

Back then they'd just drill a well, move the rig over eighty feet and drill another one. They put forty oil wells on his forty-five acres that were producing two hundred thousand barrels a month. The oil company did the drilling, producing fifty thousand barrels a month, and Daddy got 25 percent of it. Today oil is roughly $25 a barrel, but in 1930 oil was selling for ten cents a barrel, which would hardly pay for the trucking to haul it to the refinery. Finally it went up to about $1 a barrel, and that was a lot of money back then.

So in 1936 when I was six years old, my daddy bought 155 acres at 1801 West Bow Street in Tyler, about a mile and a half from the courthouse and the town square. He gave $100 an acre for it and thought he was getting robbed. Built a beautiful two-story brick home with a sunken garden on the land, a great big barn and a roping arena. Fixed up a pasture and bought some horses. Daddy was from Oklahoma, always had been a cowboy at heart, and liked to rope calves. Now he could practice his cowboying without having to worry about being on the oil rig at six o'clock every morning.

When Mother and Daddy moved into the new house, Pappy Wolford, my daddy's daddy, moved in with them. He was eighty-six years old and still spry. Pappy wore a patch over his eye—a guy had shot it out on a riverboat in New Orleans and Pappy killed him in self-defense. He had been a Texas Ranger, a frontiersman, an Indian fighter, and knew Frank James personally. Led two covered wagon trains to California. Showed us where they had the last Indian fight in Wichita Falls, Texas and took us right to the spot beside a big hill. "When the Indians got closer to us," he said, "they tried to save their ammunition, started shooting them bows and arrows." The Texas Rangers museum in Waco honored Pappy Wolford for helping capture Geronimo. Pappy told us that Geronimo was as smart as a lobo wolf and as sly as any fox that ever lived. He knew Wild Bill Hickok and all the famous old West people that you read about. He was sort of a celebrity himself although he never got the publicity that the others got. Pappy Wolford was a quiet man.

My daddy joined the Elks Club in Tyler where all the oil men hung around. They had a few drinks together, discussed oil leases and deals, and played a helluva poker game. He enjoyed fellowship. Brady Gentry (he had been a congressman for eight years) and a lot of other important people lived in Tyler. Every year about a dozen of them went deer hunting together down in south Texas. They'd stay about ten days, hire a cook, set up tents, play poker, and kill some deer to bring home.

On this one particular hunting trip, nobody killed a deer the first day out. They all had those high-powered rifles with telescope sights. Pappy Wolford oiled up his old rifle, the one he'd had for forty or fifty years that only had one sight on it, and took it along with him. He was a sly frontiersman, knew what to do, where to sit, how the wind was blowing, and where they were running. Pappy killed two big bucks before noon and when he came dragging them in, they couldn't believe it —nobody else had even seen a deer! Some of those Elks Club guys would've killed fifteen deer if they could've just to say that they'd done it, but not Pappy Wolford. Two was enough for him; he didn't kill them for the sport, he killed them to eat like he'd been raised to do. Finally somebody else got a deer, so they strapped the deer on the fender of the car and hauled them back home, just showing off a little bit.

When he got home from that hunting trip, Pappy Wolford went over to visit Uncle Slats and Uncle Gene, who were still working in the oil fields in Barbers Hill and living in "shotgun" houses, shanties where you could open the front and back doors and shoot a shotgun straight through them. My uncles hadn't struck oil like my daddy did. One night Pappy was feeling pretty bad and went to bed early in the evening. Died in his sleep without a rumble. Maybe the good Lord had a new frontier in heaven and needed Pappy Wolford to help tame it as he had done in the old West.

★ Roxy 'n' Me in the Arena ★

Some of our friends in Tyler—Jeff and Glenn Bracken who were in the oil business, and Frank Kitchens who was the president of Citizens National Bank—got together and started roping calves as a hobby on the weekends in my daddy's arena. There were some little bitty rodeos near Tyler on the weekends in Lufkin and Jacksonville where they'd have jackpot roping. Everybody would put up a $10 or $15 entry fee just like you do in poker tournaments these days.

Daddy bought me a solid black Shetland pony named Roxy, a saddle, and a nice little bridle, and started teaching me how to rope. I started off by roping the little milk-pen calves that were still on the cows, the calves that you'd let in after you'd milked the cows so they could get the rest of the milk. They were smaller than the ones that Daddy and his friends roped. I started roping these little calves off of ole Roxy when I was six years old and the more I roped, the better I got at it. Had good coordination and boy, was I good at it!

The big guys roped the big calves off their big horses and I'd take ole Roxy and tie the little ones faster than they could tie the big ones. They got to be a little bit jealous, I think, but they still loved me and pulled for me. Daddy started making it to the rodeos around East Texas and sometimes as far away as Oklahoma and I'd go with him. We had a '41 Ford coupe and on the way home from the rodeos, I'd lay down in the front seat and rest my head on my daddy's lap. The next morning I'd get up real early and go to school.

Sometimes I would put on what you might call a roping exhibition at the rodeos. After all the rodeo events with the men roping and bulldogging, I'd ride out on Roxy and they'd let loose a little milk-pen calf and I'd rope it in front of the crowd. I usually tied the calf a lot faster than the big guys did, and people really liked seeing me do that. Sometimes they'd give me $20 to put on this calf-roping exhibition, a lot of money back then. By the time I was about nine years old, I was entering the wild cow milking event. A cowboy would rope a cow, usually an older cow, and then a guy called a mugger would grab a hold of it. Then I'd run in and get some milk from the cow in a Coke bottle and run back across the line with it.

One time when I was about eleven Daddy took me to a jackpot roping and I won $18, so one day I asked him if I could quit school. "You know, Daddy, if I can make $18 or $20 a week, I don't need to go to no school," I explained to him. I thought I was smarter than anybody, what the hell could I learn there? "No, I want you to finish school, son," he said. (I sometimes tell my friends that my teacher threw me out of third grade because I wouldn't shave every day.)

I got to be pretty good at roping, roped every day when I got home from school, twenty or thirty calves a day, and turned professional when I was fifteen years old. Back then you legged the calves, you didn't flank them (flanking is two seconds the best of it). When you leg a calf, you have to step over him and string and tie him. I'd tie them till my hands got bloody and I'd have to wrap them with tape. I could tie a calf faster than anybody—in fact, I became the fastest man in the world.

The reason that I was so good at tying a calf was this: I had read in the newspaper that when soldiers were on the battleground and their machines guns jammed up, they could fix their guns even when they had powder in their eyes and couldn't see them, just like they'd been blindfolded. So I started blindfolding myself, taking a calf by its leg, stepping over him, putting a piggin' string on him and tying him blind. Probably roped a hundred or more calves a week. I practiced it so many times that my hands got blisters but I kept on tying blindfolded until I could do it naturally. And that's why I became the fastest man at tying a calf that ever lived—not bragging, you can ask any of the old-time cowboys about it.

★ My First Big Rodeo at Age Fifteen ★

The first big rodeo and calf roping I entered was at Shreveport, Louisiana in 1945 where they had a big rodeo by the standards of those days. There must've been about fifty of the top ropers in the country there, along with Don McLaughlin, five-time world champion trick and calf roper. You could win the day money for the best time of anybody who roped that day and then there was the day money for the next day that you roped. To cap it off, there was the best time overall on the average for two calves—you'd be the champion calf roper if you won that one. And I won it. Got paid $600, quite a bit of money back then.

When I went up to get my money from the rodeo secretary, she asked, "What's your name, son?"

"Byron Wolford." I was feeling mighty proud.

"Well, your daddy'll have to come get his money," she said, "I can't give it to *you*."

"But my daddy didn't win it—I won it," I explained.

She was real surprised that some little ole fifteen-year-old boy had beat all those top calf ropers. That's when I turned professional. From then on when I roped, I roped with the big guys, didn't make no difference to me. What I call the big guys were all the top ropers, but to me they didn't look no bigger than anybody else.

On the way back from Shreveport to Tyler we stopped at a little cafe in Longview for dinner. My dad, the Brackens, Papaw and I were all traveling together and since I'd just won so much money in the roping, I picked up the check. For five of us eating all that we wanted, the bill was about $11. "I'll just big-dog 'em a little bit," I thought, so when I went to the cashier to pay the check I gave her one of the $100 bills that I'd won at the rodeo figuring she wouldn't have change for it. She looked at me funny, whipped open the cash register, and bam! Gave me the change in two seconds flat. That's the last time I ever tried to big-dog it with a $100 bill.

Papaw was our nickname for my mother's daddy, Charley Cannady, who had a sixty-five acre farm near Tyler in Arp. He'd been a sand-land farmer all his life, getting his water out of the well, barely scratching out a living, bless his heart. Didn't know nothing else. Oil had gotten to be a dollar a barrel—can you believe that?! Hell, Daddy couldn't spend it all, so he asked Papaw to lock up the old farm and come live with us.

★ Turning Pro on the Rodeo Circuit ★

After I won all that money in Shreveport, I joined the Turtles Association and turned professional. Today it's called the PRCA, the Professional Rodeo Cowboys Association. Approximately twelve hundred cowboys in the world belong to it and I've got my gold card. When you reach the age of fifty, you get a gold card if you've been a professional cowboy for twenty-five years. Some special privileges go along with it, one being that you get free admittance to all PRCA rodeos.

I started out making rodeos that were within one hundred miles of Tyler—Fort Worth, Mount Pleasant, Lufkin, and Gladewater, Texas. All the top hands turned out for the big rodeo every June in Gladewater. When I was seventeen years old, I entered it roping off my daddy's horse, Dunny. Boy, what a horse! Daddy bought him off some guy riding down the highway on him, gave $125 for him. When Dunny died, Daddy would rather for it to have been him. He loved that horse and everybody loved him. Dunny ran the place. I tied my last calf in Gladewater in 10.04 seconds, the all-time record there. Won the roping by more than four seconds against every top hand in the country.

I decided to make the rodeos up in Nebraska and Kansas that summer and asked two of my buddies to go with me. One of them was a boy who lived right near me in Kilgore, Texas named Johnny Handy, a roper like me, and the other one was Neal Eddie Woods who lived about sixty miles out of Tyler in Carthage. Neal Eddie was a bareback rider, weighed about 155 pounds, and the wildest sonnabitch I've ever known, but he was a good guy, giggled and laughed all the time. And he was the best street fighter I've ever seen. It didn't make any difference if a guy weighed two hundred pounds, you could bet what you had that Neal Eddie would beat him. Johnny had a '36 International panel truck and we got us a two-horse trailer and got ready to take off for Kansas, Nebraska, Illinois, and Soldiers Field in Chicago where they play football today.

Momma and Daddy decided that the only way that we could go was to take Papaw along with us. Hell, Papaw was ready to go, hadn't had a wife in years, always wore overalls, and knew how to take care of stock and his money too. So we got everything together, loaded up the horses, kissed all the folks good-bye, and pulled out of 1801 West Bow Street.

Papaw, Neal Eddie, Johnny, and I packed a Coleman stove, our bedrolls, and a big grocery box that looked like a chuckwagon box in the back of the truck. The horse trailer had a side compartment near the front of it where we stored the horse feed, water buckets, grooming brushes, roping saddle, and roping can. Camping out, cooking breakfast and dinner, and telling Wild West stories by the campfire was fun.

Of course, I usually was shuffling cards and thinking of ways that I could make some money at poker. In fact, I've been to many a rodeo, found a good poker game, and stayed there a week or two after the rodeo if I was winning pretty good. If you could make $500 or $600 at a rodeo, that was good (of course, you might have had to drive a thousand miles to win it). But if you won that much in a poker pot, it sort of spoiled you, you know what I'm saying? In fact, I always carried two sets of clothes along with me—Levi's, tennis shoes, and a cowboy hat to rope in, plus slacks, silk shirts, a sport coat, and alligator boots to play poker in.

The first few years that I rodeoed, we camped out during our road trips to save money, but when I got to be a little older and was winning pretty good at the rodeos and at poker, I didn't like to camp out anymore. It was hard to start a poker game out in the middle of nowhere, you know. So I began checking into hotels or motels where there was a little action around and you'd be surprised how many poker games I got into that way. My idea of roughing it became slow room service and unpressed sheets.

The first rodeo that we hit was Strong City, Kansas where Ken Roberts was putting on the rodeo. He had been a world champion cowboy but had retired from cowboying and was raising stock and managing rodeos. It was really something when we got there—we were far away from Tyler, on our own, and the world was our oyster.

That was the first time that I ever saw Casey Tibbs from Fort Pierre, South Dakota—the best saddle bronc rider who ever lived, a living legend. (A big statue of him riding a bronc is at the Cowboy Hall of Fame in Colorado Springs and he was the only cowboy ever to be featured on the cover of Life magazine.) Ole Casey was standing right there in front of us, wearing a neckerchief with his shirt open, slender and kinda pale looking, about eighteen years old.

"I wonder who that sissy lookin' sonnagun is?" I asked the boys standing around me.

"That's Casey Tibbs."

"So what?"

"He's a helluva bronc rider," they said.

The first time I saw him ride a bronc, I had to admit that they were right—he was the best saddle bronc rider in the world. Casey and I later became good friends. He used to go home with me after the rodeos in Madison Square Garden and Boston Garden and stay during the wintertime. I'd practice roping and he'd try to rope, but he wasn't really good at it. Always drove a Cadillac convertible, liked to party, liked the girls, liked to high-roll, and dressed like a movie star.

Johnny, Neal Eddie, Papaw, and I arrived in Strong City about three days before the rodeo began and slept in the panel truck. Papaw laid out his bedroll and set himself up a nice place in the ticket office; he was always neat in his habits. We had heard that there was a dance downtown that night, so Johnny and Neal Eddie and I wanted to get on down there, drink some beer and chase the girls. We started dancing around with those country Kansas gals and after the dance was over, we bought a case of beer and invited them to go out to the rodeo grounds with us. The stars were out, the sky was clear, and they were drinking and giggling, saying, "We're sure glad you Texas boys are here." The girls were ready.

So we all went to the grounds together, drank some more beer, and made some love. The cake was all dough—and it was downhill and shady.

"You know," I said to the girls, "I sure feel sorry for Papaw."

"Who's Papaw?"

"He's my granddaddy, he's asleep over there in the ticket office. His wife died years ago, bless his heart, makes a lot of money, but he ain't had no lovin' in right near twenty years. He's kinda timid, you know, so I was just wonderin' if one of you girls would give him some lovin'."

"Well hell, if he's that kind of a guy, I will," one of them piped up. They'd had a good time, you know, and we'd made some good love to them.

"Okay then, just go over to the ticket office and knock on the door, tell him you've come to visit with him."

The next day Papaw was the happiest old man I've ever seen in my life. You'd think that he had hit the lottery. He was tickled pink, probably thinking about what a wonderful time he'd had. We had him right where we wanted him.

★ Papaw Loses His Teeth ★

We didn't make any money at Strong City so we took off for a little four-day rodeo over the Fourth of July in Pecatonica, Illinois on our way to Chicago. Along the way we pulled off by a creek to make camp, exercised the horses, fed and brushed them, and set up a Coleman stove and the groceries, beer, and ice we'd bought at the store—it was the life. Every day was a holiday; every meal was a banquet.

We cooked up some chicken-fried steak and pinto beans, sliced some onions and cucumber, and drank some cold beer— a real feast. The next morning we were planning to pull out and drive another couple of hundred miles on our way to Pecatonica. Along about six o'clock in the evening, the horses started nickering, patting their feet and looking around.

"What the hell's wrong with them horses?" I asked my granddaddy.

"It must be gonna come a rainstorm," Papaw answered. "You know, animals can tell about them things." In that part of the country it was likely that a blowhard could come at any time and then be over within an hour's time.

Papaw went on to bed down by the creek where he had laid out his bedroll under a tree and Johnny, Neal Eddie, and I went to sleep all scooched up on the mattress that we had set up in the panel truck. Wasn't long before the wind came up and the rain came down, started blowing and raining so hard that I guarantee you couldn't see fifty feet in front of you.

And here came Papaw running barefoot in his long nightgown (slept in one every night, bless his heart). Started banging on the side of the panel truck in the dark with the wind blowing and the rain pouring down.

"Get outta there and help me!" he yelled. "It's comin' a flood!"

"What you want us to do for you?" we yelled back.

"I picked up my cot down there by the creek and my false teeth was under the pillow and they fell out. I'm afraid they're gonna wash away."

"Well hell, I'm afraid to go out there," Neal Eddie said.

"Why?" Papaw asked, shivering in the dark soaked to his bones.

"I'm afraid I'll step on them teeth and they'll bite my foot off!" he answered.

Man, did Papaw get mad over that! But we crawled on out there in the mud and found his teeth. Papaw got in the truck with us for the rest of the night, the storm got over in a couple of hours, and early the next morning we drove up to Pecatonica. We got there three or four days before the rodeo started, put up the horses in the barns, and waited. Papaw would earn a few dollars at the rodeos taking care of horses and stock, working the gates, saving his money, not spending any of it. But hell, with what little money we had we'd pay our entry fees, buy beer, chase the gals, whatever. And right then we didn't have any money at all.

Clyde Miller from Rich Hill, Missouri was the rodeo producer. The producer is the one who hauls the stock to the rodeo and charges the town so much for furnishing the stock to put in the rodeo. I didn't know him.

"Mr. Miller, my name's Byron Wolford," I told him. "My grandpa and a couple of friends are up here from Tyler, Texas fixin' to enter this rodeo." He didn't seem too impressed. "Johnny and Neal Eddie and me, we're kinda short on money."

"Well, I ain't got nothin' you can do to earn it," he said.

So I came up with a proposition for him. "I'll tell you what I'll do," I said. "I'll dress up like a girl, sit in the grandstand, and during the bull riding you can ask over the loudspeaker if there's any ladies out there who want to try to ride them bulls. Then I'll come down over the fence and get on one of the bulls. That'd be a thrill for the crowd."

"All right," he said, "how much you want for doing it?"

"Just what I need to pay my entry fee, $25." Of course you had to pay in advance, so Papaw had already put up my fee for me but I needed to pay him back.

"I'll give you the $25 if the crowd likes it and if they don't like it, I won't pay you nothin'."

The first night I won the $100 day money, so we were back in the chips but I still had made that deal to ride the bull. Theo McClaine, a roper and bulldogger, and his wife Pat had come in from Lufkin, Texas. I only weighed one hundred thirty pounds so Pat put one of her dresses on me, painted my face with lipstick and rouge, tied a bandana on my head, and made me up to look just like a girl. It was an amazing transformation.

I got up there in the grandstands and after they'd ridden a few bulls the announcer says, "Any of you ladies out there want to try this?" I stood up and hoisted an empty V.O. bottle over my head. "There's a lady who wants to try it!" he said. All the crowd was standing up looking at me as I crawled down from the stands and went through the side gate. Ole Clyde put a black bull in there that weighed about eighteen hundred pounds, a rank sonnagun, guess he wanted to get me killed.

The gate opened and that sonnabitch jumped out about eight feet high and turned back and then twisted the other way and threw me off. I must've flown about ten feet in the air and when I landed, that bull tried to hook me and sweep me along the ground. I crawled to a fence as fast as I could to get away from him. All this time the crowd was clapping and hollering for me. It was the best event in the whole show.

"Well, how'd you like *that*?" I asked Clyde.

"That was the greatest thing we've ever saw!" a couple of guys standing around answered. And you know what Miller said? "Hell, they didn't like it at all!" and he wouldn't pay me my money. Never did pay me.

I wound up winning the day money all four days and Johnny won a couple of seconds. But poor ole Neal Eddie broke his leg riding a bareback horse, had a cast put on it, and couldn't hardly get around on his crutches. Had to lay down in the back of the panel truck while we were getting ready to pull out for Soldiers Field.

★ A Sucker Loses His Money ★

Papaw and Johnny had everything loaded just waiting for me to get my horse out of the barn and load him into the trailer. I had about $270 on me that I'd won and boy, was I in the chips. Started down the aisle in the barn and noticed that they had a craps game going, shooting dice on a cot. I stopped for just a minute to watch.

The guy shooting the dice says, "Ten! $10 I make it." I knew the odds were 2 to 1 against so I said, "That's a bet!"

He made the ten. Then he says, "I'll bet $40 I can make it with two fives."

"Well hell, you've got me," and I called him. Danged if he didn't make it again! Come to find out later that he was picking up the dice acting like he was shaking them, but he was sliding them so that they never would turn over. He could make any number he wanted. In ten minutes, I got flat broke. Flat broke! How sick I was.

Somehow I ended up driving the truck with Papaw sitting next to me in the front seat and the two other boys in the back. I had to pull into a station down the road a piece to get some gasoline, twelve cents a gallon. While an ole boy was filling it up, I looked over at Papaw and said, "Granddaddy, I hate to tell you this but I got broke a while ago."

"What the hell you talking 'bout?!" he screamed. "You had might near $300."

"Well, I was going through the barn and they had a craps game and some sonnabitch was betting even money that he could make ten. Then he got to betting he could make it with two fives. He won every one of them bets and I got broke."

"You're the silliest bastard that I've ever saw," he said.

"Well, I can't help it. I guess they was doing something but

I thought that I really had the best of it and I know now that I didn't."

The ole boy filling the tank overheard all of this and tried to help me out by saying, "Oh hell, Pop, give him a break."

"Pop, my ass!" Papaw shot back. "He's kept me broke all summer." Boy, was he mad! We sat there arguing with me sweating it out wondering if Papaw was going to pay for the gas, but he finally did and we headed out for Chicago.

★ The Setup at Soldiers Field ★

Got to Soldiers Field a couple of days before the rodeo started, set up our own camp right there on the grounds. Listened over and over again to the most popular song on the radio back then, "Peg O' My Heart." Rained every day. And we didn't have a quarter to our name.

Somehow Johnny and I got into the roping events, but Neal Eddie couldn't do anything because he was still laid up with that broken leg. Of course when one of us made money, we all made money—that's the way it was back then. And Papaw was working the gates and taking care of a few horses, making some money.

All the top hands were there. I roped about five or six calves, tied them in seventeen or eighteen seconds, placed in two or three of the day moneys. Come the last day, I won the day money and took second place in the average. None of the big dogs knew who I was, weren't paying no attention to me, but they ended up thinking, "Well hell, this kid can really rope." I wound up winning $1,700, a big score in those days.

The rodeo didn't get good crowds at Soldiers Field that year because of the rain and the producers lost a lot of money on it. After it was over, all the cowboys were standing in line at the rodeo office waiting to get their money. Back then the producers didn't have to deposit the money in a bank before the rodeo started like they do nowadays.

"We can't pay you off," they told us, "because we didn't make no money and got broke." So there we are a long way from home in Chicago and they aren't gonna pay us off. I ain't got any money, Johnny ain't got no money, and all that Neal Eddie's got is a broken leg. It was pitiful.

There was an ole boy from Chicago there, a bulldogger who went to some rodeos during the summer. Always had plenty of money, drove a new car, had a good horse, and dressed well. His name was Speedy Dinsmore, a good guy. "What's the trouble?" he asked.

"They ain't gonna pay the rodeo off," I complained.

"You've gotta be kidding!" he said. "They owe me some money, too. Oh, they'll pay us off all right, just wait and see. We'll have our money in two hours."

Speedy got on the phone and in about an hour and a half, two guys showed up at the rodeo office dressed up real nice, black hair, looked like they'd just walked off the screen of a picture show. Within an hour the money arrived in paper sacks and they paid everybody. Come to find out that Speedy collected money for the mob, just rodeoed for a hobby.

So we drove back to East Texas. I finished high school, Johnny went back to roughnecking in the oil fields, and Neal Eddie went back to Carthage to try to heal up. Papaw stayed in Illinois through the winter to work in the stables for somebody he'd met at the rodeo. Came home around Christmas with his pockets full of money.

Johnny didn't ever rope with us again. He was working up high in an oil derrick, slipped and fell out of that sonnabitch, hit the floor on his head and was paralyzed for life. Wound up marrying the nurse who took care of him. That's the break he got in life—makes you feel lucky to be around.

Neal Eddie's leg healed up and he ended up working as a rodeo clown. We'd be at a rodeo up north somewhere sitting in a bar and he'd say to one of the locals, "You all sure are lucky up here."

"Why? Where you from?" one of the cowboys would ask.

"Texas," Neal Eddie would answer, "and we been taking care of you sonnabitches up here for years." Then some ole boy would jump up and they would go outside and fight, Neal Eddie would whip him, and then they'd come back in and Neal Eddie would pat him on the back and buy him a beer. Back then there wasn't any cheating, just a fist fight on the square and whoever won it, won it. The fighters might come back all beat up and bloody, but they'd wash up and then all drink a beer together. I never saw Neal Eddie lose a fight, didn't matter if it was with a wrestler or a football player or a Kansas farmer.

★ Lookin' for My Papaw ★

The next summer Papaw and I took off, just the two of us, heading up north for the rodeos. By then I was a real veteran, a professional cowboy, eighteen years old and in good shape. I'd already broken the record at Gladewater, Texas and had won calf ropings at Shreveport, Pecatonica, Soldiers Field, and a lot of smaller rodeos.

I had a station wagon with a mattress in the back of it, a one-horse trailer, and a good horse. About six o'clock one morning we were driving through Strong City, Kansas where the boys and I had set Papaw up with that country girl the summer before. He had been sleeping in the back of the car, woke up just as we got past town, grouchy like he always was every morning. As he was rubbing the sleep out of his eyes, I told him a little story.

"Papaw, I seen the damnedest thing I've ever seen in my life a while ago when we were driving through Strong City."

"What the hell did you see?" he grumbled.

"Well, when we came through Strong City there was this little ole biddy guy, I guess he was about a foot and a half high, had on overalls just like you and a dip of snuff. And he was carryin' a suitcase with a sign on it, 'Going to Texas Looking for my Papaw.'"

"Bose," he says, "you're the silliest man that I ever saw." He was so mad he wanted to strangle me.

"Yeah," I repeated, "had a sign saying 'Looking for my Papaw.' Wonder what that meant?"

We had some helluva times, me and my grandpa. We'd go to a rodeo, set up our own craps game, give the cowboys a $5 or $10 limit, and break them all. Then Papaw would loan some money back to all of them—$10 for $12 and pay it at the next rodeo. He was a smart operator, really loved rodeoing and taking care of everybody's stock. Papaw was as famous as the cowboys!

When he became aged, Papaw went to live in a rest home in Jefferson. My parents had sold their place in Tyler and moved to Jefferson with Papaw, where my dad took a job supervising some oil wells. Papaw and I had so many good times together; I really missed him when he died.

Although my father had become fairly wealthy in the East Texas oil boom, he eventually ran out of spare money because he had given so much of it away to kin folk and so on. Of course he had put some money into a savings account for security, but he took the job in Jefferson to meet daily living expenses. Daddy died in 1984 of emphysema. He was a good man and I loved him dearly.

My mother had a different type of personality from my dad, not nearly as outgoing, but she was good to people. She was only four feet ten inches tall, but she wouldn't give a bear the middle of the road. And she was a great cook; she could cook or can anything. Every now and then she'd have a few drinks and then she was a dandy. Mother died in 1998. She was a good woman but it was my daddy that I was the closest to. We were the best of friends, we rodeoed together and everything. When Daddy and Papaw passed on, I lost two of my best friends.

★ Raisin' Hell with Johnny, Ray, and Bernie ★

Johnny Wheeler and I lived right across the street from each other and began the first grade together. Johnny and I started gambling when we were six years old, playing tops and marbles and some poker. Another boy who lived near us was Robert Smith, who was a couple of years older than we were, tall, black-headed, and tougher than a boot. Robert liked banty roosters, had a few that he thought were the best fighters in the county. His favorite things in the world were hunting, fishing, and messing with those roosters.

When I was about twelve years old, I went into the rooster business myself but I left it in a hurry. Robert had this banty that was a good little fighter, so good that he thought nobody could beat it. I decided to find out just how good he was, so I went down to the poultry house in Tyler, bought a little black rooster for a quarter, and carried him over to Robert's house.

"I've got me a little rooster here and I wanna see if he can lick yours," I announced to Robert.

"He's got no chance to whup my rooster," he bragged.

"We'll see," and I threw my rooster in with his. They went at each other in a dead run, fighting and crowing and clawing. My rooster whupped Robert's rooster easy—and then Robert whupped me! And that's why I got out of the rooster fighting business.

When Johnny and I were about eighteen years old, he had a twenty-five-cent ante poker game with a $10 change-in in his garage. Back then there wasn't any such thing as limit poker so you could bet whatever you wanted to. One Saturday night we were playing and Robert decided to join us. Pretty soon he had lost his $10 buy-in. Never was much of a poker player. By eight o'clock in the morning the only players left in the game were me, Johnny, and Robert. Robert was $80 loser and he was in shock.

"Well, I guess we oughta quit, boys, we've been playing all night long," I suggested. Johnny agreed with me.

"If anybody quits this game, I'm gonna whup their ass right here and now, both of you," Robert warned. Johnny and I looked at each other. Neither one of us moved an inch.

"Go ahead and deal me in," I said.

"Me, too!" Johnny agreed. Robert won back $30, leaving him only $50 stuck. Seemed like a small price to pay for me and Johnny.

We had some great times together, the three of us. Johnny is gone now, but he always had something going later in life, a Vegas-style craps game or a blackjack game or whatever. He did very well before the riverboats opened up in Bossier City, just a hundred miles from Tyler. A lot of his regulars lived in Longview or Corpus and they'd only have to drive fifty miles to play. Johnny owned a big spread in Tyler and I always admired him because he took care of his family so that they didn't have to worry about anything, no difference how he was doing, and when he bought something he fixed it up perfect, no matter what it cost. I'm happy to say that he was inducted into the Seniors Poker Hall of Fame a few years ago.

Dick Melvin from Henderson, Texas, was another childhood friend. He's dead now, too, but he used to make a bunch of money at bookmaking and he played a lot of poker with us in Dallas. I miss Johnny and Robert and Dick and a lot of the other guys that I used to do things with. It seems like it was only yesterday that we were all together back in Tyler.

My two brothers, Ray and Bernie, and my sister Patsy and I had a good time growing up together and we're still the best of friends to this day. I'm the oldest by four years and my two brothers both were born on the same day, June 9, just two years apart. In our early years at home in Tyler when I was about fourteen years old and Ray was ten, he and I used to go squirrel hunting together. One time in July during the hottest part of summer, wearing shorts and no shirts, we walked about three miles to an area where there were a lot of squirrels. Between us we had one rifle, three shells, and fifty cents. Along the way we stopped at Nickels Grocery Store and each bought a Dr. Pepper and a candy bar.

When we got to the woods, we found a squirrel running up a tree. Ray shot at him and missed. That really pissed me off because we only had two shells left. Then we found another squirrel. "You can get this one," I assured Ray and gave him the rifle. He missed that one, too! Now I was really hot—we only had one shell left. The next squirrel we saw, I shot at and I got him.

Now we're leaving the woods, I'm carrying the gun and Ray's walking behind me carrying the squirrel in his back pocket to take the load off during our hike. But by the time we reached the highway, he had lost it. Boy was I mad! Here he had missed two squirrels and I'd finally got one and he'd lost it. We might near fought it out right there.

We were strung out on the highway three miles from home with Ray walking in front and me walking behind him, when an ole guy in a pickup stopped and asked me if I wanted a ride. "Yessir, I sure do," and got in the truck.

"What about that other boy?" he asked, pointing to Ray.

"No sir," I answered. "He lives right there on the side of the road." As we drove past Ray, I waved at him.

When I got home, I went down to the watermelon patch, got me a big ole melon, and sat under a big tree eating it. About an hour and a half later, here came Ray dragging himself home, madder than a wet hornet. I knew we were gonna have a fight, so I started running with Ray right behind me. Suddenly something hit me hard in the middle of my back. Ray had pulled up a buzzard weed with big clods of dirt on its roots and when it hit me, it felt like a bullet. "Oh my gosh, he had another shell and he's shot me!" I thought. We would've fought it out, but I was laughing so hard I couldn't fight. Ray and I fought each other every day until we were twenty-one years old but always ended up hugging each other afterward. Guess that's why I love him so much.

We had a great big barn on our place in Tyler and Daddy rented it out to a rose packer named W.W. Dice (Tyler is the rose capital of the world). About fifteen black guys worked for Dice and they knew that Ray and I fought all the time, so we devised a little scheme just for them. "Let's go down to the barn in front of all those guys sitting on those rows of benches packing them roses and pretend to get into a big argument," I told Ray. "Then you take out the gun and fire. I'll cup some ketchup in my palm and when you shoot me, I'll hit my forehead and it'll look like blood." We removed all the shots from the shells in our gun and I went on down to the barn around the rosebush packers. Pretty soon, here came Ray holding that two-foot long gun acting like he was looking for me

"There you are!" he yelled.

"What is it this time?" I asked disgustedly.

"I'm tired of messin' with you! I'm gonna shoot you!" he yelled. As he pulled the trigger, I hit my forehead with the ketchup. When the workers saw me fall over like I was dead, they dropped everything they were doing and ran like hell from the barn and didn't come back for the rest of the day. Our little shenanigan disrupted the entire packing process, shut everything down. Ray and I got a pretty good whipping from Daddy over that little caper.

I'll bet you've never heard of a "dumb bull." To make a dumb bull, you take a nail keg and get a piece of fresh cowhide. You knock one end out of the keg and stretch the cowhide over the other end and staple it. When the hide dries it gets hard as a rock. Then you punch a hole right in the middle of the cowhide, take a long string and put rosin on the string. Then you stick the string through the hole, putting a stick behind it so that it won't come loose.

There used to be a place about twenty miles from Tyler near a lake down in the bottoms named Big Eddie. Ray or Johnny and I would make a dumb bull and take it down there where people were camping out and fishing on the weekend. We'd get about a hundred yards from them in the woods, set up the dumb bull, and run our fingers up and down the rosin string making the damnedest sound you've ever heard—weird sounds like a lion roaring. It was pitch dark and the folks in the campground couldn't tell exactly where the sound was coming from or whether it was a dinosaur or a lion or what—but in just a little while, they all headed for home. We cleared out the whole place with our little prank and had lots of fun doing it.

Years later after he graduated from college, Ray lived in Lafayette, Louisiana, where he was in the oil well mud business during the boom and made a mint. He threw off more money than a lot of people will ever see. They had a poker game in Lafayette in the back of a bar and one day he called me, saying, "Man, we've got a poker game down here like you've never seen. All these oil guys are just giving their money away." So I hightailed it down there and met everybody, had a beer and some conversation, saw that they were playing poker real high, and told Ray, "I'll take 50 percent of your play and you take half of mine."

To make a long story short, I won $70,000 off the game in four days. Then I drove on home to Houston, where Ray had a second place that he stayed in when he wasn't doing business in Lafayette. We stopped at the country club and had a few drinks before I drove the rest of the way to my place. On my way home the police stopped me and hauled me off to jail. They thought that I was drunk, but I wasn't about to admit it—wouldn't take a breath test. When they checked me into the pokey, they took everything out of my pockets, including the money I had won in Lafayette.

"Where did you get all this money?" they asked.

"Well," I answered, "me and my brother are in the oil business and we're drilling some wells up in Kentucky. The only way they'll deal up there is in cash, you know." They went for my story and I was released the next morning.

Ray has always been a poker player and today he owns a Red Men's Club in Dallas. My baby sister, Patsy Ruth, who is eleven years younger than I am, used to be a building contractor in California and now she is a job estimator in Houston. Say that somebody has a $20 million budget to construct a building. Patsy estimates what the job will cost from the ground floor up, from its first nail to its finish, what it will cost to build it and put everything into it—that's how smart she is.

My brother Bernie owns Papaw's old farm today, bought it off Papaw years ago and built a beautiful townhouse on it, plus a big pond with catfish that weigh twenty pounds. We call it the Arp Arms. When Bernie graduated from Kilgore Junior College, Delta Drilling sent him to Libya in North Africa to solve a repair problem. He only weighed one hundred thirty pounds and when he got off the plane this guy looked at him and said, "There must be a shortage of men in the United States."

Bernie was a helluva diesel mechanic and engineer and later became one of the main men in Delta, the second biggest independent oil drilling company in the world back then. Sold his stock just before the oil business went down and went in with Dan Lester's drilling company in Jefferson, Texas, which they sold for $20 million when oil was selling for $50 a barrel. Before long the bottom fell out of the oil business and the new owners couldn't get ten cents on a dollar for it. Everything Bernie's done has turned to gold. He used to build oil field roads and take a piece of the well in exchange, and had a small interest in a hundred gas wells. There's $80,000 a month in the mailbox, but he still works every day like Jack Binion does, like he ain't got a quarter.

One time Delta sent Bernie to Salvador, Brazil for five years; his kids even learned to speak Portuguese. While he was there, I was rodeoing all over the country and playing poker wherever I could, hadn't even talked to him during all that time. Well, the word got around that Bernie had won $1 million playing poker in Salvador with all those rich oil people. Hell, I'd never seen him bet fifty cents on anything, he was one of the tightest guys I've ever seen, wouldn't gamble on nothing. And here they were saying that he had won $1 million. "If he's won $1 million, I'll go down there and in a couple of months I'll win $10 million," I thought. I didn't know exactly where he was in Salvador and ended up spending $100 trying to get him on the telephone. Finally I got a hold of him.

"How you doin', Bernie?" I started out slow and easy.

"Oh, fine, how's everything going with you, Bose?"

"Oh, everything's good, but let me ask you something. You all playin' any poker down there?"

"Yeah, we play about once a week."

"Well, what if I flew down there and played some poker with you all? You can have any part of my action you want."

"Oh hell, it wouldn't be worth your while."

"Whattaya mean? I heard you won a million dollars."

"No, Bose," he laughed again. "I won a million *lire*."

"A million lire? How much is that worth?"

"About $75," he says.

"Well hell, I've done spent more than that trying to get a hold of you!"

He cracked up. I'd blown my money on the telephone so I sure wasn't going to go to Brazil. To this day Bernie still laughs every time I tell that story. And he still never bets more than fifty cents.

RODEOIN' AND HUSTLIN' AT THE GARDEN

*"Rodeo is an athlete's crap game. A man pays his money
and takes his chances, knowing that there can
only be a few winners and a lot of losers."*
— *Fred Schnell, "Rodeo! The Suicide Circuit"*

I've been a gambler all my life—a cowboy, a gambler, and a road hustler—skills that came in mighty handy the first time I went to the big rodeo in Madison Square Garden in 1949 when I was nineteen years old. Don McLaughlin, five-time world champion calf roper before it was all over with, kinda liked me and knew that I was a good roper so he asked if I wanted to go to the Garden with him. He and his wife Jeannie and I drove up there in his station wagon hauling his horse Red, a great big ole horse that I planned to ride in the rodeo.

When we got to New York City we checked into the Belvedere Hotel, where a lot of the scenes from "The Maltese Falcon" starring Humphrey Bogart had been filmed and everybody made a big deal of that. The hotel was right across from Madison Square Garden. You stored your car and trailer in the hotel's basement and they never came out for the thirty days that you were in the rodeo. I'd never been to a town that big and it was all new to me.

You got about ten calves while you were there. They paid day money on each calf and paid average-money to whoever had the best time on all ten calves. You were allowed two loops to rope a calf and if you missed both of them, you were out of contention for the average. If you tied one and he got up before the time limit, you also were out of it and then you just had to do your best to try to win the day money.

I didn't win very much money at the rodeo, but I did get a hold of a little money at the Belvedere. The cowboys had a craps game down in the basement of the hotel just about every afternoon before the rodeo started, and Buddy Steele and I won a couple hundred dollars in the game. About 90 percent of all cowboys back then were natural-born gamblers, you know. In my day they all liked to play poker, shoot craps, drink whiskey and chase women. Rodeo was a pretty good life, a happy-go-lucky thing, and most of us were a little wild. We didn't bother nobody, though, mostly stayed to ourselves. We were a breed of our own. Rodeo is the only sport that I know of besides poker where you have to put up your own entry fees, you're not guaranteed a quarter, and if you don't win, you don't have any money in your jeans. (It's different now—the cowboys fly here, fly there, hardly speaking to each other. It's strictly a business deal.)

Buddy and I had always heard of broiled lobster. Down there in East Texas where I'm from and in Arkansas where Buddy was born, they never served lobster but we had heard that it was really good. So when Buddy and I got a hold of that $200 in the craps game, we put on white shirts and clean

Levi's and took off to find us some broiled lobster. Of course, we didn't want to get too far away from the Garden because if you went too deep into the city wearing a cowboy hat and boots, they thought you were crazy and were liable to jump on you. We came across a place on Broadway near the Belvedere named the Turf Bar with a sign over the door that read "Fresh Broiled Lobster," so we went in and sat down.

An old gentleman came over to wait on us and we ordered some beer. I was nineteen years old and Buddy was seventeen, but he never even questioned our age. Then we told him that we wanted the broiled lobster with all the trimmings, we'd always heard that it was something special. So he sat the napkins down, the forks, the knives, real careful like. A little while later he came back and sat two bowls down and some Saltine crackers. We figured he'd brought us some soup to eat while they were cooking the lobster so we both crumbled up our crackers and put them in our bowls. I tasted it and said to Buddy, "I'll bet the lobster ain't gonna be no good here. This is the weakest damned soup I've ever eaten. Tastes like lemon juice."

"Hell, I like it," he said and ate all the rest of mine. Then I called the old gentleman over.

"Sir," I asked him. "What kind of soup is this?"

"Oh, uh, sir," he fidgeted, "that's the finger bowl."

Hell, we didn't know what a finger bowl was, nobody used them where we were from. Later on he brought us the lobster and it tasted good, a real treat to Buddy and me.

★ Playing Poker at the Garden ★

After my first couple of times at the Garden, I always had a poker game going at the Belvedere Hotel during the rodeo. I would rent two adjoining rooms, one for playing cards and the other for my living quarters. We played no-limit ace-to-five lowball, no joker, check and raise. Everybody had to pay me a dollar an hour to play, which added up at the end of the month when the rodeo ended, but nobody seemed to mind because the game was full around the clock. In fact, if a guy's name was on the list and he was called to take an open seat, even if it was three o'clock in the morning, he'd get up out of bed and rush over to the game because he knew that it might be three or four more days before he could get a seat again.

Nobody bothered us, we did whatever we wanted. At the Garden we'd play "red dog" in the clowns' room before the rodeo started and shoot craps in the basement while it was going on. Very few cowboys in those days didn't gamble at all. Some of the top hands were big gamblers. Clyde Burk, the world champion calf roper, was the biggest gambler I ever saw—he'd bet on anything, shoot dice for $500 a roll back when $100 was $100. Toots Mansfield, seven-time world champion calf roper, was a good poker player. We played high poker, considering the times, with pots that sometimes had two or three thousand in them. The entry fees at the Garden were only $100, but hell, you might win as much in one pot as you would in the whole rodeo. Of course, you could lose it all in one pot, too. That's how I got started playing high poker.

Jimmy Whaley from Comanche, Oklahoma was a boy that I'd known for a long time; we'd roped with each other for years. His daddy, Slim Whaley, was one of the best horse trainers in the world (even when he was in his eighties, he was still getting up early in the morning and working with horses). Slim and his wife Rose used to travel all over the country in a covered pickup truck with beds and a stove set up in the back of it. Slim also worked as a pickup man at the rodeos and would enter the roping events if the competition wasn't too stiff. He also had a bulldogging team, and made 25 percent of the win on it. Slim celebrated his one hundredth birthday in 2000.

Jimmy and I ran around together. He was one of the wildest guys I've ever seen—loved to drink, would drink all day and all night, and was a natural-born gambler. I might have a few drinks sometimes but the next morning, the last thing I wanted was a drink. I did a lot of the driving and kept him out of a few storms that came up while we were traveling all over the country entering rodeos and playing poker. In fact, we had just about all of them cowboys so broke, they started calling us "Frank and Jesse."

Four rodeos were held back to back in the Northwest. Everybody called them the Big Four—Lewiston, Idaho; Walla Walla and Ellensburg, Washington; and Pendleton, Oregon where the rodeo was held just after Labor Day weekend. After the Big Four, we drove to Pine Bluff, Arkansas. Hit the road in Jimmy's Buick and only stopped once in two thousand miles for a few minutes to give our horse Sonny some exercise. Sonny was a good little horse that could stand the trailer and the hauling during long trips but he was ganted up from riding for so long, bless his heart. I won both day moneys and the average and tied two calves in twenty-three seconds flat.

In the fall of 1957 we planned to make a few rodeos before we drove up to New York for the rodeo at Madison Square Garden, so we decided to go down to the rodeo at Texarkana, a four-day show, and then to Memphis for the Mid-State Fair Rodeo. Everybody was sort of getting keyed up for the Garden, which was only about a month off, so they'd make all the shows along the way to New York. Jimmy and I had been doing pretty good so we got a hold of a two-horse trailer, put Sonny in one side of it and set up a poker table and a craps table in the other side with a light that hung down over the tables. At Memphis we ran into Junior Vaughn, a calf roper that Jimmy and I used to play poker with. We didn't do any good at the rodeo there, just about ran out of money.

"Hell, I'm going on up to New York now," I told Jimmy and Junior. "We've been on the road about nine months and I'm tired, man. I just wanna drive on up to New York and rest up a while before the rodeo starts."

"We ain't got enough money to go up there and rest. Hell, it's two weeks before it starts."

"I know it, but we can get checked into the Belvedere and set up the poker room so we'll be ready by the time the others get there."

"No," Junior said, "let's all go on down to Evansville and make the rodeo there. There won't be a lot of hands there and hell, we're a cinch to win the ropin'. Probably win about five or six hundred and then we'll have enough for New York."

"Well, you all just go on ahead," I answered. "Jimmy, you can ride with Junior to Evansville and I'll drive the horse and everything else up to the Garden." And that's what we did. Ten days later, Jimmy and Junior came to realize what a mistake they'd made by not going with me.

★ Hustlin' a Big Game at the Belvedere ★

As soon as I got to the Belvedere, I rented two adjoining rooms and started getting the poker and craps tables out of the trailer. Eased them up the stairs, set them up in the room, hung the light, set up the chip rack over there, put a pad and pencil here, and got the bellmen to take out one of the beds and bring up some chairs from downstairs. Of course, I had to bribe the bellmen to get it all done but as I've said, nobody messed with us cowboys at the Belvedere.

I hung up my clothes, what few I had, and got everything to looking pretty good. My horse was stored in the basement of Madison Square Garden with a groom looking after him and Jimmy's car and trailer were stored in the Belvedere's garage since we didn't go nowhere except the rodeo and the hotel. Then I got to thinking, "What am I gonna do now? Here I am up here ten days before the rodeo starts and all I've got is $70 to my name. The entry fees are $100 and there's my rent and everything else and there ain't nothin' to do up here. Guess I shoulda gone to the rodeo at Evansville and tried to win four or five hundred before I came up here. At least I'd have had something to do."

Downstairs in the Belvedere was a circular bar with booze and stuff hanging on shelves behind it and a big plate glass window in front of it that bordered the sidewalk. You could sit at the bar and look out the window across the street to the side entrance of Madison Square Garden about fifty feet away, the door that the cowboys used. You'd go in that door and walk back to where the rodeo secretary was set up and then to the clowns' room where all the clowns and cowboys hung out, before the rodeo started, playing red dog or some other kind of game. I hung around the bar for a couple of days looking out the window, drinking a few beers, getting bored, wondering what to do. I had thought that I needed to rest up but hell, I was young and in good shape and after about two days rest I was getting pretty hyper, ready to do something. It was September and the ball games were on. Those folks up in New York were baseball crazy, still are.

So there I was sitting at the bar about three o'clock one afternoon staring out across the street when a big white Lincoln pulled up by the side entrance to the Garden hauling a long white trailer to match, one of those shotgun trailers, the highest priced horse trailers you could buy. The driver was wearing a cowboy hat and a blond-headed lady was sitting beside him. He went in and came back out real quick with a groom following him. I reckoned that he had hired the groom to take care of his horses and then store the Lincoln and the trailer in the Garden's basement for him.

As soon as everything was taken care of, the man walked across the street and right into the Belvedere bar. He looked around and saw me sitting at the bar, the only other guy in New York City who was wearing a cowboy hat. Walked up to me and said, "I've heard that this is a helluva rodeo up here. First time I've ever been here."

"What do you do?" I asked.

"I'm from Kansas. I came up here to get in the bulldogging at Madison Square Garden. I've heard this is a wild place but there don't seem to be nobody around. Where the hell is everybody?"

I decided to make up a story to satisfy his curiosity. "Well, Jim Shoulders and Casey Tibbs, they're downtown," I started. "Just called me a while ago. They're down there partying now but they'll be here after a while 'cause they wanna play some poker."

"Play some poker?"

"Yeah, I always have the poker game up here. I'm a calf roper, name's Byron Wolford."

"I've heard of you, you're a good roper."

"Well, sometimes I am. Anyway, Jim and Casey will be here in an hour or two to play some poker."

"Where do you play?"

"I've got a place upstairs here with a poker room set up. I always have a good poker game here during the rodeos, all the cowboys play in it and we have a big time."

"Well, I've gotta take my wife down to the Mayflower Hotel and get checked in, but I'll be back in a little while." The Mayflower was a high-priced hotel compared to the Belvedere. A room there cost $18 a day. But he had his wife with him and I guess he wanted to get her away from all us wild cowboys during the rodeo. Anyway, I didn't think much about it when he said he'd be back, just kept on sitting there, drinking a beer, messing around, thinking.

In about an hour, the man walked back in the door. He was a great big guy, about six foot three, weighed about two hundred forty pounds and he wasn't fat either, just one of those Kansas farmers-turned-cowboys. "I've got the ole lady situated at the Mayflower," he said. "She's all moved in and happy, eating dinner there right now. I told her that I was going to come back here, that Jim and Casey were coming in and that we were gonna play a little bit of cards."

"Well, they just called again," I lied, "but they said for

us to go ahead and start playing and they'd be here in a little while."

"Me and you start playing?"

"Yeah, if that's okay with you."

"Sure, just let me get myself a drink first." As soon as he finished drinking, we went up to my poker parlor. It really looked pretty the way I had it set up (of course, I had a lot of experience at setting up a place to make it look good). It was eye-catching.

"Man, this is a nice place," he said.

"Thanks. We play here thirty days, sometimes the games don't ever break up." All the while I was thinking to myself, this guy's probably got a lot of money and I ain't got but $70, so how in the hell am I gonna play him? I decided to just take a shot at him anyway and if I lost I'd tell him that it would take me a couple of days to get the money to pay him. The way I saw it, I didn't have any other choice.

"Let's get some chips to start with," I told him. "Casey and them will probably be up here in an hour or so and they'll likely have somebody with them and we'll have a good game. But we'll just go ahead and start playing till they get here."

"Well, what kind of games do you play?"

"Lowball, that's what all the cowboys play. Wheel lowball, A-2-3-4-5, straights and flushes don't count against you, no-limit, and you can check and raise."

"I've never really played much lowball. I think five-card stud is the only game there is, or maybe draw."

That got me to thinking. Like I said, I've been a road hustler all my life and I knew that nobody could beat me playing five-card stud, as many tricks as I knew. If this guy beats me at five-card stud, I thought, I'll take him down the road and drive him—hell, I'll rob a bank to keep him in money.

"You're right," I said to him. "I think stud's the only poker there is, too, because it's a real game. You and I can play some stud but when the guys get here, we might have to change to lowball."

"That's fair enough," he answered. "Give me a thousand in chips to start with."

"What?!"

"Give me a thousand." So I got his chips, set them in front of him, and he gave me ten $100-dollar bills. I stuffed them in my pocket, reached over in the rack and got me a thousand in chips.

"Deal!" he said and we started playing his favorite game.

Right off the bat I could tell that he wasn't a good player. It wasn't but fifteen minutes before I broke him.

"Gimme another thousand," he said.

"Yessir," I answered and gave him the chips. In about twenty minutes, I won that thousand off him.

"I ain't doin' too good," he said. "I'm runnin' pretty unlucky."

"Yeah, you sure are," I sympathized. "Why don't we quit? If Casey and Jim get here, I'll just tell 'em that we're gonna play tomorrow."

"No, I wanna play now. Give me *three* thousand. If I win a hand, I've gotta have enough in front of me to get even."

"All right, sir," I said and gave him the chips. We kept playing along and he was losing about $1,500 when he said, "Say, where's Casey and Jim? I thought they were gonna be up here."

"I don't know, they must've got tied up," I answered. "But I wouldn't let 'em play now anyway."

"Why?"

"Well, you're three or four thousand loser and they're gonna come up here and buy $200 wanting to play lowball. What chance would you have to get even?"

"By God, you're right! They can't play."

"Well then, I'll just call the desk right now and tell them that I ain't takin' no calls, won't be in tonight, because if they come up here, I don't even want to answer the door." Of course, they weren't within fifteen hundred miles of New York City.

"That's a good idea," he agreed, so I called the front desk and made the arrangements and we started dealing. It wasn't long before he was out of chips again.

"Man, I've never run this bad in my life," he said.

"I've never run this lucky," I answered. "It's about time for you to quit," but I was thinking, $5,000— boy that's a lot of money, I'm really in the chips, I mean really in the chips.

"Look," he said, "Can you cash some travelers checks for me? I wanna play some more."

"Sure," I told him and he reached in his pocket and pulled out a wad of travelers checks, $500 apiece, and tore off ten of them saying, "I want $5,000 worth of chips." Man, I thought, if I win this I'll be rich. To make a long story short, we played and played and played until I had won all the money.

"This is the damnedest thing I've ever seen," he commented. "I've never run this bad in my life."

"I understand. I sure wish you'd quit when you were just a coupla thousand behind. We're gonna be playing during the whole rodeo, you know."

"You don't know me, I realize that, but can I give you a check for $5,000? If I lose that, I'll quit. I won't play any more poker. You don't have to worry about the check. I'll give it to you on my bank in Kansas and you can just take it down to the bank and deposit it in the morning. It's good as gold." I knew his check had to be good, a man carrying that kind of money and driving such a fancy rig.

"Okay, write the check but if I win this or if you get even, the game is over. I want to explain that to you right up front."

"Fair enough," he said and handed me the check.

It took me about two or three hours to break him. "I hope your wife won't be mad at you or nothin'," I said.

"Oh, hell, she'll be all right, don't worry about it. But don't say nothin' to her about how much I lost if you run into her, okay?"

"I won't say a thing," I assured him. "I don't say nothin' to anybody about anything."

"I'm goin' back to my hotel now," he said.

"We'll be having a game here every day," I assured him. "You're welcome to come around any time you want to," and I shook his hand as he closed the door. His name was Stuart Boucher; I'll never forget him.

There I sat with $15,000 in my jeans. The day money in the calf roping at the Garden was about $600 and if you won all ten day moneys, which is impossible, you'd get $6,000. The best average on all ten calves paid about $2,000 and you'd really have to go through a lot to win it, so if you made $2,000 for the thirty days the rodeo lasted, you'd have a pretty good month and if you won as much as $3,000 you'd be in clover. And if you were an all-around hand and worked two or three events, you'd have a fantastic month if you won $7,000 or $8,000. Here I had won $15,000 in about eight hours of playing poker, as much money as I would've made if I had won every average in all of the five events at the rodeo and all ten day moneys in the calf roping. With that much money in my pocket, I was feeling powerful good!

The next morning I decided to make a few changes. "I've been rodeoing on the road for nine months now and I'm gonna get out of these Levi's," I said to myself. "Ole Jimmy and Junior probably haven't won a quarter at Evansville and them sonnabitches will be broke when they get here, but at least I can help them out." So I went downtown to a nice store and bought me six pairs of alligator shoes, brown ones, black ones, orange ones, and even some purple ones. They had some nice shoes there all right, about $55 a pair (nowadays, they're $600). Then I bought me some slacks, silk shirts, and three sport coats. I like to dress nice, you know—I didn't wear cowboy clothes unless I was up in the roping that evening. Bought myself a helluva wardrobe, brought it back to the hotel, unwrapped it real careful and hung it all neatly in the closet. I was going to slick up and enjoy myself. Dressed up and went down to the

Belvedere bar wearing my new alligator shoes, silk shirt, and nice sport coat with my pockets full of money. The cake was all dough and it was downhill and shady. I'm telling you, I was in business.

★ Parlaying a Windfall ★

I was sitting there watching the ball game, listening to the guys talking about a game that they had a bet on and one of them mentioned a parlay bet that he'd made. I never did bet sports that much, but I'd seen those parlay cards one time down in Texas and knew that if you picked three teams, you got 6 to 1 and if you picked four, you got 10 to 1. The more teams you picked the more odds you got. So I got to thinking about those parlays. "I've got me a big bankroll here," I thought, "and I know all the ropers and bulldoggers real good—who all the top hands are, who rides the best horses, who's the leading money winner for the year, who looks like he'll be the world champion." Hell, I was a top hand myself. We'd all been around each other every week making a rodeo together somewhere or other, so I knew them all perfectly.

It was about five or six days before the rodeo started and back then you had to be entered a week before it started so that they would know how many entries they had for all of the events. I decided to go over to the rodeo office and get a list of all the ropers and doggers who had entered the events, and headed off to see Flaxie Fletcher, the rodeo secretary, who was married to the world champion cowboy, Kid Fletcher, a helluva rider.

"Flaxie, I need a copy of the program with all the names of the ropers and doggers who are performing," I told her, handing her a $25 tip. "Go out and have dinner on me tonight." She thanked me and gave me the list, probably thinking that I'd struck oil or something. As it turned out, I might as well have done just that. My idea about the parlay cards was unique; nobody in the history of rodeo had ever done it before or since.

"What I'm gonna do," I said to myself, "is make up some parlay cards on these ropers and doggers and then I'm gonna let these cowboys bet—hell, they'll bet on anything. And I'm gonna handicap them myself because I know them all so well."

So I sat down and started handicapping this roper against that one, like Don McLaughlin against Toots Mansfield, Buddy Groff against Byron Wolford, Glen Franklin against Olin Young, just like football teams. I knew how good they roped and whether it would be close or not, but there wouldn't be no such thing as giving or taking points. Then I handicapped the doggers. When I was done with it all, I wrote on the top of the form "Calf Roping Parlay Card, Must Pick Three" and the same kind of thing for the bulldoggers. I dropped the odds a little on each one of them: "Three Pays 5 to 1, Six Pays 9 to 1."

I knew that picking three ropers in one go-round would be just as hard or maybe harder than picking football teams because so many things could happen—a cowboy could break the barrier, a calf might get up too early, one guy might draw a good calf and the other might draw a bad one. If you had a bet on the best roper and he drew a bad calf, the other guy was bound to beat him 90 percent of the time. The next morning I went to a printer and had two thousand of my parlay cards printed, half on the ropers and half on the doggers, just knowing that these cowboys were going to love betting on them.

A couple of days later I was sitting at the bar all dressed up with a pocketful of money and here came ole Jimmy and Junior walking in looking like they'd just gotten out of jail. "How did you all do in Evansville?" I inquired.

"Man, we didn't win a quarter. We only had a $10 bill coming through that Holland tunnel with our horse and trailer, thought we were gonna run out of gas right there in the middle of it. We were lucky to get here."

"Well, why don't you all just sit down and have a drink on

me," I suggested, pulling a big wad of bills out of my pocket.

"Where the hell did you get that?!" they asked.

"Bartender, give these suckers another drink. They're ropers, been down in Evansville beating all them other cowboys," I ribbed.

"Looks like you're doin' pretty good," they said.

"Yeah, I'm doin' some good," I said, pulling out a couple of hundreds. "Here's some money for your entry fees, you all can pay me back later. And take $50 apiece for walking around money. And try to get your clothes clean, okay? I don't want to be hangin' around with no bums like you."

"Tell us what happened. How did you get all that money?"

"I've been downtown today getting some parlay cards printed," I said, evading their question. "I'm gonna book the roping and the dogging, just like football. It's gonna be a big deal and if you all want to go to work for me running these parlay cards, I'll give you a percentage of it."

"Hell yeah, we'll do anything you say."

"All you have to do is get the bets on the parlay cards and write them down right. You'll make some money 'cause I guarantee you that we'll get a lot of action on these things." Then I reached in my pocket and showed them the cards.

"Hell, I see a couple here that I like," Jimmy said.

"I see some that I like, too," Junior chimed in. "This is gonna be okay."

"You all can bet, too, don't make no difference to me, but where it really is is getting other people to bet. I'll give you 25 percent of what business you turn in. Then as soon as you make some money, you all can hit it a lick yourselves and bet whatever you want."

"Sounds good to me," Jimmy said, "but where did you get all this money?" Looked like I couldn't avoid the issue any longer, so I made up a story especially for the occasion to put the rib on them.

★ Putting the Rib on the Boys ★

"Well, the other night, don't know why but I just felt like eating some Italian food," I began, "so I went out to get me some spaghetti. Found a real nice little ole Italian place with checkered tablecloths, a nice bar, and some tables over by a big ole wide window that looked out on the street. I just wanted to enjoy myself, eat a little something and drink some beer to kill some time. So there I was sitting at the bar drinking a beer when this limousine pulled up in front. The chauffeur opened the back door for an old gentleman, looked to be about seventy-five or eighty years old, dressed up real nice, a real slender little guy wearing a nice hat, a suit and tie and all. He must've had a table reserved by the window because when he came inside, the owner ran over and pulled up a chair for him and the waiters started bending head over foot to wait on him. 'Wonder who that guy is?' I was thinking. 'Must be some kind of a big figure up here.'

"In a little while a guy comes walking through the door, a big rough looking sonnabitch. He run over to that table and started arguing with that ole man, reached back and slapped him. You know I wouldn't want nobody that was that young and big slappin' my daddy, so I jumped up off my stool and hit that sonnabitch in the eye and run him out of the joint, telling him that he'd better not ever come back in there because that ole man was a friend of mine. I was a hot sonnagun for him slapping that ole gentleman." Jimmy and Junior knew that I was a pretty good fighter, that I had been the AAU boxing champion in high school, and wanted to know what happened next. They were hooked on my story.

"Well, they took the ole gentleman in the washroom and cleaned the blood off his face and when he came back, he walked up to me and said, 'Son, I don't know who you are, but you saved my life.' Everybody was standing around listening with their mouths hangin' open, you could've heard a pin drop. 'If it wasn't for you, that guy probably would have killed me. You'll never have to worry the rest of your life.'

'Well, sir, I sure wouldn't want some big ass bully like that jumpin' on my daddy. I'm from Texas, I'm a cowboy.'

'Yes, you look like a cowboy. I could tell by the way you hit that guy that you're something. I'm not gonna tell you exactly what my name is but I'm very well known. How you doin' at the rodeo?'

'It don't start for a week. I'm just hangin' out at the Belvedere Hotel till then.'

'I'm gonna come there in the morning to see you and I'll bring you some cash so that you'll have plenty of money for the rodeo. And after it's over with I want you to stay here and work for me.'

'What kind of job you want me to do, sir?'

'I just want you to go around with me in case something comes up like it did tonight. You won't never have to worry about money.' And he stuck a hundred-dollar bill in my shirt pocket as he was leaving.

'Thank you, sir,' I said and moved on to my plate of spaghetti." By now the boys were on their third beer, hanging on my every word, wondering how this story was going to wind down.

"The next morning at nine o'clock my phone rang," I continued. "It was the ole gentleman asking me to meet him in the lobby. He was sitting in a lounge chair waiting for me.

'How are you this morning, sir?'

'I'm doing good. Pretty rough deal there last night but I'll be all right. He didn't hurt me, thanks to you.' And then he handed me a briefcase. 'Byron, I want you to keep this, it's yours. And here's a phone number in case you need to get in touch with me for anything. After this rodeo's over I want you to stay here in New York.'

'Well, I might stay up here for a while.'

'You might stay up here a long time with the deal I'm gonna make you. I'll see you later,' he said and his chauffeur opened the door for him and they left. Well, what do you suppose was in that briefcase?"

Jimmy and Junior couldn't wait for me to tell them.

"There was $20,000 in it."

"Cash money?!" Their mouths were hanging open.

"That's the damnedest thing I've ever heard of," Jimmy said. "No tellin' who that guy is."

"I checked around at the restaurant and I think he's the head of one of these mobs up here, but he's a nice guy and he's got millions they told me."

"Man, he must have millions if he gave you $20,000 just for that one thing. Do you think that when the rodeo's over, you could get us on with him and we could stay up here, too?"

"I don't know, the way you sonnabitches look. If you'd get cleaned up a little bit, I might get you some kind of deal. Of course, I haven't made mine for sure yet, but I imagine I could get you something." They seemed thrilled with the prospect. "But there's one thing. My clothes have to be kept good all the time 'cause I'm gonna be busy runnin' that poker game and handlin' these parlay cards. I want my shoes shined and my dirty shirts put in the cleaners so that if this man does come around and I have to go somewhere for three or four days, I'll have some nice stuff to take with me."

"Oh, don't worry none 'bout that. You've done paid our entry fees for us, gave us some walking-around money, and you're gonna try to get us a job. You just get some rest and we'll take care of everything."

"Bullshit, I ain't gonna rest. We're gonna have a big poker game up here and we're gonna book the ropin' and doggin'. It's gonna be a big thing, you just wait and see."

They took my shoes to the bell stand and had them shined, put my shirts in the cleaners, took care of me like I was a big boss. I really had them ribbed up. Of course I wasn't sure what I was gonna tell them later when they found out how I really got the money.

★ A Hitch in the Parlay Plan ★

Sure enough, all the cowboys came into town about three days before the rodeo and we started putting the parlay cards on them. I had the inside pocket of my sport coat full of them. "You can make a bet with me, boys," I told them and they'd look at the odds, see their names on the list, they just loved it—and boy, did they start betting! Might near every one of those sonnabitches placed a bet before the rodeo started. Of course they had to bet in advance, they couldn't bet just ten minutes before an event started after the stock had already been drawn because if one guy drew a good calf and another one drew a bad calf, you'd know who had the best of it. Jimmy and Junior were putting out cards like crazy and damn, I'm telling you that those cowboys were betting, really betting.

But then I noticed something strange happening on the bulldogging tickets. I had handicapped a guy named Nick Panzello, a Saturday night cowboy from New Jersey who dogged in the rodeos there every weekend. He'd been at the Garden a couple of years and I'd seen him bulldog but he really wasn't a top hand, just made the rodeos in Cowtown and a few other little rodeos in that part of the country. I knew Nick and just about everybody else, but I didn't know this guy on the program named Don Huddleston (like I said, I'd been up in the Northwest all summer), so I just went ahead and matched Panzello with Huddleston in the bulldogging. Everything else I had in pretty good shape.

It didn't take long for me to notice that if the cowboys bet on two or three things wheeling their tickets, they'd usually bet on the Huddleston-Panzello match-up. Then they started asking me if they could make a straight bet if they laid me 11 to 10 like they do in football when you just bet on one team. "No," I told them, "you'll have to lay me 12 to 10 if you wanna make a straight bet." Well, just about every sonnabitch started betting this Don Huddleston against Nick Panzello. I couldn't figure it out.

"Something's wrong here," I thought. "I'd better go check on this deal." I went over to the rodeo office and talked with Flaxie and a couple of cowboys about it.

"Who in the hell is this Don Huddleston?" I asked.

"Oh, he's that new bulldogger that Willard Combs has been training. He's a helluva hand."

"A helluva hand, you say?"

"Yeah, he might even be better than Willard."

Willard was the world champion back then, riding Baby Doll, that famous horse of his, the best bulldogging mare that ever lived. It seems that Willard had been training this Huddleston guy all summer at his ranch in Oklahoma where he had a big doggin' arena and some horses. Willard didn't rodeo up in the Northwest like we did every year, he'd just make New York and Fort Worth, places like that. He had plenty of money anyway, so it didn't make much difference to him.

Huddleston was about six-foot-five, weighed about two hundred fifty pounds and he wasn't fat. And when I started checking further, I found out that he might even be the rookie of the year. "Oh man, what a trap I'm in!" I thought. "This is pitiful. I'm gonna get flat broke. Hell, I ain't even gonna have enough money to pay off."

It looked like they had the nuts on me. I had about $15,000 but hell, it looked like I was gonna lose more than any $15,000, the way they were betting. I had to close up shop on the Huddleston-Panzello ticket. Wouldn't let anybody make no more bets on that match, told them I'd had all I wanted and that was it.

"I want Huddleston and I want it straight up at 12 to 10," they'd say.

"No, I'm sorry, sir," I'd answer, "you can't bet on that team. The quarterback's crippled and that one's been scratched, but you can bet on any other match-up you want to."

On the night of the rodeo when Huddleston and Panzello were up in the bulldogging, it was coming right down to this: A lot of the cowboys had all the parlays going for them and if Don beat Nick, I was going to lose just about every bet, in addition to all of those straight bets that I had taken at 12 to 10. I'd done good on the ropers because, like I said, it's hard to pick three winners but this deal was another story. It's coming down to the last bunch of doggers and goddamn, I'm really gonna get drowned on this bulldogging proposition. I never will forget how miserable I felt waiting for them to perform.

★ A Miracle of Sports ★

There were as many cowboys in the arena that night as there were people in the grandstands. It was the middle of the week, kind of a slow night, and there wasn't too big a crowd. All of them gamblin' cowboys were sitting down around the fence and boy, were they grinning—they knew that they had the nuts. And there sat Jimmy and me down in the arena up against the fence looking glum.

"Boy, ain't this a helluva way to get broke?" I asked.

"It really is," he agreed. "Goddamn, you're a goner."

"Yeah, I reckon I am," I said and I wasn't smiling.

Nick was up first. At the Garden you come down at the other end of the arena from the ropin' and doggin' chutes and then after you rope or dog, the calf or the steer goes back down in the basement with the other stock and you also go out that way with your horse. Then another performer comes riding in from the other end of the arena when it's his turn to dog or rope.

And here comes Nick. I hadn't seen him for a year or two and hell, he couldn't hardly ride his horse, looked like a plow horse. He just came over to the Garden every year so that he could tell everybody that he had performed there. He'd never won a quarter at the Garden in his entire life against all the top hands. It was depressing.

Here he came into the doggin' chute holding his horse by the rein and this ole horse had his head up and kinda turned to the right with ole Nick sitting up there like a monkey on a football. He called for the steer.

It was a big one, about seven hundred pounds—like I said, they had big steers and calves at the Garden because the Humane Society liked seeing us cowboys get eaten up—and in some unbelievable way, his horse jumped out of the chute and Nick fell off him and right onto that big ole steer. As fat as the stock was back then, if you threw one in eight or nine seconds, you were a cinch to win the day money. Nick turned that steer back and threw him in seven flat! I'm telling you, it was a miracle. All them cowboys sitting down there by the fence turned white as ghosts.

Now here came Don Huddleston riding Baby Doll. He was so rattled he missed his steer the first time, jumped back on his horse, ran the steer around the arena, and threw him in about thirty-nine seconds to stay in the average.

We didn't have to cash a single ticket. Didn't have one losing bet, won every quarter we could. It was a miracle of sports, something like SMU beating the Dallas Cowboys. Those cowboys couldn't believe it. There wasn't change for a $20 bill.

Nick Panzello not only beat Don Huddleston, he won the day money at Madison Square Garden. So after the rodeo was over that night, Nick and about eight people who had come over from New Jersey to watch him perform were all gathered around a big round table in the Belvedere bar. When I walked in, there they sat celebrating Nick's victory.

"This man is gonna be the greatest bulldogger in the world someday," I told them. "He's the only one up East here that can beat them Texans and Oklahomans at bulldogging. That was a great run you made, Nick, you're one of the greatest." Then I pulled a $100 bill out of my pocket, saying, "I want you to treat all these nice people to drinks and dinner tonight on me." Man, they thought that was really something. Nick thanked me and boy, he was just glowing with pride.

★ The Daily Double ★

The next morning the phone started ringing at six o'clock, jangling off the wall with all those cowboys who had made bets and had never won a single one of them. They were really pissed off at me—you could hear them hollering and screaming on that phone from two blocks away. I had to think of something fast, some proposition that would keep them coming.

"Well, you can bet on the daily double," I said.

"What's that?"

"You put up five bucks. The winner of the ropin' and the winner of the bulldoggin' at the night performance is the daily double. All the money goes into a pot at the clowns' room and I take off 20 percent for handling it. If nobody hits it the first time around, all the money goes back into the pot until somebody hits it."

They liked that proposition and started betting right away. One time it went for three or four days before it hit and paid about $1,100. They really did like that deal, my latest gimmick. So everything was going good, we had a pocketful of money, a helluva poker game, and plenty to play with. And it all started when Stuart Boucher came walking across the street asking, "What the hell's goin' on? I heard this rodeo was a wild sonnabitch—where's everybody at?"

About two days later, Jimmy and Junior and I were sitting at the Belvedere bar when Stuart came in. Walked right over to me and said, "You're the luckiest sonnabitch playing poker that I've ever seen." Suddenly, the boys—who had been getting my shoes shined and my shirts ironed for about four or five days—realized how I'd gotten hold of the money. There wasn't any old man from the mob, that was just a bullshit story I'd made up. Man, were they pissed!

"Boys, reckon I'm gonna have to go back south with you this winter," I said. "Looks like the mob man ain't around no more. Of course, you all can't be too mad because you've got about $2,200 coming from that deal on Nick and Don. That'll cool you out a little, won't it?"

"Yeah, boss, we're cooled out, don't worry about it."

"Okay, you all got your percentage still going, but I want you to start movin' some of these cards. You sonnabitches ain't gettin' no action. Hell, I could hire a little girl off the street to get more business than you all are gettin' selling these parlay cards." They assured me that they'd try a little harder.

The three of us had a big time together with things like that, but this parlay card deal and the Nick Panzello story is one of my favorite stories of all time. It truly was a miracle of sports when Nick, riding that ole plow horse, beat Don Huddleston riding Baby Doll, the world champion doggin' horse, trained by the world champion bulldogger. All the old cowboys still talk about it.

Just goes to prove that you never can tell what's going to occur in a sports event—on any given day anything is liable to happen. Sometimes all you need is a chip and a chair.

A ROPER AIN'T NOTHIN' WITHOUT A GOOD HORSE

"Seventy-five percent of any roper is his horse."
— *Will Rogers*

A roper ain't nothin' without a good horse. Of course a horse ain't worth much without a good roper either. You might go through your whole life and have only two good roping horses, really good ones—if you're lucky. If you don't have a good one, you'll have to ride somebody else's horse and give him a percentage of your win.

Good roping horses are so hard to find because they get burned out after a while from being hauled around so much. I've seen some good roping horses that work perfectly at home—they know where they are, there's no big crowd making a lot of noise, no loud music blaring, no rodeo announcer on the loud speakers. Then you put him in your trailer and haul him a thousand miles to your first rodeo, and two days later you haul him six hundred miles to the next one and he doesn't perform nearly as well. A horse will come along now and then that isn't bothered by all that pressure, and I've been lucky to own a few of them.

Not all the calves perform well either. There are always three or four in the rodeo pens that are "good" calves, the ones that don't give you too much trouble. If you draw one of them and you're a good hand, you'll probably win. But even if the calf you draw isn't as good as some of the others, you can make a good one out of him if you're fast enough, have a good horse, and get to the calf just right. I've tied some rank calves in my day and broken the record on them. You have a far better chance of making a good calf out of a bad one than you have of making a bad poker hand into a good one.

To be a good roper you also have to have good coordination, a good eye, and be able to judge distance. When we were just little boys, most of us would practice our roping around the rodeos while we were there with our daddies. We'd sit a bale of hay up on its side, stand about eight feet behind it, and rope those bales time after time until it became natural. In fact, we roped just about everything we saw. I can't count how many of my mother's chickens I've roped or how many whippings I got for doing it. That practice came in handy later on when I won a lot of money betting a bunch of poker players in Dallas that I could rope a chicken.

The modern style of roping a calf is different from the way it was when I was on the circuit. Today ropers get off the right side of the horse after they've roped a calf. Then they "flank" the calf by reaching over the animal, grabbing it by the neck and belly, and throwing it on its side. That way, they don't have to step over the calf to tie him, which saves them about two seconds.

In the old days, we didn't flank the calves—we "legged" them down. I got off the left side of my horse, held the rope around the calf's neck with my right hand and reached down with my left hand to get a hold of a foreleg so that I could tip him to the ground. Then I stepped over him, jerked my piggin' string out of my mouth, and tied any three of his legs together. A piggin' string is about six feet of quarter-inch rope that has an eye in it. You flip the looped end of the string over a foreleg, cross the calf's hind legs over his foreleg, take a couple of quick turns with the piggin' string, and finish the wrap with a half hitch (a hooey). Then you raise your hands in the air to let the timers know that you're finished. All the while, your horse is pulling against the rope to keep pressure on the calf and keep him from getting up.

★ Good Eye, My Best Horse ★

I was fortunate in my roping days to have several top-notch horses. Just after I finished high school I made quite a few rodeos in Kansas, Nebraska, and Oklahoma. In 1950 when I was nineteen years old I stopped off in Chickasha, Oklahoma, on my way home from Madison Square Garden and ran into Skinner Smith, a roper who trained and sold horses for a living. Skinner had several horses for sale but he wanted anywhere from $1,500 to $2,500 apiece for them, a lot of money back then. Then I noticed a big bay horse in the corral and asked him about him.

"That's a practice horse," he answered. "Only has one eye." You saved your good horses, kept them in top shape, but you didn't practice a whole lot off of them.

"Well, can I saddle him up and rope a couple off him?" I asked. He agreed, so I saddled up the one-eyed horse and roped a few practice calves off him. I could tell right off the bat that Good Eye was the best horse that Skinner had and he didn't even know it, so I didn't rope too much in front of him, just took a few "lucky" runs.

"What'll you take for this ole horse?" I asked.

"Oh, you don't want that ole horse."

""Yeah, I want him. How much do you want for him?"

"Hell, I'd have to have $600," he said, thinking that he was really doing something.

"$600?! That's an awful lot of money," I protested. I knew he was hijacking me but I didn't care. Daddy had been training a couple of horses for me but they weren't ready, so I called him and said that I was planning to buy this horse, wanted to see how he felt about it. He told me to go ahead with the deal. Like I've said, Daddy could train a horse or a dog to do anything. I wasn't really a good horse trainer, didn't have the patience to mess with it. All I wanted to do was get on them and rope, try to get the money, get out of there and get on to a poker game somewhere. I just roped because I wanted to eat. Ole Good Eye was perfect for me.

I took Good Eye home and showed him to Daddy. After he'd roped a few calves off him, Daddy said, "Boy, you got yourself a deal. That's a helluva horse." He was right. Riding Good Eye was like driving a car—you could let him out or ease him up, and when you roped a calf he would stop and jerk that calf six feet high. I'd be there waiting for him when the calf got up, leg him down, string and tie him. Nothing to it. I roped off Good Eye for a couple of months that winter before Daddy and I drove up to Denver for the rodeo in 1951. I didn't do any good on my first calf but I tied the last one in thirteen seconds flat. Didn't look like I was going to place in the money, they were tying them pretty fast. I was up in the first part of the go-round and after I roped, we left. Got back home and found out that I'd won second in the day money, $1,300, and I was happy to get it.

After the rodeo in Denver we went to the Fort Worth Fat Stock Show, which always comes right on the heels of Denver. Didn't do no good at all, roped one right over the line, drew a bad calf and he kicked me. What I mean is that sometimes you draw a calf that just kicks and there's nothing that you can do about it. Of course I always treated a calf like he was made out of glass, handled him with kid gloves so that I wouldn't upset him trying to get a wrap on him. Hell, if I could get a half hitch around its legs, I could hold an elephant.

From there we went to the Houston Fat Stock Show in February. Bill Boyd, "Hopalong Cassidy," was the star of the rodeo that year. He rode around the fence and signed autographs for all the kids, saying, "I don't sing and my horse don't do tricks." Got paid $30,000 while all us cowboys were sleeping in horse trailers and trying to win $800.

They had the biggest calves at Houston that anybody's seen in the history of roping. Everett Colburn and Gene Autry, the men who supplied the stock for Madison Square Garden, had some heifer calves there that weighed three hundred twenty pounds. They were wild as the wind, just waiting to eat up all one hundred sixty of us ropers. I drew one of the biggest calves I've ever seen, tied that sonnagun in 19.8 seconds, a pretty slow time for me, but the calves were so big and wild that my time was good enough to win the first day money. Tied my last calf in twenty seconds flat and won the average for the 1951 Houston Fat Stock Show. Hadn't owned Good Eye but four months and already I had won second in the day money at Denver and the average at Houston with him. I knew he was a helluva horse.

Then I drove Good Eye way up to Wisconsin, where they had a rodeo inside a building. Not many rodeos were held in buildings in the old days, just Fort Worth, Houston, San Antonio, Madison Square Garden, and Boston Garden. All the rest of them were held outdoors. The fella who put on the rodeo had a couple of ropers who worked for him driving trucks hauling the stock and things like that. Then they'd perform in the rodeo, all the while being on a salary. They had a good deal and got the best of anything that came up because they worked for the producer. I'd been around long enough to know that they didn't draw those calves just right.

The night that I was up in the roping, I tied my calf in 10.04 seconds. The officials had never heard of anybody roping a calf inside a building in that kind of time, so they figured that the stopwatch hadn't worked. "I don't know why you think the watch didn't work," I complained. "Hell, a lot of times I tie them in nine practicing at home." But they insisted that the watch hadn't worked right and told me that I'd have to rope the calf over again after the show that night.

"All right," I bragged. "I'll tie that sonnabitch in ten again." The calves weren't that big, you know, so that was right down my alley and I had a good horse. In fact, Good Eye was one of the best roping horses that I ever had. You could haul him five hundred miles, get him out of the trailer, and go with him. He knew how to rest while he was traveling, he was just a natural.

So after the show was over, they got the calf back in there and they got the stopwatch and the time keeper and the flag judge all ready to go. This time I tied the calf in 9.06. They were amazed!

"Well, did the watch work right that time?" I ribbed them. "If you all ain't pleased, why don't you run the calf back in there. I believe I can tie that sonnabitch in eight flat." They couldn't say a thing to that. This is just the type of story that ole cowboys like me remember for years.

Troy Fort was the world champion roper at that time. Troy and I were sitting around playing poker during the rodeo in San Antone, just passing time until the roping started that night. About six o'clock we drew the calves.

"What'd you draw?" Troy asked. When I told him the number I'd drawn, he said, "You ain't got a chance! I was forty-four seconds on that ole heifer at Houston."

"Well hell, there's a lot of difference between my roping and yours, Troy," I cracked back at him. "I won't be that long." Everybody just laughed.

I backed ole Good Eye into the chute and they let loose that big calf. I roped him, Good Eye jumped him down, I waited for the calf to get up, legged him down and tied him in 12.1. Broke the all-time record at San Antone on the same calf that the world champion had roped in 44.0. Made Troy eat his words.

Ole Good Eye and I went back home after San Antone, did a few local rodeos and then headed out for San Angelo, Texas. Just me, my Cadillac, a trailer, and Good Eye—hell, that was all I needed in the whole world. When we arrived, Junior Vaughn from New Mexico was already there. He had a ranch, raised calves, and drank quite a bit.

"Whatcha doin', Wolf?" he asked.

"Hell, I just got in and I've gotta go find me a place to stay."

"Well, lookie here, me and so-and-so have two beds in our room, so why don't you just stay with us?" That was fine with me, so we all went to their motel room to get cleaned up before going out to eat supper.

"Hey, I've got an idea," I cracked. "Why don't we play some poker with our change and the winner buys supper?" They liked the idea so we took all the change out of our pockets, got a deck of cards, and started to play lowball poker on a bed in the motel room. They might not have known that I'm a helluva lowball player.

Pretty soon they got broke and started digging for more money. I started playing with about $2.80 and by the next morning, counting what money they had and what they owed me, I had won $10,000! That was mighty near more money than you could win in a year at rodeoing. They were in shock. Never did go out to eat.

I didn't do any good at the rodeo, so ole Good Eye and I drove on over to Baton Rouge, Louisiana for a big rodeo on the college grounds at Louisiana State University. There I was at LSU with all this money that I'd won off those two yaps, and damn, I was in business! Both of them came to Baton Rouge to rope, couldn't hardly wait to find me. Somebody told me they were looking for me and I didn't know if I was going to have to fight them or what, but as it turns out they just wanted to play some more poker to try to get even. Hell, I drowned them again, won about $5,000 more off them.

When ole Good Eye and I got back home in Tyler, I had plenty of money. Took care of my folks and then partied for about ten days in Gladewater before I took off again. Went up to Phillipsburg, Kansas where ole Good Eye won the roping for me on about four calves. We traveled from there up to Burwell and won that one, too. I'd had Good Eye for a little less than a year and already had won close to $20,000 off him.

We finally made our way back home for some rest. Like I always did, I took care of ole Good Eye as soon as we got there, put him up in Daddy's barn. The next morning he was sick, wouldn't get up. I didn't know what the hell was wrong with him, so I called the vet. Everybody knew Dr. Terman. He was kind of a family doctor for all your stock. But even he couldn't help my horse.

Damned if ole Good Eye didn't lay down and die! I couldn't believe it, he just laid down and died. I would rather for my wife to have died than Good Eye because I made my living off him. I was crazy about that horse—he was my bread and butter.

There I was again without a good horse. The one that Daddy had been training for me was still too inexperienced. You have to haul a horse for a year or so to get him used to the lights and the hauling, so if you can find a "natural" like ole Good Eye that knows how to take care of himself and doesn't get hurt when you haul him, it's a blessing. You might only have one or two horses like that in your lifetime. There wasn't anybody in the country that could beat me while I had Good Eye with me. But now my horse was dead—the best roping horse in the country. Boy was I sick. I didn't know what the hell to do.

★ Along Came Buddy ★

Buddy Steele, my friend who ate that finger-bowl soup with me at the Garden, had a little blaze-faced horse named Buddy Boy (never did know why they both had the same name). Buddy Boy only weighed about nine hundred fifty pounds (Good Eye had weighed about twelve hundred), but that little horse was fast. He would stop but he wouldn't jerk a calf down, he'd just switch around and back up so that the rope was always tight and you could really get a hold on a calf. Buddy and I decided to travel together and take his horse up to the big rodeo at Madison Square Garden. It was 1951 and I was all grown up at age twenty-one.

The calves up there that year were wild sonnaguns, weighed about three hundred pounds. Of course Colburn and Autry had furnished them, just like they did at Houston. The fastest time that anybody had tied a calf in thirty years at the Garden was twelve-something because the calves were so big and wild. And because the Humane Society had gotten a rule put in that if you jerked a calf down, you got a ten-second penalty so that even if you tied one in ten seconds, your time would be listed as twenty. Hell, I've known those big calves at the Garden to kick so hard they'd split a pair of Levi's.

On my first go-round in the roping event, I drew the same calf that Don McLaughlin, five-time world champion, had taken thirty-two seconds to tie, she was that wild. I almost missed my chance at getting to rope her because I got the program mixed up somehow and didn't know that I was up for the roping that afternoon, so I was sitting at the Belvedere Hotel bar right across the street from the Garden drinking a beer. You'd walk about fifty or sixty steps from the hotel, go in the side door and turn left and you'd be right there by the bucking chutes. The roping chutes where the calves and steers were penned up were at the other end of the arena. You'd ride your horse to that end of it, rope your calf, and then the calf would go back into the basement with all the other stock and you'd take your horse to the basement where he would stay until your next roping.

The rodeo had already begun when the groom who was taking care of my horse came running into the bar looking for me. "Byron, you're up in the roping!" he shouted.

"What?! I'm not up till tomorrow."

"No, you're up now and there ain't but twenty minutes before the roping starts." Well hell, the bareback event was all over with and so was the Rin Tin Tin act, so I barely had time to make it. "I've got your horse saddled and ready to go. You'd better slip on your boots and get on over there. You drawed that calf that McLaughlin was thirty-two seconds on. You're probably wasting your time, but you'd better get over there anyway." So I ran upstairs right quick, slipped on my boots, and headed for the arena.

The ropes we used in those days were made out of manila. If the weather was cold or damp, they'd get stiff; if it was hot and dry, they'd get limber. In New York the weather was kind of damp so you kept your ropes in the boiler room. During the rodeo, the boiler room would be full of ropes that each cowboy had hung in his special place so that his ropes wouldn't get stiff. You'd go get your rope about thirty minutes before the roping started knowing that it would be in pretty good shape, but I didn't have time to go get mine.

I was mighty glad to run into Bill Rush, who had just roped his calf off a real good horse named Rowdy.

"Bill, loan me your rope and your piggin' string," I said. "If I mess it up, I'll pay you for it."

"That's the best rope I've got," he answered, hesitating. Cowboys don't really like to loan out their ropes.

"Hell, I'll be right be right back," I said with a little bit of brag. "I won't be very long." So he agreed to let me borrow them and I rode up to the other end of the arena planning to rope just so I could stay in the average.

I got a good start out of the chute and roped the calf. Somehow or other he got his right foot in the rope so that it was around his neck and his right foot and I was real lucky that I didn't jerk him down. Ole Buddy kinda switched the calf around and I got there just in time. A lot of times I would get to the calf before he would even start to get up. By the time he turned around I was there waiting on him—caught him just right, legged him down, stepped over him and put one of my famous ties on him. Tied that calf in 11.03. Broke the all-time record at Madison Square Garden, a record that stood for thirty-eight years (1959 was the last year that they had the rodeo in the old Madison Square Garden).

J.B. Harris from Shreveport shot a picture of me breaking the record that I still have hanging on the wall in my den at home. Harris went around to all the rodeos taking pictures of the cowboys when they performed. Then he would develop eight by ten prints in black and white and sell them to you for $1.50 apiece. In the photo I've already tied the calf, I'm holding my arms straight up in the air, ole Buddy has the rope as tight as can be—but the flagman has never dropped his flag. I don't know whether he was trying to flag me slow or I tied the calf so fast that he was stunned or what, but he must've beat me out of at least a second. It's such a rare photograph that I'm planning to put it in the Cowboy Hall of Fame some day.

Whatever happened, that was the best run that I or anybody else has ever made on a calf that wild. Frank Moore, the manager of the Garden had a belt buckle made for me, a silver and gold buckle with genuine rubies in the corners. "Calf Roping Fastest Time, Madison Square Garden Rodeo, Byron Wolford, 11-3-1951."

Yes, Buddy Boy was a good little horse. We went back home to Tyler with him after the rodeo, put him up, and took off for Summerfield about thirty-five miles away where they had a poker game going. Buddy and I called the guys there "Cabbage Farmers" because they raised cabbage plants in hot houses. I could hardly wait to play poker with them and we wound up playing there for about two weeks.

When I got back home from the poker on Saturday night, I told Daddy, "Let's go on up to Eunice for the roping." You see, before the invention of the National Finals Rodeo, the movie star Audie Murphy and Ray Woods, a big car dealer in Fort Worth who had an arena at Eunice, Texas, ran an event to determine who was the best roper that year. The top fifteen ropers in the United States put up $500 entry fees, with added money by the sponsors, and roped eight calves each for the championship title.

"You've been playing poker and haven't even saddled up your horse in two weeks," he said. "You ain't got a chance."

"The hell I don't!" I answered. "That's got nothing to do with anything."

"All right, we'll go," he said, "but I don't think much of it."

We had an ole cherry-red International pickup and called it the Lone Ranger because it was so rough riding, loaded Buddy in it, and took off for Eunice. All the big dogs were there—Toots Mansfield (seven-time world champion), Troy Fort, Jack Skipworth, Lanham Riley, Don McLaughlin, and Audie Murphy. The roper with the best time overall for the eight calves would be named the champion. In short, I never made a bad run—tied them in fifteen, fourteen, tied one in twelve—beat them all by eight seconds. Won $5,000 and the title of Champion Roper for 1951, the equivalent of winning the National Finals today. There also was a jackpot roping with one hundred ropers in it. I tied my calf in 11.2 and won second place in that.

Before the championship roping started, they held a Calcutta like they do in golf tournaments. All fifteen ropers were auctioned off and the money went into a central pool. Daddy and I, we were just two country bumpkins and didn't even know what a Calcutta was. Toots Mansfield and Don McLaughlin brought $700 or $800 each in the auction, a lot of money back then. I brought $50 in the thing. If we had put up the $50 to buy ourselves, we could have won $7,000. But anyway, the guy who had bought us and won the Calcutta gave me $500.

So here I was the Champion Roper of 1951 and I also had won two other championships that year—the AAU boxing title and the Texas hold'em championships back-to-back. Buddy Tureman, a heavyweight fighter that I'd gone to school with, was always asking folks around Dallas, "Do you know who the only guy is that ever held three championship titles at one time in the state of Texas?" When they couldn't come up with the answer, he'd reel off my three titles for them, kind of like he was bragging for me. Buddy probably could've been the world champion boxer but he partied all the time and didn't train. He fought Roy Harris in Tyler and the winner was to get a match with Floyd Patterson. It was a helluva fight, but Buddy wasn't in shape so Harris out-pointed him and went on to fight Patterson for the championship.

The no-limit hold'em championship was put on every year by Milton Peale, who had a poker room in Waxahachie, Texas. I booked it two years running. When you book a poker tournament, you make a price on everybody just like a bookmaker does when he books the money line on a football game. Say that I made Curtis Skinner 6 to 1, big Ken Smith 6 to 1, and Everett Goulsby 5 to 1. If you bet $200 on Goulsby you would get $1,000 back, five times your money, if he won. Almost everybody bet on themselves if they thought that they could win it because that way, they'd make some extra money on their bet. I won the tournament both times I booked it, so I didn't have to pay off any bets. I hadn't booked myself, just all the other players, and never had to pay anybody a quarter. I got a kick out of that, but nobody else did.

★ The Horse I Lost in a Poker Game ★

I rode Buddy Boy for a couple of years at the rodeos, playing poker when I wasn't roping. I had another horse named Glass Eye, a blaze-faced mare that I was planning to take to San Antone for the rodeo in 1954. We called her Glass Eye because she had one white eye. She could see out of it just fine, it was just a different color than her other one. I had a week to kill before the rodeo started so I took a little side trip up to Idaho to play lowball. I'm up there playing poker with all the locals—those fellas had more cards in their boots than they had on the table—and I lost all my money, every quarter of it. Even lost Glass Eye! Boy, did I hate to go home. I had to drive clear back to Tyler with an empty horse trailer trying to figure out how to tell my daddy that I'd lost my horse in a poker game. I decided to drive real slow.

Took me three days driving home—I wasn't in any big hurry. My daddy had trained Glass Eye and I hadn't seen him for three months. When I pulled into the driveway that evening, Daddy was outside walking under a pecan tree, just like he had been waiting for me. He walked up to the car, looked in the trailer, never even asked how you doin' son or anything. Just said, "Where's ole Glass Eye?"

"I hate to tell you, Daddy, but I lost him in a poker game."

"Do you mean to tell me that you lost your horse in a *poker* game?" He couldn't believe it.

"No, I didn't put her up in the middle of the table and bet her, I sold her and lost the money."

"Boy, you're a dandy!" he said and strode off. I'd rather for him to have whipped me than to say that. I knew he wouldn't but I didn't want to stay around the house too much, so the next morning I got up early and headed out for the rodeo in San Antone. I figured that I'd probably run into somebody along the way whose rig was broke down, load his horse up, and we'd hit the rodeo together. But that's not exactly the way it turned out.

★ My Ace in the Hole ★

In the old days you seldom saw a white horse or a painted horse in the rodeos because it seemed like they just didn't have the breeding to make good roping horses. One of the few that I ever saw belonged to a fella that I used to rope with who had a white horse that scored pretty well in the chute and would give you a good loop. But he didn't have a stop on him. You always trained your horse to stop hard and fast after you had roped the calf and jerked him down so that you'd be right there by the time the calf got up. You had to let the calf get back up on its feet before you could throw him and tie him, and if you were ready for him you had a big advantage. At Madison Square Garden there was a ten-second penalty if you jerked a calf down because the Humane Society had decided that it was cruelty to animals. The same ten-second fine applied in Calgary.

Anyway, I'd seen this fella rope off his white horse and I knew that the horse was a pretty good one except that he couldn't jerk a calf down. He just sort of bounced when he stopped and then switched the calf around. He worked the rope pretty well, backed up and kept the rope tight after you had roped the calf so that you could get a good hold on it and pull the calf toward you. If your horse doesn't keep the rope tight, the calf can run anywhere it wants to.

This fella was at the rodeo with his white horse when I got there. I knew that he liked to play poker, so he and I started playing heads-up, thirty minutes of lowball and thirty minutes of high draw. It wasn't too long before he got broke and wanted to borrow some money.

"I'm not in the loan business," I told him. "You're playing unlucky so why don't we just quit and play some more tomorrow? Maybe your luck will be better then."

"I'd sure like to keep on playing," he answered, "so I'll tell you what I'll do—I'll put up my horse."

"That's okay with me. What do you want for him?"

" $800."

"Well, why don't I just give you $800 worth of chips for him. If I win them back from you, the horse is mine. If you win, you keep the horse."

"Fair enough. Give me the chips and let's play."

I gave him the chips and we started dealing. Pretty soon this poker hand came up that I'll never forget. We were playing high draw and he dealt me three aces, a deuce, and a seven. I opened the pot for $50 and he raised me $100. I called him and drew two cards, an eight and a nine. He also drew two cards. I led off with a $100-bet and he raised all the rest of his money. I took a little extra time to think it through. "He drew two cards," I was thinking. "Surely he wouldn't be drawing at a flush or a straight, so he must have trips. I hope he didn't catch the fourth one or make a full house because I haven't helped my aces." I called him. He had three kings and got no help on the draw, so I won the pot—and the horse of course.

"Well, now you own the horse," he said, being a good sport about it.

"Yeah, but I'm gonna have to feed that horse and I don't have to feed money when I win it," I said, laughing it off.

I named my white horse "Ace" because I'd won him with three aces. The next morning I loaded Ace in the trailer and headed back to Tyler. When I came into the house late that evening, my daddy asked, "Where'd you get that sorry lookin' gray sonnabitch?"

"Won him in a poker game," I answered with my chest stuck way out.

"Well, it's about time you won one. You've sure lost enough of them," he quipped.

After I got cleaned up, I went out on the town that night. The next morning when I came downstairs for breakfast, Daddy was sitting at the kitchen table drinking coffee. I knew that he'd been up at daylight and already had roped off Ace.

"Well, how'd you like my new horse?" I asked.

"I wouldn't give a quarter for him," he answered. "He can't even jerk a calf down. He gives you a pretty good loop and scores in the chute, but you won't win a nickel on him."

"Well, I'm going to Canada with him. He's gonna be perfect for the stampede because if you jerk a calf down up there, you get a ten-second fine. He's just what the doctor ordered."

"Good luck to you, son, but don't call me for no money."

ROPIN' AND GAMBLIN' AT CALGARY

"I've always played cards. I can't remember when there wasn't a gambling game going on somewhere, even if it was a craps game in a wheelbarrow on the backside of the arena."
— *Wilford Brimley*

Canada was a long way from home for a piney woods boy like me, so I called Buddy Steele and asked if he wanted to go up there with me and my new horse, Ace. Buddy was about twenty-one years old, a little bit younger than I was, and I had taught him how to rope. He was ready to ride, so we looked in the rodeo schedule to see what we could make before the big one in Calgary and found that the first rodeo we could do was at Lloydminister, Saskatchewan. Boy, that's a lot of miles from Tyler, Texas!

I had a '50 Chrysler and a good horse trailer and we started driving north with Ace in tow. Seems like we drove for a year before we finally arrived at the border, got through customs, and headed north to Saskatchewan. Lloydminister is way up there in the sticks; in fact, the roads weren't even paved for the last hundred miles of the trip.

Finally we pulled into town (the streets weren't paved there, either) and noticed a big wooden hotel with a few other buildings around it. We rented a room for $7 a day and then went back to the car to drive Ace to the rodeo grounds to get him settled—but the danged car wouldn't start. Neither Buddy nor I could figure out what was wrong with it and neither could the town's mechanic.

"Well, hell, where's the rodeo grounds?" I asked him.

"About two miles out of town," he said, pointing north.

"Okay," I told Buddy. "I'll ride Ace out to the grounds and I'll be back here in a little while. Ain't no need to watch the car while I'm gone—hell, it won't even run, so nobody's gonna steal it." Actually, I was wishing that somebody would steal the no-account sonnagun.

I hopped on ole Ace and loped him on down the road to the fairgrounds. I went into one of the barns, found an empty stall, watered Ace, and planned to score for a bucket of oats for him later in the day. Down at the end of the barn some cowboys were playing poker on bales of hay with a gallon of wine sitting between them. They were one tough looking bunch of sonnaguns, sitting there drinking that wine and playing some sort of two-card game in which you can draw one.

"What are you all playin'?" I asked.

"We're playing stuke," they explained. "It's something like blackjack." A lot of green, yellow, and other colors of Canadian money was on the table, money that was worth five cents more on the dollar than U.S. currency.

"Care if I play?"

"Nope, you're welcome to play. Where you from?" They looked at me, just a little guy from the states, and sorta laughed.

"Tyler, Texas. I'm a calf roper and this is the first time I've ever been up here to Canada." Right off the bat I saw that they couldn't play a lick, didn't have much card sense. After a while when the deal got to me, I said, "Well, you all been dealin' this stuke game, so I'm gonna deal some Chicago."

"What the hell's that, Tex?" Reckon they called everybody from Texas by the same nickname.

"You get one card down and two up. You bet on the first card down and then you bet each time you turn a card up. The high spade in the hole splits the pot with the high hand."

"We've never played no cards like that," they said.

"Oh, it's a real action game," I told them. "You might have the worst hand but you can still win half of the pot if you have the high spade in the hole." They agreed to try it, so we played a few rounds and they really liked it.

Of course I could see that they didn't fully understand how to play it—they didn't know how to bet and would call with the ten of spades in the hole when I knew that you needed a higher spade than that to win. All you had to do was wait until you got the ace of spades, then maybe pair the ace, and you'd end up scooping both ends of the pot. In about three hours I had broken every one of them. I must've had about $1,500 of their money—they didn't have a quarter left—and they were pretty perturbed with me. They were still drinking pretty good, so I just eased up, put the money in my pocket and said, "Well, boys, I've played awful lucky today. The rodeo don't start for a coupla days and I reckon we can play some more tomorrow, but right now I'm going back to the hotel. Nice meeting you all."

It's a wonder that I got out of there with the money—I found out later that my poker pals were chuckwagon racers. The rodeos in Calgary and Cheyenne usually featured chuckwagon races, really wild events in which they race each other around a big oval track. The guys who competed in these contests were rough sonnabitches, tougher than a boot. They usually stayed off to themselves gambling and drinking and fighting when they weren't racing.

It wasn't long before somebody came knocking on our hotel door. Nobody knew that I was in town except the chuckwagon guys that I'd played cards with, so I was wondering who in the world it might be. It was Bob Flaker, a bareback rider from Colorado.

"Byron, I'm here to warn you," he said.

"Warn me about what?" I asked.

"Well, you know them guys you played cards with out at the barn today?"

"No, I don't know 'em. I've never seen them before in my whole life."

"They're chuckwagon racers, the toughest bunch in Canada" he said. "And they're really mad because they think you cheated them."

"Man, I didn't cheat them," I said. "They just can't play a lick, that's all."

"It don't make no difference what you did," he explained. "They're really hot about it and they're looking for you. In fact, they're downstairs in the men's parlor waiting for you."

"The men's parlor? Where the hell is that?" I didn't know that in Canada in the old days, men and women couldn't drink alcohol together in public places, so most of the hotels had a men's parlor on one side of the lobby and a ladies' parlor on the other side. "I guess I've just gotta go downstairs and face them," I told Buddy. "I've either gotta bluff at them or take a whipping 'cause I'm not leaving. I like it here." I put on slacks, alligator shoes, a sport coat, and a silk shirt buttoned up to the collar—and stuck my pistol in the back pocket of my pants.

When I walked into the men's parlor, about eight of them were sitting at a big round table drinking beer. In Saskatchewan they served you two glasses of beer at once, both at room temperature. As I walked up to their table, they all got quiet as a pin and I decided to try to put a bluff on them.

"I heard you guys are looking for me," I announced.

"Yeah, Tex," one of them answered, "we think you done something to us out there in that card game where you won all our money. You weren't supposed to win it all—ain't nobody that lucky."

"Let me tell you all this," I replied. "I can't help it if I'm lucky, but I'm sure glad that I am."

"Don't matter, we still think you done something to us."

"Let me get something straight with you all right now," I said. "I know that you're a tough bunch and I can't whip all of you, that's for sure, but I come from a pretty tough bunch myself down in East Texas. Sure, I'm an ole watermelon raiser but let me tell you something—the first one of you sonnabitches that tears a button off my shirt is the first one that I'm gonna shoot. I know you'll hit me, but I'm gonna get the first one or two of you, don't worry 'bout that. So whatever the hell you wanna do about it, let's just goddamn get it on right now and get it over with one way or the other."

That shocked them. Those eight big sonnabitches just kind of froze up, looking at each other in disbelief. Finally the biggest one—a guy named Phil Gooch who weighed about three hundred pounds and looked like Burt Lancaster—spoke up saying, "Aw hell, Tex, you're all right. Sit down and have a beer."

Boy, he didn't know how glad I was to hear him say that! I pulled up a chair and told the bartender, "Bring all my friends a beer!" We got to talking and drinking beer and I became friendly with Phil.

"You know, Phil, you all might not believe it, but I'm one of the best ropers in the world. I was wondering if you can mug one of them ole muley white-faced cows?"

"Hell, I can hold one of them sonnabitches left-handed!" he bragged through his beer.

"Well then, I'm gonna enter us in the cow milking event and we'll split whatever we win fifty-fifty. If you can mug one, we'll win every day money and the average."

"I can damn sure mug, I just hope you can rope."

"Don't be worrying 'bout that," I reassured him.

A wild cow milking is an extra event that rodeos used to have. You rope a cow from your horse, but you don't tie your rope to your saddle, you "dally." Instead of tying the rope to your saddle's horn, you wrap the rope around the horn a couple of wraps and hold it. That way, after you stop the cow, you can let it go. Your mugger then comes running into the arena and grabs the cow around its head or ears and holds it. Then you get off your horse, take the Coke bottle that you have in your pocket and get just enough milk (we called it "leche") into the bottle to pour, and run like hell back across the line.

When you enter a cow milking event, you have to list the name of your mugger and I proudly wrote down "Phil Gooch" (who later became a close friend of mine). They drove up a bunch of cows with the calves on them from the open pasture, penned them up, and the cow milking was on. These were not gentle milk cows—each one of them weighed eight to nine hundred pounds and were wild as coots. I'd rope one of those big ole muley cows, dally, and they would might near jerk my horse down they were so heavy. Then here would come ole Phil—he'd grab that cow, sit down on her, and get a hold of her ears. I'd catch some milk in my Coke bottle and run fast as I could across the line. Phil and I won every day money and the average in the cow milking by six or seven seconds—nobody else was even close to us. I also won every day money in the calf roping. The chuck wagon racers thought I was the greatest guy in the world. They didn't get outside of their own bunch, but they kind of took me in so that I could drink and gamble with them—hell, it was just what the doctor ordered.

From Saskatchewan we went to Cardston, Alberta where I won the calf roping, and then we headed for Calgary. Boy, the stampede was a big place—rows of barns, hundreds of pens, it was huge. All the top hands were there and, unlike most American rodeos, lots of Indians.

The Indians set up a campground in Calgary with hundreds of teepees and bonfires burning at night. Some of the Indians competed as ribbon decorators in the rodeo, but they also had their own special rodeo events that were separate from the rest of us. They rode wild broncs and wrestled steers, and the various tribes would dress up in their finest native costumes to compete in dance contests. They put on exhibits for the tourists showing them how they tanned hides and things like that. At the end of the rodeo the Indians had a grand powwow that featured a feast that included their favorite delicacy, cooked dog. Those Indians were so wild that everyone was afraid of them—they were truly wild, it wasn't just an act.

One of them was a bareback and bronc rider nicknamed "Okinagan Paul." Paul got his nickname because he had fought on Okinawa during WWII where he would sneak across the line into Japanese territory and cut a few throats—that's how tough he was. After the war he was playing poker one night in Chicago when two guys tried to cheat and take a pot away from him, a fatal mistake. Okinagan Paul slipped out his knife and killed one of them and he cut J.D. McKenna, a champion cowboy at the time, across his stomach so that his intestines fell out in his hands. Luckily, J.D. didn't die. A suit was filed against Paul over the knifing and killing, but a general who knew him from Okinawa and liked what he had done in the war stood up for Paul and helped him get out of the mess.

After the rodeo in Calgary I planned to drive south to Cheyenne, Wyoming to one of the few American rodeos that the Indians appeared in. At the Cheyenne Frontier Days they put on a show, a reenactment of some of the Indian-American battles with the Indians surrounding stagecoaches whooping and hollering. Then the United States army, all decked out in blue uniforms and blowing bugles, would come racing in on their horses and start shooting the Indians, who had trained their horses to fall down and play dead like they did in the movies. This was a very big production, one that isn't done any more in rodeos today, and the fans loved it.

In Deadwood, South Dakota, the Indians performed dances during the halftime show. All of them were relatives of Sitting Bull in the Black Hills where they got Custer. In the early '50s when I was there, some of those Indians were eighty years old and actually had fought in Indian battles.

In the calf roping at Calgary I won second in the first day money and third in the second day money. For the best time on two calves, I was leading the average and it looked like I was going to win the Calgary Stampede my first time there, but then something almost unbelievable happened. A roper named Cliff Vandergriff had to tie his last calf in 17.8 to beat me. He was a big heavy man who wasn't too fast on the ground and it looked like I was the favorite to win it all. When ole Cliff roped, he threw a loop as long as a bed (I never used a real long loop myself). If he missed the calf, he could run him back through the loop—hell, he could run a pickup truck through it! He came out, scooped up the calf, got the rope around its neck some way or another, fell off his horse, didn't jerk him down, and tied that sonnagun in 17.7 to beat me for the average! I finished second by one-tenth of a second.

Somehow or other, I thought that they might've gotten me on the watch because I figured that they wanted a Canadian to win the roping—not one of the cowboys from the "south" who were the best ropers in the world and who had traveled all the way up to Calgary to try to win the Canadian calf roping title.

Of course, I vowed to return to Canada the next year. I had seen the beautiful bronze trophies that they awarded at the Calgary Stampede. They weighed about twenty pounds and were sculpted by Charles Beil, who was Charles Russell's protégé, and I wanted to win one of them real bad.

★ No More Second-Bests at the Stampede ★

In 1955 I went back to Calgary with Wayne Garrett, a cowboy from Oklahoma who had a really good horse. Ole Ace had been a good horse for the stampede, but he had hurt his leg up there and got crippled. I didn't want to ruin him, so I retired him when I got back home. Luckily, Wayne had a really good horse, one that I eventually made famous.

We headed for Canada in Wayne's pickup truck with his horse in the trailer. Wayne was a bulldogger as well as a calf roper and we both used his roping horse to haze steers and rope calves. The first rodeo that we made was at Clear Lake, South Dakota, where I tied four calves in forty-three seconds, an average of just over ten seconds a calf. I was mighty proud of myself because that was the fastest that four calves had ever been tied in a rodeo. Then we crossed the border to Cardston, Alberta, where I won the roping for the second year in a row. From there we headed directly for Calgary to compete in the 1955 stampede.

There were so many ropers there that year that we each got only two calves. I drew a spot in the first go-round and took second with 16.2 in the first day money against about a hundred ropers. I wasn't up again for three days when the second go-round started—then they would take the top ten ropers and let them rope the last day to finish off the show.

That year they didn't have a bulldoggin' event—they had steer decorating instead because the Humane Society wouldn't allow the cowboys to twist the steers' necks and bulldog them. In a steer-decorating contest, a cowboy has a rubber band with a ribbon attached to it wrapped around his hand. After he jumps on the steer, he "decorates" it by slipping the rubber band on its horn and then he gets away from the steer as fast as he could. Some of those Canadian Indians would get drunk before the steer-decorating and come out with their horses running fast as they could and just dive at those steers trying to get that ribbon on their horns. There were some real wrecks in that event. It was so wild that I don't see how some of them kept from getting killed. All the chuckwagon racers that I had met in '54 were there for the biggest races in the world, so we got to do some visiting and a little poker playing.

Slim Pickens was the rodeo clown in '55 and '56 at the Calgary Stampede and we became good friends. Later on he started making so many movies that he didn't have any time for rodeo clowning. Slim was a really nice guy and a natural actor, talking and acting on the screen the same way he did off the screen.

With one of the top ten times in the calf roping, I was up for the last performance. I didn't want to take any chances on breaking the barrier in front of the chute because if you started too fast and broke it, you got a ten-second fine. Of course, you also would get a ten-second penalty if you jerked your calf down. Being real careful, I tied my last calf in 14.7, which was a very good run considering the jerk-down rule. With that time, I won the day money and the average and was awarded a big silver and gold belt buckle inscribed, "Champion Calf Roper, Calgary Stampede."

Of course I also won the beautiful bronze trophy sculpted by Beil that I had been aiming for. The sculpture depicts a horse saddled up with his head hanging down as though he's tired. Beil later became famous on his own merit and these trophies have become collectors' items that are worth a lot of money today. I'm proud to say that I own two of them.

★ Calgary in '56 with a Horse Named Bill ★

Daddy had been training a horse named Bill for a year. He trained ole Bill just right and boy, was he a good horse! So in 1956 I took Bill to Calgary with me. As soon as I got there, I unloaded ole Bill at the big barn on the grounds of the rodeo and started walking down the aisle through the barns when I noticed that they had a craps game going. Damnedest thing I've ever seen—the chuckwagon men were shooting the dice and a big guy in a suit was betting me even money that he could make ten. Right away I thought about Pecatonica and how I had been cheated in that game. I knew that this might be another trap, but I figured that I had wised up since then. I could see that everything was all right—he just didn't know the odds, and was betting even money that he could make nine, $40 here, $50 there. Making a long story short, in two hours I didn't have one nickel to my name!

Bill was standing in the barn and I was standing alone by my car with just $20 in my jeans. Took $10 of it to rent myself a little room and got up the next morning, broke, to go see what I could do about it. Went out to the rodeo grounds and found some cowboys who loaned me $500. I had met a fella named Ernie Walters in the craps game, a really nice guy who owned a car business in Calgary. With some dice that I bought at the drug store, I went down to Ernie's car lot to pay him a visit.

"How ya doin', Ernie?"

"Hello there, Byron, what're you up to?"

"I came down here to shoot some craps with you."

"Sure, we'll play some," he answered.

We shot the dice right there on the desk in his office. With my dice he was betting even money on nine, ten, five, everything. Damned if he didn't win all my money—he was lucky and I was sick, just sick. Had to borrow some more money to pay my entry fees.

I was unlucky at the dice, but the rodeo was a different story. The first day I took second in the day money. I won the day money the next day, won the short day money, and won the average. In fact, I won every nickel that I could win at Calgary except for $137. Tied my last calf in 12.5. I broke the all-time record getting off the left side of the horse and took home $4,500 in prize money.

After I'd won big at the rodeo and had money in my pocket, I called Ernie again. "I've got a bankroll now, Ernie."

"Where you going from here?" he asked.

"I'm leaving for Shelby, Montana in the morning. Say, why don't you come on down to the hotel and we'll have a drink and shoot some craps before I leave?"

"I'll be right down!"

I had some whiskey in my room, set a suitcase on the bed, and we started shooting dice on top of it. Ernie was still betting even money on ten and nine and all that. I was shooting $20 and he was shooting about $100. He'd take the ten and I'd say, "A hundred you don't make it." The tide had turned. I beat him out of $10,000 cash.

"Let me have $200 and I'll send it to you at Shelby," Ernie pleaded. I gave him the dice and he rolled ace-deuce. He didn't want to borrow any more money after that. Ernie was such a pure yap that I should've turned my car around, driven back up there, and won myself rich off him, but I was too busy doing nothing. When I got to Shelby there was a $200 money order waiting for me in the rodeo office. I found out later than Ernie was killed in a car accident that Christmas. What a shame—he was a nice guy. And thanks to him I left Canada in '56 with might near $15,000.

It's funny how I can remember names like Ernie's after forty or fifty years. Seems like it was yesterday. A lot of times I'll be going down the road with my wife and I'll say, "Ole so-and-so lives here, used to rodeo with him years ago."

"When's the last time you saw him?" she'll ask. I'll answer, "It doesn't seem so long ago. Maybe forty-five years or so."

I've even stopped to see if some of them were still in the phone book so I could call them. When I get a hold of one of them, they'll say, "Byron Wolford! I can't believe it's you." Sometimes one of the old-timers will meet me at the cafe for a glass of iced tea and a bite to eat and we'll talk just like we'd seen other a few days earlier. Of course, everybody's changed and we all look different, but that don't make no difference to us, you know. I think I'm lucky to be able to remember all these things.

And of course, there are some famous people I've met in rodeoing that nobody, no matter how bad they are with names, could ever forget. One of them was Dean Oliver.

ROPIN' WITH THE CHAMPIONS

"Mental attitude is probably one of the most important things in rodeo, next to the luck of the draw."
— *Larry Mahan*

In the old days, the rodeos at Madison Square Garden and Boston Garden were the big ones, but today the biggest rodeos in the world are the Calgary Stampede, Houston Fat Stock Show, Cheyenne Frontier Days, and the National Finals Rodeo in Las Vegas, which has put rodeoing on the map. At the National Finals, the top fifteen cowboys in each event get ten head of stock apiece. Every time the fifteen compete, the rodeo pays out four or five places in day money. At the end of the rodeo the cowboy with the best overall time in calf roping or bulldogging, and the cowboy who scores the most points in the riding events, wins the average and is crowned rodeo champion.

I wish that the National Finals had been going on when I was in my prime. It's such a big event for the cowboys because they can win $60,000 to $100,000 at it—you couldn't make nearly that much money when I was rodeoing. Of course, expenses are a lot higher these days. If you can find one, a good roping horse costs $50,000, and a good car and trailer run another $50,000 or more. A cowboy who comes in tenth at the NFR probably won't even make his expenses for the year. That's one reason why I think that we might have done better in the old days when if you won $15,000 to $20,000 a year, you were doing really well.

Dean Oliver was the eight-time world champion while I was rodeoing in the old days. I'll always remember the first time that I met him, before he won his first world championship. Jimmy Whaley and I were up in Idaho for a rodeo. We got there about three days before it started and wandered into a bar for a beer.

"Where you guys from?" a fella drinking at the bar asked.

"We're from Texas."

"What you all do down there?"

"We're calf ropers."

"Calf ropers, huh? We've got a calf roper up here in Boise named Dean Oliver."

"I've heard of him," I said, "but I've never met him."

"You wanna rope him in a match roping?"

"I'll rope anybody from Idaho. Hell, I've never seen a potato digger that could beat me ropin' calves," I bragged. I'd had a couple of beers by then and was feeling mighty powerful. By now there was a crowd of cowboys gathered around us, and boy, did that make them mad!

"How much you wanna rope him for?" the fella asked.

"I don't know. First, where we gonna rope at?"

"We'll rope out at my ranch," he answered. "I've got an arena, fresh calves on the cow, everything. How much do you wanna bet?" The fella's name was Moe Sager, owned an eight thousand-acre ranch there. I didn't know that Sager was Dean Oliver's backer at that time.

"Hell, I don't know how much we have, but we'll bet whatever we've got," I answered kind of cocky. "Gotta save enough out for our room and eats, that's all." Jimmy and I started counting our money and including the $200 we had hidden in the car, it added up to about $2,400. So we got it all together and started talking deal.

"How many calves you wanna rope?" I asked.

"Eight," Moe answered.

"That suits me. What time?"

"Eleven in the morning."

Pretty soon the word got around the whole town that Dean Oliver and Byron Wolford were gonna have a match roping the next morning. I would be riding Jimmy's sorrel horse Sonny and boy, he was a good one. Jimmy's daddy Slim was one of the best horse trainers around and he'd done a good job training ole Sonny. He used to smoke Prince Albert and drink a little whiskey and take his roping horses and dogging team around to the rodeos, sleeping in the back of his truck. And now he's over one hundred years old!

The next morning when we got out to Moe's ranch, there were more people gathered around to watch us rope than there were at the rodeo. From this nice arena that he had, we looked down into the valley with the mountains rising all around and way down there we saw cowboys driving a herd of about three hundred white-faced cows. As they got closer and closer, we could see that every one of them had a calf. A calf that's still on a cow and has never been roped is a wild one. They're fresh, they're stout, and they're wild as can be.

Then Dean Oliver comes into the arena. He's about six foot four, weighs two hundred-something pounds, and he ain't fat. When Dean exercised his horse, he didn't ride him—he took the sonnagun by the halter and ran three miles leading him!

We started picking out the calves that we were going to rope. The way it's done is this: You pick out four and he picks out four. You rope four, he turns around and ropes your four, and then you rope his four. Well, I picked out the four smallest calves I could find, weighed about two hundred seventy apiece. And Oliver picked out the four biggest sonnabitches he could find; some of them weighed three hundred fifty pounds. Big as Dean was, it looked like I was caught in one helluva trap.

But luckily, Sonny was one helluva horse. He'd jerk one down and I'd be there waiting on him, leg him down and string him. The way I worked a wild calf was to ease him up like his legs were glass, get a wrap on him, and then tie him—hell, I could tie a giraffe that way. When Dean roped a calf, he would try to grab him and push his legs up, but that way the calf would start kicking. I beat him by seventy seconds on the eight calves. Everybody was amazed. Moe Sager was hotter than an onion. Dean Oliver was in shock. And I was $2,400 richer.

So Jimmy and I gathered up the money, made the little rodeo there, and then headed for Caldwell, Idaho where they have a rodeo that was called the "night rodeo." We're sitting in a bar a couple of days before the rodeo and who shows up but ole Sager, the millionaire who was backing Oliver.

"You wanna rope Dean again?" he asked.

"No, I don't," I answered, "but I'll tell you what we can do. We'll lay a calf down and start the watch over him and I'll tie Dean ten calves for whatever you want to bet."

"Well, I don't know about that," he answered.

"I don't either," I said, "but I'll tell you what we can do— I'll play you some heads-up poker and if you beat me at the poker, I'll rope him for whatever you beat me out of."

"Hell, you've got that one on!" he answered.

"Just go buy some cards," I said, "and we'll start playing right now."

After he'd had another drink, Sager and I went up to his hotel room to play some heads-up lowball, along with a whole bunch of cowboys who came along to watch us. By the time the game was over about two thirty in the morning, I had beat him out of $10,000.

He wrote me a check for it—didn't bother me because I knew that he had plenty of money. I asked Jimmy to drive the two hundred miles to Sager's bank to cash the check for me. "Be there when the bank opens," I said. "This is a whole lot of money and I just have a funny feeling about this sonnagun Moe."

Jimmy had a new Buick and could travel pretty fast, so he and a buddy got themselves a six-pack, jumped in the car, and took off for the bank to get the money. They were there when the bank opened at nine o'clock. When they walked in they saw Earl, a boy they knew who worked in the bank and did some bareback riding at rodeos during the summer.

"Jimmy, guess what?" Earl said. "That sonnabitch Sager called the president of the bank last night and stopped payment on that check." We couldn't believe it. At the end of the rodeo I saw Moe on the grounds.

"Hey, you sonnabitch," I yelled. "What about my $10,000? You haven't paid me." He never answered me and he never paid me either although he had as much money as anybody in Idaho. But I guess I broke him of the habit of betting on Dean and playing poker.

★ A Match Roping Disaster ★

In 1951 I went to Del Rio in Ozona, Texas and roped Walter Pogge. He was a big-time roper, went around with Toots Mansfield, seven-time world champion. I had Buddy with me, the horse that I had broken the record with at Madison Square Garden that year. Walter and I each roped four calves. I tied my first calf in 9.8 seconds.

"These Texas boys are something! Two-tenths off the world record—what a great run," the announcer said over the loud speakers. I think Walter did about 15.0, a good score considering the kinds of calves we were roping. Tied my next calf in 9.6.

"Ladies and gentlemen, this piney woods boy from East Texas has just tied the arena record here. What a show!" the announcer screamed. And boy, everybody was clapping and hollering. Came back into the arena and tied my next calf in 9.4. Nobody there had ever seen three calves in a row tied in nine seconds apiece.

"Ladies and gentlemen," the announcer yelled, "this is unbelievable. He's just broken the arena record!" The crowd went nuts. I was so far ahead of Walter that it looked like it was all over with.

So here comes my last calf and all I have to do is rope the sonnabitch. It was a cinch. I roped him perfect. Then my horse Buddy stepped over the rope, which buggered him, and he ran away with the calf, drug it all the way around the arena! By the time I caught up with him, I'd picked up sixty seconds. That was the worse break I've ever had. Walter Pogge beat me. Somebody even wrote an article in the paper about the piney woods boy who set all the records and then lost it all when his horse ran away with the calf.

After the roping, Daddy and I started getting ready to drive the four hundred miles back home. We'd bet $500 and lost it all on a fluke. Boy, were we two depressed cowboys. But I guess there's a silver lining in every cloud. While we were packing Buddy and our belongings into the pickup, all the ranchers started coming around putting $20 bills in my pocket, saying that they had never been entertained as much as they were by that roping match and just wanted to show me their appreciation for the good time that I'd given them. Even though I'd lost, they thought I was really something and they understood how unlucky I'd been.

Daddy and I had been on the road a while before I started counting all the money the ranchers had given me—$700. This time it was me who was feeling the gratitude.

★ Match Roping with Don McLaughlin ★

In 1956 just before I went up to Calgary, they had a big calf roping at Snyder, Texas. Don McLaughlin was there and so was Buddy Groff from Bandera, Texas. Pat B. Snyder, a lawyer who was at the rodeos all the time and drank a lot and played poker, got on the microphone at this jackpot roping and announced, "Byron Wolford can beat anybody here for whatever you wanna bet!"

No sooner had the words come out of his mouth but here came Don and Buddy. "I hate to go against you, Byron," Don said, "but it's on account of your horse." He was talking about Bill, the young horse that I wound up winning a lot of money with at Calgary, Great Falls, and New York. Pat B. was rich and he bet Don $2,500 that I could beat Buddy.

My style of roping was different from Don's and the others. For example Don would sit on his horse and let him stop. But the way I roped was that I kicked both feet out and was there waiting on the calf. I was there for the money, I wasn't trying to work my horse. Like Dee Burk said one time at the National Finals in Las Vegas, "You know, Byron roped in the old days like we do now. We didn't know it back then, but that was the right way to do it and that's why he tied so many fast calves and broke so many records."

Buddy Groff and I roped eight calves and I never made a bad run—roped every one of them perfect and beat him by about eight or nine seconds. Later I won the jackpot roping at the rodeo. "Well, the only reason that I bet against you was because of that horse. I didn't think he looked good," Don told me afterward. That's one time he was dead wrong.

★ The Greatest Match Roping of All ★

The best match roping that I ever roped turned out to be one of the greatest matches in history. Right after I won the Calgary Stampede in 1956, Wayne Garrett and I traveled south to Wolf Point, Montana on our way to Cheyenne. Glen Franklin, a boy from House, New Mexico, was at Wolf Point. Glen was about three years younger than me, a helluva roper, who later won the PRCA championship in calf roping several years in a row. When we got to Montana, all the cowboys were talking about Glen and me, how good a roper Glen was and what a good roper I was. One thing led to another and they decided to have a match roping between the two of us.

We each were to rope eight white-faced calves that weighed about two hundred fifty pounds apiece. Wayne wanted us to rope for $2,000, but nobody else wanted to bet that much so the prize money was set at $1,000. Wayne gambled a little bit and thought that I was the nuts at roping. He was hauling and entering me for half of what I won and if I played poker, he got a half of that, too. Wayne really liked doing business with me because I was making a lot of money for him. So we roped for $1,000, but a lot of side bets also were made.

The stock producer put up the calves and the timekeeper and flagman who worked the rodeo did the same jobs for our match roping, knowing that the winner would give them something for their work. We decided to score the calves twenty feet, which means that we gave them a twenty-foot head start before we could come out of the chute to rope them. I've seen a lot of match ropings, but this was one of the best ever. The old cowboys still talk about it to this day.

I would tie a calf in fourteen or fifteen seconds getting off from the left side and then Glen would rope one. He got off on the right side and flanked them, which is two seconds the best of it. By the time we got to the seventh calf, there wasn't more than a second's difference between our times. Glen missed the seventh one on his first loop. Of course you get two loops so you always have an extra rope on your saddle in case you miss your calf the first time. Regardless of what your time is with two loops, the betting is done on the average time for all your calves, so you have to tie him to even have a chance at winning. As soon as he missed his calf on the first loop, he grabbed his second rope and roped and tied him in 17.9, one helluva run with two loops.

On the eighth calf, I was first up. "All I've gotta do now is just rope this last calf in fourteen or fifteen seconds, being sure not to break the barrier, and I'll win this roping," I told Wayne. He agreed that was the smart thing to do. I got out of the chute perfectly being careful not to break the barrier, roped my calf, and tied him just right in fourteen-something. I could've tied him a little faster, but I just made a good solid run without taking any chances.

Now it was down to the last calf for all the money. I had forced Glen to the wire—he would have to tie his final calf in ten seconds flat to tie me and 9.9 seconds to beat me. It looked like a football game where you're fourteen points ahead with only a minute to go, a cinch. You might rope one hundred calves as strong and wild as these calves were and never tie one in 9.9.

Glen went into the chute and called for the calf. He laid the barrier back perfectly—it was on the horse's chest, but it didn't break. You couldn't have gotten it any better with a computer. He reached right to the end of his rope, roped his calf, jumped off on the right, ran out to the calf, reached out to flank him, and the calf fell perfectly flat for him. Then instead of two wraps and a hooey like he usually took, he did one wrap and a hooey. Tied him in 9.9 to beat me by one-tenth of a second! That was the damnedest thing anybody had ever seen—they still talk about it today.

Glen became a three-time champion calf roper and today he's a preacher. Wayne wound up training racehorses and is still running them today.

★ A Good Hand, A Bad Beat ★

Jack Favor was a bulldogger from Arlington, Texas, a great big ole nice guy who was two-times bulldogging champion at the Fort Worth Fat Stock Show. Jack had been a heavyweight boxing champion in the Navy and always sort of ran the chutes around the rodeo. At the Belvedere Hotel in New York, there weren't very many people who could handle all those cowboys when they got to drinking, so Jack worked as a bouncer at the bar. He was a powerful man and could handle any kind of trouble that came up. And everybody liked him.

I used to travel with Jack sometimes and I'll never forget the time that we drove to Denver for the National Western Livestock Show in Jack's big ole Lincoln pulling two horses in his trailer. As we came through Limon, Colorado at about four o'clock in the morning, it was fifteen below zero and snowing so hard we could barely see the highway. Took us a long time to drive from there to Denver so we had plenty of time for talk, all the while hoping the horses didn't freeze to death before we got there. Neither one of us had much money back then, and Jack started talking about it. "I wish I'd taken care of my money," he lamented. "And I wish I'd never drank. I'm never gonna take another drink," he vowed. He was repenting.

By the time we got to Denver, the horses were damn near frozen stiff, so first thing, we put them in a stall in one of the warm tents that had been set up for the stock. Then Jack went over to the rodeo office. He was always kind of a boss around the rodeos, letting the horses out of the chutes and making sure everything got done right, overseeing things like the director of a poker tournament does. When he came back, Jack told me that a big lowball game was going on in one of the tents. Naturally, I walked over there to check it out.

As usual, the game was no-limit lowball and I knew some of the guys in it. They'd been playing all night long so there was a lot of money on the table. I only had about $400 on me, but in those days there wasn't any such thing as a change-in, you just played what you had on you. I put all my money on the table, told them to deal me in, and started playing wheel lowball, no- limit, no joker with them. Making a long story short, I caught a few cards, won a big pot or two, and by the time Jack came to pick me up so that we could drive into town and get a hotel room, I was about $3,800 winner. I gathered up all the money, wished everybody luck, and we left. The poker game had made our trip a little more worthwhile.

I don't think Jack had any more than $100 in his jeans at the time, so he was tickled to death—that was more than the roping and the bulldogging paid and like always, we split the profits. When we got to our hotel, Jack got all dressed up.

"Let's go downstairs and get a drink," he said.

"I thought you were gonna quit drinking," I teased.

"Aw, I've changed my mind," he answered. Reckon he'd decided against becoming a teetotaler since he'd gotten off to such a good start from my poker playing.

Some years later Jack took one of the worst bad beats I've ever heard of. It seems that he was driving his pickup truck to a rodeo and stopped to pick up two hitchhikers. He gave them a ride down the road for a couple hundred miles—he was always good-hearted, treated everybody right. Later on he came to find out that the two hitchhikers had killed somebody. The law pinned the murder on Jack, as though he had been with them. He was framed on the rap and sent to prison in Louisiana where he did ten years flat before they found out that he wasn't guilty. When he got out of the pen he went back home to Arlington. He got in touch with me in Dallas when I had my poker joint there and we got together for a few drinks at my place to reminisce about "the good ole days." I was watching TV recently and heard Clint Black talking about making a movie about Jack Favor's life—what a story that would be!

★ Some Top Hands in the Old Days ★

There weren't as many ropers back then, maybe only a dozen top hands, and they couldn't rope as fast as they do today. I knew them all and competed against them—Troy Fort, Toots Mansfield, Clyde Burk, Dee Burk, all of them. Clyde, a four-time national calf-roping champion, owned a blaze-faced, top roping horse named Baldy. When Clyde was thirty-two years old, he was killed while hazing a steer in Denver. Jack Skipworth and Troy Fort bought Baldy from Clyde's widow for $2,500. That made headlines in the Fort Worth newspaper—nobody had ever heard of that much money being paid for a roping horse. They wound up making a lot of money off Baldy.

Just as there aren't many great left-handed golfers, there weren't very many top left-handed ropers. The two best ones that I knew were Ronnye Sewalt and Sonny Sykes. Ronnye's dad, Royce, was the world champion roper in 1946 and Ronnye was the best left-handed roper that I've ever known. Ronnye's son Rusty used to rope in the National Finals Rodeo every year in Las Vegas, so I guess roping must run in the family. Sonny was a left-handed boy that I roped with when we were both kids. In 1941 Sonny and I had a match roping at the Bear Club rodeo in Waco. We roped off ponies and tied those calves faster than the big guys did—the crowd loved us.

Toots Mansfield, Don McLaughlin, and Royce Sewalt were some of the top ropers from Texas. I'd like to think that I was in that bunch, too. Another friend of mine, Ray Wharton from Bandera, won the calf roping championship in 1956. He was a little bitty guy that we all called "Mighty Mouse," and he was tougher than a boot. Jim Bob Altizer from Del Rio was one of the top match ropers around the rodeos and won the calf roping championship in 1959.

Juan Salinas and his brother Tony also were from Texas. They were Mexicans and good guys. Tony was a fair calf roper back then and today, his son Tony lives in Vegas where he's an oddsmaker. Juan owned a famous roping horse named Honey Boy. One time while we were at San Antone for the rodeo, we were playing cards when Juan came walking by.

"Where you goin'?" we asked.

"I think I'll go downtown and see a picture show," he answered and left. About three hours later when he came back, we asked Juan which movie he had seen.

"Gone with the Grapes," he answered. He had gotten "Gone with the Wind" mixed up with "The Grapes of Wrath." We howled; it was so funny. For years afterward whenever some ole cowboy was asked what movie he'd seen, he'd answer "Gone with the Grapes." Juan later became a sheriff.

Elgin Horton, C.F. Sealey, and Dwight Graham were some of the best calf ropers in East Texas in my day. Billy Leach also was one of the top ropers in my neck of the woods and his wife, Faye Ann, was one of the best cowgirls around—she could rope, too. Annie Golightly was another good cowgirl who became a singer and entertainer.

Bob Crosby was a famous cowboy in the late '30s and '40s. One time at the Fort Worth stock show when he was older and had retired from roping, he entered the cutting horse contest. He had a paint horse named Powderhorn that he had trained to be one of the best, which is unusual for a paint. He was leading the contest, came out for his last performance, got right in the middle of the arena, and took the bridle off ole Powderhorn. That paint worked perfectly without its bridle on, but he got disqualified because of some rule they had.

Anyway, Bob was a good ole roper and bulldogger who used to go up in the northwest in the early '30s for the rodeos. They might have only seven or eight ropers back then, and they'd rope two calves each for the day money. One time Bob broke his leg and contracted gangrene. The doctor wanted to amputate his leg, but Bob wouldn't hear of it.

He was tougher than a boot, so he just let the blow flies and screw worms take care of the gangrene until it healed. This is a famous story that still goes around the rodeos. Bob wore the same black hat for forty-four years, and got killed in a Jeep accident in New Mexico.

In the old days the best ropers were from Oklahoma, Texas, and New Mexico, but these days they come from everywhere. Troy Fort, Olin Young, Glen Franklin, Sonny Davis, and Jack Skipworth were the top hands from New Mexico and I used to make a lot of rodeos around Jess and Buck Goodspeed, who were real good calf ropers from Oklahoma. Jess's son Bobby also was a good left-handed roper. We were in Chicago once for the big rodeo there and two days before it began, there was a wrestling match in the arena featuring Gorgeous George. The place was packed with seventeen thousand fans, more people than ever showed up for the rodeo, and you couldn't even get in the joint.

Jess didn't gamble but one day while he was walking through the alley between the barns, he noticed a guy running a three-card Monte game, a takeoff proposition. You'd bet all your money and then they'd switch the cards and toss you the losing card that they wanted you to have. Jess stopped to watch and a shill sitting in the game invited him to play a few rounds. Thinking that he had the nuts in this game, Jess started playing and wound up losing $700. He would rather have lost his house. When he finally dragged himself back to the barns he was in shock, white as a sheet. Poor guy, he had never gambled on anything at all except roping and here he'd gone off for a big number in that crooked Monte game.

Clark McEntire (Reba's daddy) from Kiowa, Oklahoma won the steer roping championship in 1957 and '58 and again in 1961. Everett Shaw from Stonewall won the steer roping championship three times. Marvell Rogers, a black man who was a great hand and worked all the events except roping, was a friend of mine from Elk City, Oklahoma. I won the roping contest at Russell, Kansas, and while I was out in the middle of the arena being awarded my belt buckle, Marvell was standing right there by the side of me getting four of them—he had won the bareback riding, the saddle bronc riding, the bulldogging, and the bull riding.

Marvell used to smoke cigars all the time, even when he was riding a bull. One time at the rodeo in New York, there was a really rank bull with a mean reputation for roughing up cowboys. Everybody started talking about this bull and wondering whether Marvell could ride it, so they put together a deal to get the bull in the arena the next morning before the rodeo started. All the cowboys had gathered around to watch the show, betting on whether Marvell could ride the sonnagun. I bet that he could.

He got on that big black bull, took the rope up, tightened it just right, and called for the bull. Well, that sonnabitch bull jumped out of the chute, turned back, and bucked hard trying to throw Marvell, cigar hanging out of his mouth, into the dirt. We were all amazed that he could take that much punishment, but Marvell made a perfect ride on that ton of bull—and I made a lot of money.

Jimmy Whaley also was from Oklahoma. He and I once went to Seattle a few days before the rodeo started. We only had a couple hundred dollars when we got there, so right after we checked into the motel I mentioned to Jimmy that we needed to make some money.

"Yeah, we sure do," he said. "Hell, it's four days before the rodeo starts. How we gonna get some?"

"Let's grab a sheet off this bed," I suggested. "We'll buy a piece of ply board and stretch the sheet across it. Then I'll draw a craps layout on it and we'll take it out to the barn. Then when people come in to get their stock, they'll see that we have a craps game like they do in Las Vegas."

He liked the idea. "We'll bar ace-deuce on the back line instead of two sixes, which is twice as strong. I'll drop all the hardways down to eight and six to one. People will have to walk around the table to get to their horses and they'll stop and some of them will play. We'll give them a $3 limit and hell, that's pretty nigh impossible to lose."

So we jumped up, ripped the sheet off the bed, bought some plywood and thumb tacks, and I took a three-foot ruler and a Crayola and drew a craps layout on it. I'm a good artist, you know. Jimmy stood behind our layout like a stickman and I'm in front of it like in Vegas. It wasn't long before we got the game going and started making good money at it.

After a while Bill Linderman came by. Bill was a famous cowboy in those days, a world champion from Red Lodge, Montana whose brother Bud also was a great cowboy.

"What're you all doin'?" he asked.

"We got a craps game here, Bill," I told him. He liked to gamble and had been to Las Vegas a few times. I'd never been to Vegas myself.

"What kinda limit you got?"

"Three dollars," Jimmy said.

"Three dollars?! Shit, I don't wanna waste my time."

"Bill's a Vegas player," I said to Jimmy, winking at him. "We'll give him a $10 limit."

"Well, that's different. Let's get goin'!" Bill said and started shooting the dice. Lost $1,100. He was so pissed off I thought we were gonna have to fight him, but he paid us off.

★ Benny Binion and the NFR ★

I competed in the very first National Finals Rodeo in 1959 in Dallas. Chuck Connors, star of "The Rifleman" TV show, was the celebrity star that year. After its run in Dallas, the NFR was moved to Los Angeles from 1962-64 and then to Oklahoma City, where it stayed for the next twenty years. It probably still would be held in Oklahoma if it hadn't been for an incident involving Benny Binion, founder of the Horseshoe Casino in Vegas and a close friend of mine.

For years Benny had been entering a stagecoach in the rodeo parade at the NFR. The coach had the logo of the Horseshoe Casino painted on both sides and was hooked up to a perfectly matched team of horses. It cost Benny around $15,000 or so to transport his four matched teams of horses and the coach from Montana to Oklahoma, but around 1983 or so, the officials wouldn't let him enter it in the rodeo parade that year. I don't know exactly why, but I think it might've been because all those Oklahoma Baptists didn't want anything that advertised gambling showing up in the parade.

Benny got so hot that he promised everybody that he would pay their entry fees if they'd hold the rodeo in Las Vegas. As it turned out, that was a winning proposition because the NFR has been a huge success in Vegas ever since it moved there in 1985 with prizes bigger than a barn, a lot bigger than they ever were in Oklahoma City.

The world of rodeos and horses and the whole Western entertainment scene opened the door to fame and fortune for a lot of cowboys. I knew many of them personally and met a whole lot of others during my heyday on the rodeo circuit—men such as Ben Johnson, Gene Autry, and Slim Pickens.

COWBOY CELEBRITIES & OTHER FAMOUS FOLKS

"Cowboys aren't a vanishing breed—
you just can't see 'em from the road!"
— Baxter Black

Ben Johnson got into the movies by accident. He was just a young cowboy working the rodeo circuit when he got his big break. Ben and I used to make some rodeos together and one winter we went to Newhall, California to practice our roping before the Fort Worth Fat Stock Show started. The weather was good there and you could practice your roping and train your horses. Ben had been hired to wrangle the horses for a movie that John Ford was directing in Newhall, California, which was the setting for a lot of the old cowboy movies. Dan Poor, who was a stuntman for the movies as well as a calf roper and bulldogger, and Buck Sorrels were there, too.

The female star of this Western movie was riding in a buggy when the horses ran away with her carriage, just like you see in a lot of the old cowboy films. When Ben saw what had happened, he jumped on a horse real quick, raced after the buggy, stopped it, and saved the lady just like it was a stunt. Ford saw the whole thing. "I'll never make another movie without Ben Johnson in it," he told everybody standing around him. Ben and I stayed in Newhall for about a month practicing roping and getting our horses in shape and then went on down to Fort Worth for the Fort Worth Fat Stock Show and from there to Phoenix in March.

Ben later went on to star in "She Wore a Yellow Ribbon" and other films and won an Academy Award for his role in "The Last Picture Show." Years later Benny Binion, Ben Johnson, and I were eating dinner together at the Horseshoe in Las Vegas and Benny said to me, "You know what Ben's worth now? Over $600 million!" Seems that when he started making a big salary in the movies, Ben started buying up land around Malibu, California and made a fortune on it.

One time Ben came to Snyder, Texas and stayed with me for a few days. They were having a dance at Big Springs, about fifty miles away, and I drove him over there. He was a nice guy, tall and good looking, and when we walked in that place the women thought they'd died and gone to heaven—there was Ben Johnson standing right there in front of them.

Chill Wills is another movie star that I got to know quite well. He was a good friend of Benny Binion's and used to hang around the Horseshoe in Las Vegas a lot. Chill gambled high, and would bet a quarter on roulette. Had a big car with a set of steer horns on the front of it that he used to park in front of the Horseshoe.

★ Willie 'n' the Boys ★

I met Willie Nelson about thirty years ago in Houston when he was putting on a show in a nightclub there. He's from Waco, Texas and I knew that he loved to play poker. One time Willie had played for three days straight in a poker game in Corsicana. When he was done playing, he didn't bother to rent a motel room, just went out to his car and fell asleep in the back seat.

So I invited him out to the house to join our game after the show. We set up some poker tables, a nice bar, and laid out some food, but after Willie and his crew got there, his manager wouldn't let him play with us. All the ladies were there and so instead of playing, he started singing. Sang "Turn Out the Lights, The Party's Over" before the song ever came out. He sang for them all night long but boy, about six o'clock in the morning I was getting pretty tired so I told everybody, "I hate to tell you all this, but the party *is* over."

One time Willie and Benny Binion and I were sitting in the Sombrero Room at the Horseshoe having dinner when Bunker Hunt, the big oilman from Dallas, came in.

"Benny, I'm looking for some land out here that might have gold on it," Bunker said. "Know anybody that's got some for sale?"

"No," Benny told him, "I'm lookin' for somebody that's already got the gold."

They say that Willie sold "Hello Walls" to Jim Reeves for $50 because he was broke at the time. It became a number-one hit song. Willie's a famous singer these days, but he's still just a regular guy, you know what I mean?

Glenn McCarthy, the big oilman in Houston, used to have a place called The Cork Club, a private club upstairs in a big building right in downtown Houston. Glenn staged a show every week with a big-time entertainer in it and I met quite a few famous people that way. I joined the club because they had a poker game where all the oilmen played poker for a few hours after lunch every day. I really did like that deal. That's how I met Pearl Bailey. She was something else, a really nice lady and a good singer. After her show one night, she gave us a fortune-telling reading on the cards. I also met and got to know Wayne Newton at the Cork Club long before he became famous as "The Midnight Idol" in Las Vegas where he used to pack in the biggest crowds the town had ever seen.

I've also met a fair share of cowboy movie stars. One time Richard Egan was doing a show in Dallas and rented a condominium where I lived. I had a beautiful condo with a blackjack game going in it and every night after his show, Richard would come over with his friend, Rory Calhoun, to have a few drinks and play some blackjack with us. I didn't want a lot of cars parked out in front of the place, so I had limousine service. People would call and we'd send the limo to their house to pick them up. They could play blackjack, have something to eat, drink, and enjoy themselves. You could hardly get in the place during the couple of weeks that Richard and Rory were playing there. Seemed like every starry-eyed girl in town wanted to play blackjack while those two were in town telling their stories and entertaining the crowd.

Tex Ritter used to put on shows at the rodeos and I got to know him very well. One time Tex and Bill Elliott, and Casey Tibbs and I were all at the rodeo in Gladewater. About fifteen miles away in Kilgore there was a great big dance hall with beer named the Shady Grove. You could drink whiskey there, too, but you had to carry your bottle in and buy a setup. One night after the rodeo, I took them all to the Shady Grove. All the folks around there knew me and their eyes got big when I came walking in with Tex and Bill and Casey. Everybody gathered around us and after Tex had downed a few drinks, he sang his famous song, "Rye Whiskey." Bill Elliott once tried to buy my best horse, Good Eye. Offered me $2,500 for him but I wouldn't sell him because he was such a good horse. Couldn't sell something that I was making my living on.

William Boyd, better known as Hopalong Cassidy, was the star of the Houston Fat Stock Show one year. He would come into the arena and say, "I can't sing and my horse don't do tricks," referring to Gene Autry and Roy Rogers. Then he'd ride his big white horse around the ring and all the little kids would come down over the fence and he'd shake hands with every one of them. Got paid about $30,000 for doing that while some of us cowboys were sleeping in horse trailers trying to make $800.

Dale Robertson used to put on acts around a lot of the rodeos. Starred in the "Wells Fargo" television show and several movies. The first time I met Dale was at Fort Smith, Arkansas at a rodeo that Homer Todd was producing, and later on we became pretty good friends. A few years back he sold his place in Oklahoma City. Put $680,000 from the sale into a bank there but the bank collapsed a short time later. What a tough break. He told Benny Binion and me about it one time when he was sitting with us at the Horseshoe. And I met John Wayne in San Antone while he was making the movie "The Alamo." I was playing poker there and we met in a restaurant and talked Western stuff together for quite a while.

"Old dogs, little children, and watermelon wine"—what a song! It was Tom T. Hall's masterpiece. One year I was having supper at a dinner club in Dallas where Tom was doing a show. At that time I was selling jewelry on the side and liked "Watermelon Wine" so much, I gave him a nice ring to show my appreciation. He said a nice thank-you to me during the show. I also met Elvis Presley at a big nightclub in East Texas long before he became famous. He put on a singing show for us that was second to none.

When I first met Edward G. Robinson in New York at Madison Square Garden, he looked like he had just gotten off the set of "Key Largo." Black-headed, smoking a cigar, and escorting a beautiful lady, he looked just like he did in the movies. A lot of famous folks like Edward G. liked to go to the rodeos and then sit over at the Belvedere Bar across the street from the arena, watch the cowboys drink and listen to them talk about this and that, the rodeoing and all. It was something different for them and they enjoyed it. That's how I met a lot of them. Even met Jim Thorpe, the greatest runner there ever was, at the Belvedere, and drank with him all afternoon. He was quite a guy and we had some good conversation that day.

After my rodeo days when I had the AmVets club in Dallas, Mickey Mantle would come up to my club occasionally with a friend of his who played poker. Mickey played baseball perfectly but he didn't play cards, so he would sit at the bar and drink beer for two or three hours and that's how we got acquainted. There's a joke that used to go around about when Mickey got to the pearly gates in heaven. St. Peter said, "I just can't let you in here, Mickey. You've been too wild in your lifetime." So Mickey turned around and was starting to leave when St. Peter said, "Wait a minute. Before you leave, would you sign this baseball for me?"

Jack Dempsey is another sports hero that I met. One year while I was rodeoing at Madison Square Garden, I had dinner at Jack's restaurant. He was there that evening and I introduced myself to him. Dempsey even came to Tyler once at the invitation of Bobby Mansell, a big oilman who loved boxing and had built an arena in Tyler where he tried to promote some fights. Jack came there to talk with him and I joined them one evening.

Red Bone, who had been the Northwest heavyweight champion, used to be Dempsey's sparring partner before he went into the restaurant business in Denver. Red later became a senator and I knew him quite well. In 1984 I was in Denver playing some poker near the restaurant that Red owned and I recalled a story that had made the headlines two decades earlier. Bill Linderman, a rodeo friend of mine from Red Lodge, Montana was a great big guy who was the world champion cowboy in 1950 and 1953 and served six terms as president of the Rodeo Cowboys Association. Bill and Red Bone were friends, so he always ate in Red's restaurant when he was Denver. One winter night in 1965 Bill asked Red to cash a check for $200. Bill liked to do funny things sometimes, so at the bottom of his check he wrote, "If this ain't no good, I'll see you in hell. If it's good I'll see you in heaven." The next night Bill boarded a commercial airliner bound for Denver. It crashed and killed everybody on it. Red Bones never cashed Bill Linderman's check—he framed it and hung it on the wall in his restaurant.

Another sports figure that I have met is Brent Mossberger, the sportscaster who interviewed me at the World Series of Poker in 1984 when I placed second to Jack Keller in the championship event.

"Cowboy, how'd you sleep last night after losing that $50,000 pot?" Brent asked me.

"Slept like a baby," I told him. "I'd sleep an hour and then wake up and cry for an hour." Brent thought that was funny.

Wilt Chamberlain was at the Commerce Club in California one night when I was playing there. He shook hands with me—boy, is he a tall guy. I was dressed up like a cowboy and I think that he got a kick out of meeting me. Of course, I would've had to stand on a stool to talk to him eyeball to eyeball. Wilt once bragged that he had made love to twenty thousand women—what a record.

My lifelong friend Claude Kimberlin, a rodeo man, has made quite a name for himself in Las Vegas. "Bronco Claude," as I call him, was a top-notch bronc rider and a lot of cowboys still remember his famous ride on "Five Minutes to Midnight." After he got out of rodeoing for a living in the late 1940s, Claude booked sports in Texas and Oklahoma for a while and then became a representative for the Hilton Hotel and Casino in Las Vegas steering big clients their way. He probably knows more millionaires than anybody else in the world. Claude and Benny Binion were good friends and in 1982 Benny recommended Claude to Steve Wynn, who hired him as an executive host for the Golden Nugget in downtown Vegas. Today Claude is the Southwest Regional Marketing Director for the MGM-Mirage Corporation, bringing big gamblers to the Mirage, Bellagio, MGM Grand, and Golden Nugget.

Claude and his business partner, James Harper, raise bucking bulls for rodeos. A while back they sold "Rampage" and "Jim Jam" for $65,000 each, the most money ever paid for rodeo bulls. Rampage was voted the best rodeo bull in 1999 by the Professional Bull Riders association and Jim Jam was only ridden three times in four years. Rampage was taken off the circuit because they were afraid that he might kill some cowboy, that's how rank he was. In fact, a bull rider from Canada got killed in Albuquerque in 2000 when a bull fell on his chest. Riding bulls is no easy way to make a living.

The PBR sponsors a bull riding championship every October in Las Vegas and adds $1 million to the prize pool. Claude and James furnish the bulls for the event. Ty Murray won the championship in 1999 for $504,000 and Cody Hart came in second for $400,000. The champion bull rider on the rodeo circuit that year, Mike White, only won $99,000 and he had to make all those rodeos to do it, whereas Ty only had to win one big event to take home half a million. Back in the days when Claude and I were rodeoing, $400 or $500 day money was really something.

I got to know a lot of cowboy movie stars even before they became famous. Slim Pickens started off as a professional rodeo clown. He was the clown at the Calgary Stampede and he and I became real good friends. Slim was about half cowboy but when he started making all those movies, he quit hanging around the rodeos. He appeared in "One-Eyed Jacks," with Marlon Brando. Slim's dead now and I miss him.

Some of the other cowboy stars I knew in the old days included Randolph Scott, Yakima Canutt, and Chuck Connors. I met Randolph one year at the rodeo in Denver. He was a great Western movie star and a real nice guy. He looked serious all the time but he was easy to talk with. They say that Randolph was wealthy because he knew how to take care of his money. Yakima was a stunt man who used to perform in the rodeos years ago. He planned all the stunts for the movie *Where Eagles Dare*. Clint Eastwood and Richard Burton starred in it, but Yakima did all their stunt work for them. I met Chuck Connors, "The Rifleman," at the first National Finals Rodeo ever held at Dallas and I got to know him well. He was the star of the show, quite an event for all the kids.

Roy Rogers starred in the rodeo at Madison Square Garden a few times along with Trigger and Dale Evans. Roy was a nice guy, a Christian, and he and Dale adopted a lot of kids. The Sons of the Pioneers were playing for Roy one year when he was performing at the Garden. I always had a poker game going during the rodeo in New York and the Sons of the Pioneers played in my game—lost everything except their guitars! I don't know how they could still sing and play for Roy each night. Knowing that Roy had plenty of money, I suggested, "Why don't you all bring Roy up here sometime to play with us?"

"Oh no," they answered. "He's too religious. Don't tell him we're playing."

"Well, it's not too bad to play poker," I said. "Roy might want to set in the game just to get away from everything for a while." But he never did.

I also knew Gene Autry quite well and saw him lots of times at the rodeos. One year after he had performed in New York he stopped in Louisville, Kentucky where they were having a rodeo on the football field and put on a big parade down Main Street. That night at the rodeo so many people were there, you couldn't get a seat. After his last performance, Gene came out and rode around the arena and threw his hat into the grandstand—I guess he had plenty of those big white hats that he always wore. Gene wound up owning the Angels baseball team in California.

Andy Devine, who played the comic sidekick of a lot of the stars in Western movies, used to put on acts at the rodeos and I met him once at Chillicothe, Missouri where he was performing. That was the time when I tied my last calf in 9.4

seconds, the fastest time they'd ever heard of in those parts. Grandpa Jones was a funny guy who appeared on "Hee Haw." Grandpa didn't play poker, but I met him at the Frontier Casino in Vegas when he was there with a card-playing friend of his for Jack Straus' poker tournament.

I've met a lot of entertainers rodeoing and playing poker. I've known Reba McEntire since she was a baby because I used to rodeo with her daddy, Clark McEntire, who was the three-time world's champion steer roper in the late 1950s. One time at the National Finals Rodeo, Reba was performing and when she got off the stage, she came over and sat with her mother and Clark and me and we reminisced about old childhood memories.

One year when I was flying from Las Vegas to Dallas, I sat next to Jerry Lee Lewis. Jerry was quite a piano player, a wild man who could really work up some steam on the keys. He was always in on some kind of a jackpot and so he was very interested in my poker and rodeo stories. One night Jerry was at Bob Stupak's old joint, Vegas World, during a poker tournament. The winner of the no-limit event got to play Jerry heads-up for a restored vintage Rolls Royce that Stupak had parked out front. I really wanted to win that thing, but I came in second or third. Anyway, Jerry Lewis won the heads-up match but since he was just there to help Stupak out, Bob didn't have to give him the car.

A lot of people know Gabe Kaplan from TV's "Welcome Back, Kotter." What some of them don't know is that he's also a big poker player. He has narrated the World Series of Poker video tape several times, including the last time that Stuey Ungar won it in 1997. One time after I finished playing a big lowball game at the Horseshoe, I walked across the street to the Golden Nugget where Gabe was playing. When I got there, Gabe asked me if I wanted to play some heads-up poker.

"I've always wanted to play against a movie star," I kidded. Wound up beating him out of $30,000 before he finally gave me up. These days Gabe runs around with Jerry Buss and

Frank Mariani, owners of the Los Angeles Lakers. Gabe's a great poker player and people in the poker world respect him as a player and gentleman.

Telly Savales, "Kojak," also was a helluva poker player as well as a great actor. One year in the $10,000 buy-in championship event at the World Series, he finished in the top twenty. He was one of my favorite actors, could play any part in any movie. I got to know him and his brother really well when he was playing poker at the Horseshoe.

Even though I wasn't on the silver screen like a lot of them were, most of the celebrities that I met in the old days seemed to be as interested in me and my cowboy and poker stories as I was in meeting them and hearing their tales. Most of them were just regular people and we enjoyed ourselves together. When I was in Newhall practicing roping with Ben Johnson, I could've gotten a Screen Actors Guild card for $250. As I think back, if I'd just kept hanging around Ben I guarantee you that I'd have been in the movies, too, but I was too busy rodeoing and doing nothing. You never know what might've happened in your life if you'd done this or that. But I figure that everything happens the right way in our lives and I know for sure that I have had a guardian angel looking over me all these years.

★ The Women in My Life ★

There were always a lot of young gals hanging around the rodeos hoping to make it with the cowboys, but as for me, I never did go with any of those gals because you had to be around the same people all the time at the rodeos and I didn't want to be obligated or anything like that, you know what I mean? It was like you didn't go to bed with people that you did business with. I'd rather find a girl from my hometown who didn't know anything about rodeoing.

I've had some good wives and I've had some bad ones. No, I can't say that any of them were bad—maybe the life that I lived would bear on anyone's nerves. Folks have asked me why I married so many girls, eight of them in all. "Out of respect to their mothers," I always tell them. And every woman that I married had a good mother, believe it or not. In fact some of their mothers liked me better than their daughters did. My wives and their mothers were always good to me and I was nice to them, too. If they ever needed anything and didn't have any money, I would send them some money if I had it, even after we were divorced, because like I've said before, I don't burn any bridges.

I first got married when I was nineteen years old to a telephone operator in Tyler, Texas. Just before the ceremony Daddy told me, "You know, son, two can live as cheap as one—but just half as long." Ten years later in 1959 when I came back from a rodeo in New York, I married Patricia Grambling, a real nice gal from Tyler who came from a good family. Patricia and I had a son named James Alan Wolford, one of the nicest boys that I've ever known. One of the saddest days of my life was when James Alan died in 1998. Patricia's gone now, too. Seems like all the good people are gone and I'm still around—and I don't know why.

Ever since I met my wife Evelyn, I've been a pretty straight shooter. "We got married in Reno in 1977 in between poker hands," I tell folks, and then add a joke about the years when Evelyn and I traveled together on the poker circuit that goes like this: "We had eaten dinner at some friends' house and when it got to be around ten o'clock at night, I said to Evelyn, 'Well, honey, I guess we'd better go home and go to bed now.' So she walked out to the driveway and jumped in the back seat of our car."

This little story always makes her mad. Evelyn is streetwise and she's one of the smartest people I've ever met—she can do or learn anything, and she's read every book in the world so that she can talk about any subject that comes up. She owns an antiques business in Carlsbad, California and does a lot of business on the Internet. And like I said, trying to keep up with a road gambler like me is a hard life to lead, but Evelyn has done it better than any other woman in the world.

★ Hanging Up My Rope and Saddle ★

Rodeoing was a great life. You'd just take off, throw your Coleman stove in the car, and be gone for eight or nine months. If you had a flat tire up in Montana, you'd fix it yourself with a cold patch and a hand pump because you didn't want to throw off a dollar at a filling station. All us cowboys helped each other out. If a guy was in the lead in the roping, you'd get down and kick his calf out of the chute to be sure that he got out straight even though he was beating you. I didn't know until now how good my rodeo days were—I loved rodeoing and I miss seeing the good people that were around it in the old days.

If I made $20,000 or $30,000 a year, that was real good money and I spent it on horses and girls and stuff. I never was a big drinker like a few of my friends. Most people that I know who are famous for drinking and playing poker are famous for what they lost, not for what they won. Some cowboys who made money invested it and made money off it, but I wasn't one of them. Not many of us were thinking about building a future—my future was the next rodeo or poker game. And I enjoyed it. I was my own boss and could go where I wanted to. If I went to a rodeo and found a good poker game, I'd stay for two weeks and play poker. While I was on the rodeo circuit I actually won more money at poker than I did at rodeoing.

Of course I never thought about getting old. I never think about it now either. I don't feel very old and so age doesn't bother me. Rodeoing was a hard way to make easy money but that's all I knew how to do—I was good at it and I enjoyed it, too. I've never done anything that I didn't enjoy doing. I always have to enjoy doing something or have some drive or ambition toward it in order for me to be successful at it.

Back then we drove all over the place going from rodeo to rodeo, carefree and loose, but it's a different story today. Riders fly from one city to the other and it's a serious sport with them. A good roping horse, if you can find one, these days costs $50,000; a trailer costs $15,000; and a nice car costs $60,000. Back then you could buy a good horse for between $500 and $1,000; you could get a trailer for $300; and you could buy a nice car for $1,000. Room rent was $6 or $8 a night. Sometimes I think that in the long run, we might've made as much money in the old days as they do now because our expenses were so much lower.

The poker in those days was a similar kind of deal. Players drove from town to town just like the rodeo riders, and they often traveled with a partner. People in the poker world would help you out if you played well enough. When you started going bad or got broke, you wouldn't have to ask anybody for a loan—they would just hand you some money, knowing that you'd pay them back. Making money at poker and rodeoing was quite a challenge but I enjoyed the chase.

I'd do it all over again if I could, but I wouldn't play as much poker until after I had won a few more championships. I figure that I probably could have been the world champion calf roper more often if I had just rodeoed all the time instead of playing poker, too. I was more of a go-round roper, a day money guy, because the day money paid as much as the average. When things went right, nobody could catch up with me. First I went for the dough and then I went to find a poker game. I might go to a rodeo and stay in town for several weeks after it had ended if there was a good game going on. One time in Ada, Oklahoma my horse got crippled and I stayed there for two months playing poker. Everybody in the game was carrying a pistol except me.

When I was thirty years old I quit rodeoing. The methods of roping calves had changed. Riders were dismounting from the right side of the horse and flanking the calves, getting two seconds the best of it. I wasn't winning as often as I did when we got off on the left side and legged them down. I didn't change to the new way of roping because I was thirty years old and didn't want to start anything new at that age.

I've noticed that in all sports—boxing, football, all of them—you can't beat youth. When you try to hang on, you wind up being a has-been. That's why I switched to playing poker for a living. I'd been playing the game for twenty years so it wasn't a big change for me and I didn't feel bad about quitting the rodeo—I'd won about as much as I could win anyway and I didn't want to just hang on. Like Jack Nicklaus once said, "If I'm not good enough to win, I'm not going to golf anymore." You might not be able to beat youth in sports, but you can play poker until you're ninety. It's okay to drop dead at the poker table, but it's not okay to drop dead as a rodeo rider.

But even though I haven't been a rodeo professional for more than forty years, I still dream about it. I'm in a big rodeo with Ace and I draw a big wild white-faced calf. The band is blaring and the crowd jumps to its feet, cheering us into the arena. Ole Ace and I come barreling out of the chute and then...

It's strange that after all these years, I dream about the rodeo but I never dream about poker. I reckon I'm still a cowboy at heart.

ROAD GAMBLERS

*"There are only three things to being a good outside scuffler:
knowing when you've got the best of it, money management,
and managing yourself. That third thing is the hard part."*
— *Puggy Pearson*

In 1960 I went home to Tyler and barned my roping
horse at Daddy's ranch for the last time. I had been playing
poker around rodeos since I was ten years old so it seemed
natural to me to start playing cards for a living. Of course I
already knew a lot of the regulars on the poker circuit—men
like Johnny Moss, Doc Ramsey, Morris Shapiro, and Mac
McCorquodale—because I had played with them in the '50s
at the Elks Club in Tyler or Waco during the winter when I
came home from rodeoing. In fact, during the last three years
I was roping, I played poker more and more and rodeoed less
and less.

I had heard about the good games in Corpus Christi, so
just after I quit the rodeo circuit, I went there to play. When I
walked into the Corpus Elks Club, I flashed my membership

card from Tyler and they went to get Jesse Alto, who ran the joint. "Sure, you can play in our game," he said. It was a good game; I mean it was a *good* game, a high game. They'd gamble with you. One Friday night the guys asked why everybody called me Cowboy.

"Oh hell, it's just a nickname. I used to rope calves out on my uncle's ranch and hog-tie them," I explained, wrapping my arm around a certain way to show them how I did it. That's the way a sucker would've described it, you know.

"Say, you think you could still rope one?"

"I don't know, I don't even remember the last time I was on a horse but I probably could."

"Well, every Saturday night they have a rodeo out at the fairgrounds and there's one tomorrow night. If you think you can rope one of them wild calves, why don't we enter you?"

"Well okay, but hell, like I said, I don't even have a horse." Of course I could ride any horse in the world, it was just like driving a car after you haven't been at the wheel for a long time.

"What kinda time you think you could hog-tie one in?"

"Hell, I don't know, maybe a minute."

"A minute?! There ain't no way you can tie a calf in a minute!"

"Yes, I believe I could." I forgot to mention that I had roped a calf at Madison Square Garden in 11.03 seconds, the all-time record.

"Well, how much do you wanna bet?"

"All I've got." They thought I was bluffing at them.

"How much you got?"

"I don't know, lemme see." I counted about $2,000 in front of me, $1,400 or so in my pocket, and my traveling buddy Jerry had about $200 on him. "Guess I can bet $3,600."

"Okay, we'll take that bet," they said, laughing. "If you want to bet more than that, just put up the cash." I wish I'd had $50,000 because I could've doubled it. And with that, I called the rodeo office and entered the roping contest for the next morning.

Fifty ropers showed up for the event. When a rodeo has that many ropers entered in a one-night show, ten of them perform during the rodeo and the other forty rope after the rodeo when the go-round is over. I got lucky and drew in the first ten to rope. The rodeo started at seven o'clock, but Jerry and I got there about five thirty. The first guy I ran into was Burley Fellows, a guy that I had roped with while I was on the circuit. "Byron," he said (none of the cowboys called me Cowboy, they called me Byron). "What the hell you doin' here?"

"I'm playing poker over at the Elks Club. Just got here yesterday and they've got a helluva game. I'm through with rodeoing, just got finished with the Cow Palace about two weeks ago and that's the last one I'll ever make."

"Well then, what're you doin' in this ropin'?"

"I bet all those gamblers everything I have that I can tie a calf in less than a minute. They don't know I'm a real cowboy." He just hollered at that. "I'll give you 20 percent if you'll loan me one of your horses," I added.

"I've got a horse that you'll really like," he said and showed me a pretty little bald-faced horse. "He'll give you a good ride, scores good, jumps right out there and gives you a good lope. Stops good and works the rope good." So I rode him around a little bit and he was as advertised, just perfect.

"Reckon I'll have to borrow your rope and piggin' strings and all that, too," I said, "but you'll get 20 percent." Hell, 20 percent of $3,600 was more than the calf roping paid that night, since with fifty ropers at $20 entry fee apiece, first place was only about $400.

Just before the rodeo began, here came Jesse and about eight other poker players. They sat right by the roping chute at the far end of the arena. They thought they had the nuts—they were really gonna take this sucker off, the one they called "Cowboy."

The bareback riding was always the first event in rodeos back then, followed by the calf ropers. I was the fifth roper up. The calves weighed about two hundred pounds, seemed like lightweights to me since I was used to roping those three hundred-pounders in the big rodeos. Hell, I could tie those little calves blindfolded. About the only way that I could lose the bet was to have a heart attack—it was just like finding a bird nest laying on the ground.

With all the gamblers watching, I walked out the side gate of the arena, threw the rope around my head to get the kinks out of it—kinda like practicing your golf swing before you hit the ball—and put the piggin' string in my mouth. One of the poker players told me later that they were all thinking, "Reckon that sonnabitch really is a cowboy. We're goners."

I didn't want to take any chance of breaking the barrier and getting a ten-second fine so I just let the calf get to the line, the horse jumped right out there, and I roped him clean around the neck. The horse stopped and I ran to the calf, legged him down, strung him, eased his legs up, and did two wraps and a hooey in eleven seconds flat, a fast time in a little rodeo like that. I think the next best time was 13.2. Won the thing just as easy as drinking a glass of iced tea.

Those gamblers were sick. They didn't watch another roper or another event, just got up and headed straight to the Elks Club before I could even get to them to say hello. I didn't stay to see the other ropers, just asked Burley to pick up the money for me if I won it and I'd give him his percentage of my bet with the poker players the next day.

"Byron," he said, "I wonder what these sonsabitches are thinking now about this sucker they call 'Cowboy.'" I went back to the room and showered, put on my slacks, silk shirt, sport coat, and alligator shoes, combed my hair nice, and headed for the Elks Club.

"Damn, we're lucky, boy!" Jesse said when I walked into the club. They had the money waiting for me in an envelope with all the bets clearly written on the front of it.

"Whadda you mean?" I asked.

"Hell, you coulda won $50,000 off of us!"

"I just wish I'd had that much on me!" I know they'd

have bet me that much because those guys would bet big on anything—they usually had $40,000 to $50,000 on the table.

★ The Red Men's Club in Dallas ★

The best games were at the Red Men's Club on the corner of Irving Street in downtown Dallas, so I rented an apartment and played poker there every day. The club was owned by Raymond Farrow, who also owned the liquor store downstairs. You had to walk through the liquor store and up the stairs to the club, which had about fifteen hundred square feet with a little kitchen through the swinging doors in the back of the joint near the restroom. Two poker tables and a small cage where you bought your chips were located up front. The limit games were always $5/$10 and there usually was a big no-limit hold'em game going on, too.

A lot of famous people played at the Red Men's Club. Mac McCorquodale, Bob Hooks from Wills Point, Texas, Cotton Bullard, O.T. Bounds, Morris Shapiro, Buck Winston, Bobby Chapman (the highest player in Dallas), Titanic Thompson and I—we all played no-limit hold'em. Doyle Brunson used to play with us occasionally and Doc Ramsey, Martin Cramer, Hugh Shoemaker, Blondie Forbes, and Freddy "Sarge" Ferris (he had been in the Air Force so we called him Sarge) all played there from time to time.

Before he bought the joint, Raymond had been in the liquor and food business and he couldn't play a lick of poker. No telling how much he lost in the game. One time while we were playing, Morris ordered a sandwich saying, "Put a slice of onion on it for me." At the time, Raymond was $20,000 loser in the game. A big gray-haired guy, he got up from the table to make the sandwich. After a minute or two, Raymond stuck his head out the kitchen door and said, "Morris, I forgot to tell you that a slice of onion costs a nickel extra." You see some funny things in poker—Raymond was stuck $20,000 and he was worrying about losing a nickel!

Henry Rosenberg played with us in Dallas, too—I remember once when he had two aces in a big pot and got beat with them for a lot of money. Henry raised hell when he got loser. He took those two aces and threw them way up in the air. Somehow or other, the ace of hearts hit a crack between the acoustic panels in the ceiling and just stuck there. They never did take it down. I wouldn't doubt that heart ace is still hanging there today.

Mac McCorquodale, who is in the Poker Hall of Fame, played at the Red Men's a lot and I got to know him well. Mac always dressed like a king with silk shirts that had big black pearl buttons on them. He's the one who took hold'em to Las Vegas at the California Club. He asked me to go with him, but I didn't have sense enough to do it. If I had gone, I probably would've gotten rich. Mac was a character. He would win, win, win and then every once in a while, he'd get to drinking Cordon Bleu and throw off all his money. When he got drunk once in Dallas, I drove him to a few places around town and he was the wildest old guy I'd ever seen, drinking and tipping the piano player. I didn't think I'd ever get him to go home.

One time Mac went to Hot Springs, Arkansas for the races during the days when Hot Springs had open gambling. He got there a few days early, so he went to a local place to play some five-card stud. Turned out it was a take-off joint where you couldn't win a dime. In this one hand, Mac had aces on fourth street and his opponent's highest card showing was something like a jack. McCorquodale moved in on him. "Can you get insurance here?" Mac asked. They told him no. "Can you cut the cards?" No, that wasn't allowed. "Well, can you borrow $200 to get home on?" Yes, you could do that. And sure enough, when the last card came off the deck, the other guy broke McCorquodale! Doyle and the others still talk about this story.

Mac told us about the time that he had been playing poker at the Elks Club in Waco and had been drinking a little at the table. He left the club in a taxi $30,000 winner and went to another place to play some more poker, but when he got there he couldn't find his money. That sort of sobered him up. He was sure that he'd left his wad in the taxi but the cabby told him that he hadn't found anything. Mac was sick—he offered a $2,500 reward for anyone who returned the money to him. Two days later when he went back to the Elks Club, Mac remembered that he had hung his jacket on the coat stand in the corner while he was playing poker there. He took it off the rack and in the inside coat pocket sat the $30,000, right where it had been for the past two days.

That joint in Waco was something else—it was upstairs and had a big bar in the front and a poker room in the back with windows that had been all shuttered over with plywood for years. The Elks finally decided to knock off the plywood and put in new windows to get some ventilation. Two of those old gamblers who had been playing up there for nearly twenty years keeled over dead within a month—I figure they couldn't stand all that fresh air.

The guys at the Red Men's club in Dallas called me "Cowboy" because I always wore my rodeo clothes and cowboy hat to play poker. One day somebody asked me what I used to do when I was rodeoing. "I was a roper," I answered.

"What can you rope?"

"I used to rope calves, but hell, I can rope anything."

"Anything?"

"Yeah, anything. Hell, I can even rope a chicken."

"A chicken?"

They didn't know it, but I probably had roped two thousand of my mother's chickens a year when I was a little boy—and I got about half that many whippings for roping them. I could take a lightweight rope and lasso one around its neck blindfolded, I was so good at it.

"Well, what'll you bet that you can rope a chicken right here and now?"

"I'll bet $2,100." That was all the money I had on me.

"Okay, we'll go down to the poultry house and get a chicken. And when we get back, you'll rope him on your first throw, right?"

"That's right, on my first throw."

The bet was on. We put up all the money and somebody left for the poultry house. In the meantime, I cut a sash cord off the window blinds, tied a little loop in it, and made a perfect chicken rope out of it. The poker game broke up, one of the tables was moved back to the edge of the room, and I got ready to rope the rooster. When they arrived with the chicken, they put him down on the floor—and boy, they thought they had the nuts.

He was a big ole rooster, sort of wild at first from just getting out of the poultry house and coming into a strange place, so I just stalked him around the room until he calmed down. He pranced around for a while and finally strutted over near a corner in the room. I clucked like a hen—I had it down pat—and he stuck his head up. Zing! I roped him perfectly. They were so amazed and pissed off that I could rope a chicken, that they didn't know what to say. I can still rope a chicken, don't worry 'bout that. One time last year I tried to get a bet on down in Oceanside where I work and damned near got it, but everybody "chickened" out on the deal.

★ Fadin' the White Line ★

In the 1960s when I was thirty-something, I sometimes would leave my home base in Dallas to go play poker in Tyler or Waco or Brenham, anywhere there was a good game. Everybody knew when and where the best games were going on, so you could play poker in a big game every day if you wanted to, sort of like playing the tournament circuit today.

A lot of us road gamblers faded the white line from Dallas to Houston to Waco to Shreveport to Corpus and points in-between.

We knew that the best games on Wednesday and Thursday were in Brenham at Martin Cramer's gambling joint out on the lake. Martin had $100-limit dice games and good poker games and he didn't have to worry about getting raided. No charter, no nothing, he just had it fixed up so that nobody bothered him.

In Texas in those days there was one certain guy who "owned" an area and they called him the boss gambler in that town. You could run a little poker game in the boss gambler's town but you couldn't run any craps games because the boss just wouldn't stand for it. Sam McFarland was the boss gambler in Longview, Slim Lambert was the man in San Antone, and Martin Cramer was the boss gambler in Brenham. Martin was killed one night in Houston when somebody broke into his apartment and hijacked him. The police never found out who did it.

I played with Dodie Roach, Sam Moon, and all those guys in Corpus. Played Moss, Ramsey, and McCorquodale at the Elks Club in Waco along with Bud Brown, who ran the game there. Most of these guys were in their fifties, twenty years older than I was. There weren't as many young guys playing poker in those days as there are now—guess most of them were trying to make an honest living at a day job. Back then the older guys were the best poker players in the world. If you could beat them, you could beat anybody in the world, even Freddy Ferris.

Occasionally somebody would travel with me, but usually I went by myself. I'd just throw some clothes and shaving needs in my car and take off for Brenham or wherever. Sometimes I'd come back by way of Waco where they played on the weekends at the Elks Club, just like they play poker at the Elks Clubs today. From there I might go on home to Dallas and play at the Red Men's Club, where they played poker every day. Most of the poker there was played limit although sometimes they played no-limit. All of the games in Brenham, Corpus, and Waco were no-limit and that's why I traveled to them. I always liked no-limit better because you only have to win two or three pots a week, whereas in limit you have to win eight or nine pots a day to quit winner. The no-limit games were mostly hold'em, but sometimes they'd play deuce-to-seven lowball, no joker.

The road gamblers dressed pretty nice back then, jackets and silk shirts—a lot different from how they dress today—no T-shirts or baseball caps, that kind of thing. They were a clean bunch of guys with neat haircuts, manicured fingernails, gold jewelry, a nice watch and ring.

A lot of them were married, owned their own homes, and had children. They didn't usually haul their wives around to the gambling joints with them, I guess because poker was mostly a men's game. For years McCorquodale lived at the Dorchester House, a very nice apartment house in East Dallas. Moss owned a home in Odessa, along with some apartment houses there. His wife Virgie seldom traveled with him although after he moved to Vegas, she was around him most of the time. Virgie managed the money, the house, and their children. Johnny would give her a certain amount of his win and she would invest it. They were in pretty good shape.

Some of the road gamblers traveled together and played off the same bankroll like Bobby Hoff, Carl McKelvey, and Sailor Roberts did. Everybody was aware of who was playing the same money, but that didn't bother anybody. Road partners usually didn't play in the same game, but even if they did, the other players didn't fear any collusion. Regardless of what people might think, I've seen bankroll partners playing in the same game, each man for himself, not getting anything from the other guy—they played their hands. Of course they stayed out of each other's way. But even when a man was playing the same money with his road partner, if he got broke, some other gambler usually would help him out if he had money at the time.

Very few gamblers ever drank alcohol when they were at the table. I've seen two or three of them drink a little bit and usually they threw the party when they did. I knew Bill Smith and went a lot of places with him. When he got to a certain point in his drinking, he couldn't play but when he wasn't drinking, nobody could beat him. He didn't care, really. And I guess that some of them caroused around a little bit, but I never saw them bring women to a poker game. Poker was strictly business; everybody was just trying to make some money at it.

Some poker players had problems with drugs in those days but even though I knew them quite well and traveled around them, I never participated in any of that stuff myself. I'd heard about the drugs but I never said anything about it to anybody because I figured that it wasn't any of my business. The most important thing was what they were doing in the poker game, not what they did away from the table.

Folks have asked me whether the road gamblers just played against each other, wondering how any of us could make any money always playing against the other top hands. Naturally, that's not how it was. Let's say that Mac knew somebody from Waco who had money, what we called a "producer." Mac might make a call or two and we'd drive to Waco to get in the game with him, not with the other professional players. There were always three or four men from that area who had money who weren't top players, men who just liked to play poker, and they're the ones we wanted to play with—they were the producers of the road show.

We traveled to poker games just like the cowboys went to rodeos. Some rodeos were bigger than others and some poker games were bigger than others. But still, you might go to a small game and if the right people showed up, it could become a big game. The "right people" meant anybody that didn't gamble for a living like all the rest of us. A local businessman might come in, have a few drinks, and throw a party. Some of the party throwers were oilmen. Their wells were busy producing black gold while they were producing money at the poker table.

Charlie Cannon was an oilman who lived about thirty miles from Waco and was a close friend of Noble Bates, a local gambler. Charlie just loved playing poker. If there wasn't a game going on when he walked into the Elks Club, Charlie would have a few drinks and then stake everybody to get a game started. There might be four or five ranchers there waiting around the bar and Charlie would say, "Hell, let's start a game. I'll stake you to $500 each," and the game was on. If they got broke, he'd give them more money. There he was playing against his own money—and he never did win!

Not all the road games were in gambling joints or the Elks Club or AmVets, some of them were in homes. The head of the house would run the game and his wife usually would cook meals for all the poker players. I used to play in Hugh Briscoe's home game in Denton on Tuesday and Friday nights and later on, Hugh played at my club in Dallas. And of course, Martin Cramer's game in Brenham was a home game.

★ The Road Gamblers

It would take all the audiotapes they sell at Wal-Mart for me to record all the great poker players I've played with over the years. One of the greatest was Bill Smith.

I first met Bill in Las Vegas at the Horseshoe Club where he worked in the poker room long before the World Series of Poker ever started. Sailor Roberts, Bob Hooks, and Bill were playing poker there and I went to Vegas to play with them. Bill could put a man on a hand better than anybody I've ever seen. If he hadn't been such a heavy drinker, Bill probably would have been the world champion three or four times instead of just the one time that he won it against T.J. Cloutier in 1985. Of course, Bill wasn't the violent type of drinker—he'd just sit around, have a drink and play cards. When he'd only had a few drinks, he played world-class poker but if he had too many drinks, he didn't play very well at all.

Bill lived in Dallas near where I lived and he used to play in my poker game there. He and I also ran some Vegas-style craps games around Dallas. Bill was a great no-limit poker player, a dangerous player, and it seemed like he never worried about anything, including whether or not he had any money. I don't know how many times I've been arrested for playing poker, but I guess Bill holds the record.

One morning in Lubbock while he was playing poker, the police raided the game and put them all in jail. As soon as they got out of jail that afternoon, they went to another game and the police raided again. When they got out, they went to another game that same night and the police raided them a third time! That might be the world record for getting arrested in one day for playing poker. Bill died in 1997 and a lot of us still miss him.

Another great poker player I knew was Cotton Bullard, from Wills Point, Texas where he owned a ranch. Cotton drove his Model-A Ford to the Elks Club in Tyler in the '50s and joined it because you couldn't play there unless you were a member. Cotton could hardly read or write but he had good card sense. He won himself rich in the big no-limit hold'em games at the Tyler Elks Club playing against all those oilmen— some of those guys couldn't play a lick—and just a few other good players like Bob Bryant and Bob Hooks. Cotton, his son "Catfish," and Bob Hooks play their poker in Bossier City these days. The Elks Club charged 5 percent extra when you bought chips. If you bought in for $500, it would only cost you $25 to play. Of course if you got broke and bought in for another $500, it would cost you another $25. By two o'clock in the afternoon the game would be full and you could sell your seat for $100. In fact, Jess Sweeney got rich just by selling his seat every afternoon around three o'clock.

The Elks Club closed at midnight and a lot of the regular players—Doc Ramsey, Mac McCorquodale, Morris Shapiro (we called him "Jew" Morris), Johnny Moss, George Barnes (a famous player from Oklahoma who later went to Vegas to play five-card stud with Bill Boyd and that bunch), Sam McFarland, and Freddy "Sarge" Ferris (a helluva gambler from Shreveport)—didn't like to quit playing that early. Johnny Mayfield and I had played a lot of poker in Waco and other parts of Texas and we knew them all, so in 1965 we opened up a game right across the street in a suite of rooms at the Carlton Hotel where everybody could play as late as they wanted. When the Elks Club closed for the night, a lot of players would walk across the street to play with us.

One night our game became raggedy so Sarge started a game called "Georgia skin," the gamblingest game in the world, with everybody betting against everybody else. They used to have skin tournaments in Louisiana and Sarge was quite a player. You get dealt one card and then you take a card off the deck. If you have a king and a king falls off, you lose. You can't take more than one card because if you do, the deck gets shorter and you might fall right quick. If there is a "cub" in the deck, where most of your cards are buried on the bottom of it, you can win a lot of money when you're playing high stakes. I played in a skin game in Shreveport in the '60s where the least you could bet was $50. Little Red Ashey and some black people who owned the Red Lily Cue Club in Houston were in the game. They would drive into town in their new Cadillacs with two pockets full of money and play skin for four or five days at a time. It was a big game with swings of $60,000 or more.

On this particular night in Tyler, I'd been working our poker game at the Carlton for quite a while and had just gone to sleep in the other room when Johnny woke me up saying, "We're gonna start a skin game. You wanna go in with me?" Since Johnny and I were partners in the poker game (we charged 5 percent on the chips just like the Elks did), he checked with me first.

"No, I don't wanna go in with you or anybody else," I answered. "I don't know much about skin and I don't want to tie up my money in it."

"Well, all right, I'll just go in by myself," he said and headed out the door.

The skin game started. All the boss gamblers were in it—Martin Cramer from Houston was playing big and Sam McFarland sent somebody to Longview twice to pick up $20,000 for him. Then Sarge got hot. He was catching every right card in the deck and boy, he started drowning them. Making a long story short, they played and played and played until Sarge broke every one of them, won over $100,000.

Mayfield got broke along with all the rest of them. When it was over, he came running back to my bedroom asking, "You were in with me, weren't you Byron?"

"Hell no, you know I wasn't. I don't know how you came out, but I sure as hell wasn't in with you." I still had my bankroll on me from the poker, but it all went south when I had to go in and straighten up everybody's chips in the skin game—it was a cash deal. When I paid Sarge, he tipped me $1,200. Of course, he had broken up my poker game. We couldn't get it started again for quite a while.

Another player I used to play with was James "Goody" Roy, a big tall guy from Mount Pleasant, Tennessee. One night when I was running a big poker game at the AmVets in Dallas, the action was particularly good so I called Goody. "Fly on down here to Dallas," I told him. "We've got a helluva game and I'll take 25 percent of you if you want me to."

Goody liked to "rabbit hunt" more than anybody I've ever seen, but we had a rule against it at the AmVets. After everybody's out of the hand and the pot has been pushed to the winner, the rabbit hunter says to the dealer, "Burn one so that I can see the last card." I picked up Goody at the airport and while I was driving him to the club, I mentioned that he couldn't rabbit hunt in our game.

"You can't rabbit hunt?!" he hollered.

"Nope, you sure can't. It's one of the rules."

"Well hell, just turn around and take me back to the airport right now!"

"What?! Are you serious?"

"I mean it! I ain't playing if I can't rabbit hunt." So we changed the rules while Goody was in town.

One of the shyest great poker players I ever met was Little Red Ashey, who also loved betting sports and the horses. We called him "Little Red" as a kind of joke—actually, he stood about six foot five inches tall. Not too long after Evelyn and I were married, she had a hankering to go to the races in Hot Springs, Arkansas, but I was too busy running the business in Dallas to take her, so I told her to just go by herself and have a good time. She packed up her stuff and took off in our Cadillac for Hot Springs, but when she got there that evening, there wasn't a room for rent in the whole town. It wasn't long before I got a phone call from Little Red, who was as shy as he was tall.

"Cowboy," he kind of stuttered, "I've got Evelyn here with me and uh ..."

"You all have a good time," I interrupted. "And see if you can give her a horse that'll win—she wants to make some money."

"I have one or two that might be all right for her," he said and then hemmed and hawed for a while before he got to the point. "We've got a little problem here, Byron. Evelyn can't find a place to stay tonight. I've got two beds in my room and she said she'd just stay here with me, but I don't know what to do. That's why I'm calling you."

"That's fine with me," I told him, "but in case you hurt her, just call me collect and I'll wire you $500." I thought I was being pretty humorous but Red didn't know what to make of it, poor guy.

R.D. Matthews and George McGann used to run the Sky Night Club in Dallas. One night we were all playing at the Red Men's Club in Dallas, $5/$10 limit hold'em, and George lost $2,000—unbelievable playing nickel-dime. The next afternoon about five o'clock I went out to their club and found R.D. sitting there.

"How did McGann do last night?" he asked. "Somebody said that he lost $2,000."

"Well, I think he lost pretty good all right, but he took a lot of bad beats," I answered, trying to take a little of the heat off George.

"Don't tell me that!" R.D. said. "I can turn my hand face up and still not lose $2,000 playing five and ten."

Then he and the guys started playing poker. About that time the piano player came walking in and she was drunk. "Get her outta here!" R.D. screamed, still mad about George losing the two grand.

"Oh, don't worry about it, Mr. Matthews," one of the guys said. "We'll straighten her out here in a little while. She's just been drinking, that's all."

"If you can straighten her out, our next stop will be the United Nations!" he said sarcastically. With that he walked out of the club, saying "Come on, Cowboy, let's go," and he and I drove somewhere else to play our poker.

I remember the first time that I met George McGann at the Elks Club in Longview, Texas. We got to playing heads-up hold'em and I won all his money. George had ten pairs of brand new alligator shoes in the trunk of his car, all of them size nine and ten. I won those, too, but none of them would fit so I gave some away and sold the others. Although we later became friends, I didn't know George very well at that time— if I had I would've been afraid to win his money, let alone his shoes, because he was a known underworld character. Later he and a fella got into an argument playing poker in a motel in West Texas. The other guy left the motel room, went out to his car and got a gun, came back in, and shot George dead.

Another man that you wanted as your friend, not your enemy, in those days was Henry Bowen. I first met Henry right after I retired from rodeo in 1960 when he was one of the top hold'em players on the old Texas circuit. He and I played a lot of poker around each other on the road and I can tell you that Henry was no one to get crossways with. But if you treated him right, he would do anything for you. Like Benny Binion, he was a good friend and a bad enemy. Later Henry became good friends with the Binions and acted as an unofficial bodyguard and consultant to Benny. Whenever Benny or his son Jack wanted to know about someone or something, they asked for Henry's help.

Henry spent two years on death row in Oklahoma for allegedly killing a policeman in Oklahoma, but on the night the murder was supposed to have happened, he was playing poker with all of us in Tyler. His conviction was a pure and simple frame. Thanks to the poker players who constantly took up donations to pay for lawyers for Henry, he finally got out of prison. A lot of influential people in Las Vegas also helped him. No telling what would have happened if it hadn't been for his many friends. Henry passed away a few years ago and wherever he is now, I'm sure that he's playing hold'em.

Sailor Roberts played with us in the old days, too. He used to travel with his good friends Bobby Hoff and Carl McKelvey, a couple of great no-limit and pot-limit hold'em players that I've known for years. We've played poker together everywhere from Dallas to San Antone, Corpus, Las Vegas, and California. When Bobby came in second in the World Series championship event to that novice named Hal Fowler in 1979, it was a heart breaker. Hal was a real dog to win the Series because he'd never played any big tournaments before, but he got lucky against Bobby, one of the best no-limit players in the world. Of course Bobby's still making his living at poker and nobody's seen Hal since then.

One time I had a poker tournament at one of my joints in Dallas and Mac Fisher, Tommy Grimes, Bill O'Connors, and Tony Secuse from Baton Rouge came in for it. Tommy is one of the best players in Texas and Bill is one of the best pot-limit players anywhere. Mac plays real good and real high. Tony had been a dog trainer overseas before he moved to Dallas as an older man—he could train a dog to do anything, even trained circus dogs.

Little Red Ashey knew Tony real well, used to play poker with him in Lafayette, Louisiana. One time when I went to Lafayette to play in a big game, everybody at the poker table was laughing at a funny story that they're still telling around poker tables in Louisiana. Seems that Tony Secuse was sitting in his motel room one evening shooting the bull with Little Red and some other guys. "You all want a cup of coffee?" he asked, setting up a deal that he'd made in advance with the manager of the motel's cafe. Apparently, Tony had trained his dog to carry coffee cups in a plastic tray that had slots in it so that the coffee wouldn't spill out of the cups. "How do you all want it? Sugar on the side? Cream?"

Then Tony said to the dog, "Go on down to the cafe and get the coffee for my friends." When the dog got to the cafe, the manager had it all ready for him. Those guys were purely amazed when that dog came trotting back into the room hauling a tray of coffee in its mouth!

I played poker on the road for about twenty-five years, from 1960 to 1985. During that time I also owned a few joints myself. I liked having my own game, staying put in one place and not having to travel to so many places to play poker. The rake wasn't bad either.

The first time that I had my own joint was in 1961 when I opened a place in Tyler with the most famous proposition man in the history of gambling—Titanic Thompson.

Byron Wolford winning the calf roping event at the rodeo in Burwell, Nebraska, riding Wayne Garrett's horse. Byron tied four calves in 42 seconds at Clear Lake, South Dakota, in 1955, the same year that he won the Calgary Stampede with the same horse. Note that the cowboy has dismounted from the left side before legging the calf down.

"The Violinist" often entertained his fellow poker players at Cowboy's home games in the 1980s.

Bill Nelson frequently played at Cowboy's poker room in Dallas.

The Wolfords converted the garage of their townhouse in Dallas to create one of the most popular home poker games of the early '80s. The back bar and the area surrounding the poker table were accented with vintage photos that Evelyn snapped of the road gamblers and locals who played there.

Poker players enjoying a break from the action at Cowboy Wolford's home poker game in 1982.

Top: Jack "Treetop" Straus, the 1982 World Champion of Poker (L) and Amarillo Slim Preston, the 1972 World Champion of Poker (R), with WSOP founder Benny Binion in the 1970s in a photo taken at Binion's Horseshoe by Evelyn Wolford. Bottom: Cowboy Wolford dressed to the nines to play poker in Las Vegas, 1980.

Benny Binion and Cowboy Wolford at the WSOP around 1982. The buttons on Binion's shirt are $1-dollar gold pieces. All of Benny's shirts were custom-made with buttonholes on one side and eyelets on the other side through which he attached the famous gold buttons so that he could easily transfer them from one garment to the other.

Cowboy and Evelyn pose with Carl Cannon for a publicity shot on the street just outside the poker room at Binion's Horseshoe in 1979.

Benny Binion and Cowboy Wolford in the early 80s posing in front of the $1-million-display that was a tourist attraction at the Horseshoe Casino in Las Vegas until 1999, when the money was sold by then-owner Becky Binion Behnen. The $10,000 bills, which are no longer minted, were encircled by a golden horseshoe. Patrons could have their pictures taken free of charge in front of the impressive backdrop and pick them up one hour later.

Benny Binion and the Wolfords at Benny's home in Fort Worth in 1987 when they surprised him with the WSOP quilt on their way to the World Series in Las Vegas. Benny is wearing one of his many custom-made sets of silk pajamas with matching robe. Binion and his family used to buy all their clothes at Nieman Marcus in Dallas. The chain had no store in Las Vegas when the Binion's moved there so Nieman's would fly a load of clothing to Vegas from which the family could make their selections.

Rebel, the dog who knew more poker players than any other canine in the world, poses with the Wolfords at the Horseshoe Casino in 1986. In the photo below, Rebel is sporting his craps-layout costume, one of the many outfits that Evelyn designed and sewed for him.

Amarillo Slim Preston presents the winner's trophy and money to Cowboy Wolford at Amarillo Slim's Super Bowl of Poker in 1979. Wolford beat Johnny Moss (who finished second) to win the title in the $10,000 buy-in deuce-to-seven lowball event. Cowboy is wearing the belt buckle that he won at Madison Square Garden in the calf-roping event.

Movie star Chill Wills, who was a close friend of Benny Binion, poses with legendary poker player George Barnes and Benny Binion at the inaugural World Series of Poker in 1970.

Top: Jack "Treetop" Straus and Cowboy Wolford playing in a tournament at the old Marina Hotel in Las Vegas in 1979.

Bottom: Cowboy Wolford at the 1979 World Series of Poker sporting gold collar tips and gold buttons on his tailored Western shirt.

Left: Popular poker player Seymour Liebowitz at the WSOP in the 1970s.

Right: Walter Clyde "Puggy" Pearson, the 1973 World Champion of Poker, in a classic press photo released in the 1970s by Binion's Horseshoe.

*Brian "Sailor" Roberts,
legendary road gam-
bler and the 1975 World
Champion of Poker,
posed for a press release
photo at the Horseshoe in
the 70s.*

*Johnny Moss, the Texas
road gambler who was
elected World Champion
of Poker by his peers at
the inaugural WSOP in
1970. Moss went on to
win the championship in
$10,000 buy-in, freeze-
out tournaments in 1971
and 1974.*

Top: Carl Cannon, who played in the WSOP in the early days, was known for his colorful Western garb as well as his poker prowess.

Bottom: Kenny "Whatta Player!" Smith in the early '80s. Smith was also known as "Top Hat" because he often wore the handsome black top hat he is sporting in this photo (taken by Evelyn Wolford) of him dealing a round of poker at Cowboy Wolford's home game in Dallas.

Top: Bobby "The Owl" Baldwin, the 1978 World Champion of Poker. A noted road gambler from Tulsa, Baldwin went on to become the President and CEO of Mirage Resorts, and was inducted into the Poker Hall of Fame in 2003.

Left: Doyle "Texas Dolly" Brunson, the 1976 and 1977 World Champion of Poker, in a Horseshoe press release photo in the early 80s. The most famous road gambler and poker player in the world, Brunson went on to win 10 WSOP bracelets and write the classic poker books, Super System and Super System 2.

Top: Claude Kimberlin (R), Cowboy Wolford's long-time friend, with his partner James Harper (L) and Don Gay (C), eight-times world champion bull rider.

Right: Cowboy Wolford sits in his golf cart wearing signature overalls that match the cowhide motif on his cart. An avid golfer, Wolford won many wagers on the greens of Texas, Nevada, and California.

Cowboy Wolford at the 1984 World Series of Poker where he placed second in the $10,000 title event to Jack Keller. His shirt has his "hand" pictured on it. Just before he came to the Series, Cowboy had his hair permed to change his luck. "A lot of country-Western and rock stars were getting their hair permed at that time," he explained. "I'm just glad that Grandpappy Wolford wasn't alive to see it."

Cowboy Wolford flashed a victorious smile when he won the $5,000 buy-in limit hold'em championship at the World Series of Poker in 1991. He is holding the coveted gold bracelet, to which he later commissioned a jeweler to add "Cowboy" in diamonds. Wolford's winning cards, a pair of black jacks, are nestled amid the $210,000 in prize money that Evelyn is helping him count.

This ad featuring Cowboy Wolford ran nationally in 1996.

Jack Binion, who hosted the World Series of Poker from its inception in 1970 through 1998, and Cowboy Wolford at the Horseshoe in 1979 in a photo snapped outside the vintage Horseshoe Casino in 1979 by Evelyn Wolford.

A TITANIC PROPOSITION

*"I can't relax for a second. I treat everything like playin' roulette.
And the only way to win at roulette is to own the wheel.
I tell you, gambling is hard work." — Titanic Thompson*

Titanic Thompson was one of the best proposition men
that ever lived, smart as a fox. The first time I met him was in
San Antone a year after I retired from rodeoing. I went there
to play some poker and visit Tony Salinas, whose daddy used
to be a calf roper. Tony and I went out to a poker game and
there sat Titanic. Ty was slim, wore a snap-brim hat, and sat up
straight as an arrow in his chair. And his eyes—you could tell
that he knew what was going on at all times. Whatever came
up, he was ahead of everybody else and knew what was about
to happen.

The next time we met was at the Red Men's Club in
Dallas. Ty always had a little trick or two to show us. One time

he came in with a bag, sat it down by the side of his chair, and bought some chips to play in the limit hold'em game. "I've lost every hand I've ever had at this sonnabitch club. I just can't believe the way they draw out on me here!" he ranted, putting his act on real thick. Everybody was looking at him thinking how crazy he was. "I oughta just blow up this sonnabitch and take everybody with me!" he hollered, as he picked up the bag and slipped out a ball that looked something like a bowling ball with a dynamite fuse stuck in it. Then he struck a match to it, lit it, and threw the damned thing under the table. Looked like Ty was trying to bomb the place.

Damned near scared us all to death! We jumped up in unison leaving our chips scattered on the table, and scrambled for the front door—almost tore it off trying to get out of the joint. We hovered out on the sidewalk for a while waiting for the damned thing to go off, but it never did. Somebody finally walked back up the stairs to see what was happening. There was Ty still sitting at the table laughing like a hyena.

Titanic's christened name was Alvin Clarence Thomas and he was the son of itinerant farmers. His father liked gambling better than farming and he disappeared when Ty was only six months old. Ty spent his childhood on a farm in the Ozark Mountains where he lived in a three-room log cabin with his mother and stepfather and four stepbrothers and sisters. His granddaddy and uncles worked a farm near there and liked to gamble at mountain games like shooting at targets with a .22, pitching to a crack, checkers, dominoes, and penny-ante poker. By the time Ty was fifteen years old, he could beat them all at their own games. "All I ever wanted to do was gamble," he said. And now here he sat in Dallas as an older man playing poker with us.

After we had gotten to know each other a little better, Ty and I were playing poker at the club one night when he said, "Cowboy, let's go to Tyler and open up a Red Men's Club down there." At the time I was thirty-one years old and Ty was almost seventy, although he looked like he was much younger than that. He had moved around a lot during his life and kind of liked Tyler, where he had rented a house. Ty liked me because I was a cowboy and a pretty good poker player, and I got along with everybody real well. I had all the contacts; I could get the players. The idea was that we would go into business as 50-50 partners. I would run the place, and he wouldn't have to work too hard at it.

We got a charter and opened a club upstairs in the old Elks Club building on the corner right across from the courthouse in downtown Tyler. We both put up a pretty good sum of money for the venture and in exchange for his interest, Ty wanted his piece of the drop. Sometimes he would come to the club during the day for a little while, but Ty was mostly a night person. Even at seventy years old, he prowled around at night to the bowling alleys and other joints, always working on some kind of a proposition. He never looked his age and most people thought Ty was younger than he was.

Every Wednesday night Ty and I would take off and go to the Elks Club in Longview to play in a big no-limit hold'em game with Sam McFarland, the boss gambler in East Texas. There were some weak players in the game so we had some good nights there. The poker game didn't start until about six o'clock at night, so one afternoon about four o'clock Ty and I were sitting around the bar in the club waiting for the game to begin and watching a couple of Elks Club members shoot pool. One of them was a pretty good pool player who had beaten just about everybody in Longview. Ty could play pool and any other game that required good eye-hand coordination, so when the game was over he said, "Hell, I'll play you a game or two."

"What do you want to play for?" the guy asked him.

"I can't really play that good," Ty lied, "so you'd have to spot me a little." The fella agreed and they started shooting for about $50 a game. After Ty had let the man beat him out of about $200, he said, "Man, you're really good. You oughta be on the circuit. I've never seen nobody play nine-ball as good as you can. I think I'm gonna have to quit, I've got no chance to win."

"I understand," the guy said, sticking out his chest. "Don't worry 'bout it, that's just the way it goes sometimes."

"I've got a nephew over in Tyler where I live who works at the Texaco station," Ty continued, "and he thinks he can shoot pool pretty good. I might just bring him over here next week and let him play you."

"Oh, hell, bring him on! Bring anybody you want to and we'll play for whatever you wanna play for."

That night while we were driving home I asked Ty about this "nephew" of his. "He's named Cornbread Red," he said.

"Who's that?" I asked.

"He's the best nine-ball player in the world. He's in Chicago right now, but when I get home I'm gonna call him and fly him down here. Then we'll go back to Longview and I'm gonna take 'em off in the pool." I figured it was gonna be quite a show.

Cornbread Red flew in to Dallas a few days later and we drove one hundred miles from Tyler to pick him up. Driving home I just listened while Ty explained to Red how the deal was gonna come down. The next day he went to the filling station and bought a Texaco uniform for Red. A few days later we took off for Longview with Red dressed up in his Texaco uniform, grease on his hands, hair uncombed.

About three hours before the poker game started, the three of us walked into the Elks Club at Longview. The bartender was setting up the bar and the pool shooters were all hanging around.

"I brought my nephew over from Tyler," Ty told the mark. "He was able to get off work from the station today."

"You think he's pretty good, do you?" the guy asked.

"Well, I play him sometimes and he's pretty good, but I don't think he can beat you. We'll have to spot him pretty good."

"What kind of spot do you want?"

"I believe we should start off by giving him the eight, nine, and the break."

"That's a helluva spot."

"Well, let him play a couple of games and we'll adjust if it's too much."

"How much do you wanna play for?"

"Oh, I'll bet a coupla hundred to start with."

The guy agreed and they racked up the balls. Cornbread Red had his own pool cue out in the car, but he didn't bring it into the club because that would've looked sort of bad so he picked out the straightest pool cue he could find on the rack. And the games began.

Red let the guy win the first one. Then Red won one and the mark won the next two, with the limits rising. Red won the next one, he let the guy win one, and then Red won the next two.

"Hell, I can't spot him the eight, nine, and the break no more," the mark said.

"Well, I told you we'd adjust. We'll just take the eight and the break," Ty said.

"All right, I'll try that," the man agreed and they resumed play with the bets at $400. Red let the guy win the next one, then Red would win two and let the man win another one, and then Red would win the next three. "I can't beat your nephew giving him the eight and the break," the man complained.

"Well, hell, let's bet something and I'll give you a chance to get even," Ty suggested. "In fact, we'll just let you play even." They upped the bets to $700 a game and started even, no spots. They seesawed back and forth for a few games. It had taken quite a while to put down the "stall" and get the mark to play even. Now that the time was right, Red turned on the steam and started eating him up. Finally the man said, "I can't beat him. He's just too good for me."

"Well hell, I want you to get even," Ty said. Then he turned to Red, saying, "Son, I didn't know you could shoot that good."

"Well, Uncle Ty, I just feel good today, that's all. You know, I've been working every day at the station and then going home with them kids of mine all hollering and my ole lady griping. But today I'm off work and relaxed, drinking a beer or two and playing some pool. Hell, I don't get time off like this but every two years. I'm just glad my ole lady let me come over here today."

So they started shooting some more, this time giving the pool sharp from Longview the eight and the break. All the suckers from around town who all had a lot of money from oil were betting on their local hero, thinking he'd make a big comeback at any minute. All the while Red was drowning them. The final bet they made was that Cornbread Red would get the break and even if the mark moved the nine ball to the rail twice and didn't make it, he still would win the game. They went for that one to the tune of about $2,000 more. Of course, Red would take the break, make the first ball, and then run the table. Ty wound up beating them out of $10,000. The Longview hotshot was in shock and the locals were a lot lighter in the wallet after that episode.

★ Titanic Bowls 'Em Over ★

Ty was quite a character, a scratch golfer left- or right-handed and, in general, a proposition man. Any time it looked like you had the nuts, don't worry brother, you couldn't win! One time Ty won $10,000 off a guy at a bowling alley. Dick Cooper owned the alley and he was the best bowler in that part of the country. "You know, I've got arthritis but I used to be able to play pretty good," Ty told him. "I'll bowl you if you give me back all of my splits." To make a long story short, Ty beat him at this and beat him at that, making every kind of proposition in the world.

The last bet Ty made him was for $1,000—he bet that Cooper couldn't break 100 if he bowled a game blindfolded.

As soon as they got the bet on, Ty told everybody to be real quiet so that Cooper couldn't keep his bearings. The last ball he rolled, Cooper threw it straight at the front door because he had gotten turned around.

Ty had all sorts of propositions on almost any game you could name, including horseshoes. While we were partners in the poker game in Tyler, he rented a house just out of town on the Troop Highway. Every day he stopped on the highway at a little grocery store that had a gas pump to fill up his new Lincoln with gasoline. One day Ty says to the owner, "What's that out there?"

"Oh, I pitch horseshoes," he answers.

"Boy, I'd like to learn to do that," Ty says. Of course, Ty could ring one blindfolded with a sheet up.

"What do you do for a livin'?" this guy asks Ty.

"Oh, I'm in the oil business up in Indiana. I've made so much money I'll never be able to spend it all." They talked for a while and finally, getting friendly, Ty says, "I sure wish you'd show me how to pitch them horseshoes."

So the guy takes him out to the horseshoe pit and says, "Now, you hold it like this..." And Ty would turn the horseshoe around sideways and ask, "Like this?" The guy would answer, "No, no, like this."

Ty got to throwing the shoes around and one day he says, "You know, I just can't do anything unless I gamble on it. I don't know what it is with me 'cause I've got plenty of money."

"You wouldn't have a chance of beating me," the guy answers.

"Oh, I know you've got kids and everything," Ty says, "and you probably don't gamble, but it won't hurt me to lose some money. Like I told you, I've made so much money up in Evansville in the oil business I'll never be able to spend it." Somehow, he finally got the guy to betting. Ty ended up winning $6,000 off him, just a square guy that didn't even hardly gamble, you know what I mean? "You'll be lucky if they don't run you out of town," I said to Ty, but nothing ever came up about it.

That's the way Ty was. He'd just run around all over the place making propositions. In another deal, he had a checkerboard down at our club. A lot of those ole East Texans think they can play checkers—that's all they've done for half their life. I forget exactly how this deal went, but Ty would give you all the checkers and he'd just take two kings. If you got just one of your men to the king row, you'd win the game, but you never could do it. Ty had deals like that going on all the time.

★ Titanic's Poker Psychic ★

Then there was the deal with the "poker psychic." Ty would be sitting around a poker joint that he'd never been to before and say, "Hey guys, I know this woman who's a psychic. I'll tell you just how good she is. You take a card out of that deck and put it on the table in front of us. She doesn't live in this state, but I'll bet that if you go call her, she'll tell you what the card is." Back then there wasn't any TV, no short-wave stuff, and Ty had been right there with them all the time, hadn't gone anywhere. Mighty near anybody would go for that deal.

Then he would bet $1,000 that if they called this woman who was a psychic, she could tell them over the telephone exactly what that card was. Somebody would take a card and put it on the table. "Okay," Ty would say, "here's the long distance number. Just ask for Miss Brown." They'd call and say, "Is Miss Brown there?"

"Just a moment," someone would answer. In a minute another voice said, "Hello?"

"Miss Brown, we're down here in so-and-so and we've got a bet on. This gentleman says you're quite a psychic."

"I think I am," she'd say.

"Well, we've taken a card out of the deck and laid it in the middle of the table and he bet that you could tell us what card it is."

"Give me a moment," she'd answer. Then after a short pause, she'd say, "The four of diamonds," and the guy would almost faint dead away. Of course, Ty had a different name for every card in the deck. If it was the four of diamonds, he'd tell them to ask for Miss Brown. If it was the nine of hearts, it might be Miss Ruby.

But one of the funniest stories about Ty happened one year when he was at the races in Santa Anita, California. After the track closed he'd take the train to the races in Hot Springs, Arkansas, which used to be an open gambling town; it was a real nice place. There was an old waiter at Santa Anita who always waited on Ty and after the season, the waiter would travel on to a big gambling joint down in Hot Springs where he waited tables during the races. All the gamblers and the bookmakers and proposition men from around the world would meet there—I was there myself back in '55. They'd gamble high on poker and the races and just about everything else they could think of.

Ty asked the waiter if he'd like to go with him on the train to Hot Springs. This waiter, they say, was a big ole dumb-looking guy. He was kinda like me in that he could hardly spell a word. But all the way to Hot Springs, Ty drilled him on how to spell rhinoceros and hippopotamus, and the ole waiter learned to spell them perfectly during the five-day trip. Well, Ty was going to win a big bet on this deal—he was out there every year and he knew that all the gamblers would bet on mighty near anything.

As soon as they arrived in Hot Springs, Ty started setting up the deal. They were all sitting around at the racetrack and this ole waiter was waiting on everybody. Ty had arranged for a guy in the crowd to bring up something about spelling and then Ty said, "I wonder what two words are the hardest to spell?"

"Well, I would imagine they'd be rhinoceros and hippopotamus," the shill answered.

"You're probably right," Ty agreed. "I don't think I could spell those two, but it's hard to tell who can spell and who can't. Look at that ole waiter over there—I tell you what, I bet the hell he could spell either one of them."

"Oh, Ty, you're crazy," the gamblers said. "Hell, he don't even know what town he's in."

"Well, you can't tell by looking at a guy whether or not he can spell," Ty answered. "I've just got the feeling that as dumb as he is, he might be a good speller." So, Ty bet them $3,000 that the waiter could spell both words perfectly. In advance, they all picked out rhinoceros for him to spell.

They called the ole waiter over and Ty says to him, "Don't get in no hurry now. Got a little bet on you and if you win it, I'm gonna take good care of you. You think you can spell rhinoceros?"

"I think I might," answers the waiter.

"Just take it easy now, no hurry," Ty says. "Okay, go ahead and spell it."

And the ole waiter spells out hippopotamus! He'd gotten the two words mixed up. Ty wanted to kill him right there on the spot.

★ Titanic Plays a Satellite ★

Even after Ty had gotten way up in age, he still would go to the World Series of Poker. In 1973 when he went to Binion's Horseshoe for the Series, it had been several years since I'd seen him. Of course, he knew everybody there and they all knew him because he was a living legend. A couple of the players were talking to him one day and teased him by asking, "Ty, do you think you could play poker in this World Series and win it?"

"Hell yeah," he answered. "Nobody can beat me playing poker. Of course, I'm getting at the age where I can't play for no fifteen hours like I used to, but if it wasn't for that, hell I probably could be the world champion every year." As he was putting down this story, they were all listening real close and laughing. "Yeah," he continued, "if it wasn't for my age, I'd be the world champion every year, but I just can't play as long as these young guys can."

"Well, why don't you play in one of the satellites?" someone suggested. "You'll only have to play for a couple of hours and if you win the chips, we'll make a deal where you can cash them out and won't have to play in the big tournament."

"Hell, there ain't nothing to that," he bragged. They talked about it some more and Ty told them that he might go for the deal later. Then he left.

He went out into the casino and found nine players, giving each one of them an entry fee into the ten-handed satellite. And he gave them an extra $300 apiece to dump the money off to him in the satellite in the trick that he was setting up. I was the only person that Ty told about it. The idea was that they could play legitimately against each other if Ty wasn't in the pot, but if he was in the pot they would dump the money off to him.

After he got the deal set up, Ty rejoined the men that he had been talking with earlier and said, "I've been watching one of them satellites and hell, I thought these guys in Las Vegas were real good poker players, but they can't play worth a damn. Sure, they might get lucky once in a while but they can't play a lick. I sure wish I could last fifteen hours in a big tournament 'cause I know I could beat 'em all." They were all laughing at his big brag.

"I can tell you one thing for sure," Ty went on. "I'll play one of them satellites if I can get the right price, and I'll bet you that I can win it. But if I have to play for more than three hours, win or lose, it's no bet. I just can't play for over three hours and I'll have to play like hell to do that." They all knew that the satellites didn't last for three hours. "Of course, I'll have to get some kind of a price," he repeated.

"All right," they agreed, grinning, and proceeded to the satellite area. All the while Ty was still laying down his story. "I wish they'd had these satellites a long time ago when I was young—hell, there's no telling how many championships I'd have won." They were eating it up.

In the early days the poker room ran a few satellites but they weren't as popular as they are now, so people weren't standing in long lines to play them like they have to do these days. When they got to the satellite area Ty announced, "Come on, fellas, let's get us a satellite going. I've got a little bet on it." One by one, the nine players Ty already had made a deal with signed up for the game.

"Well, we've got a satellite table put together," Ty told the group. "Now let's settle on a price." Sid Bernstein and a few other famous gamblers finally agreed on 5 to 1 odds. And hell, they were betting something—$1,500, $2,500, $3,000—so Ty ended up with about a $10,000 bet on it.

The satellite began—no-limit Texas hold'em for a seat in the championship event. The guys started off playing against each other and then Ty would get in a pot, one of them would bet, another would raise it, and Ty would call the raise. Then on the last card, Ty would bet and his "opponents" would throw their hands away. In short, they dumped the money off to him—and they did it pretty smoothly so that you couldn't really see what was going on.

Ty won the satellite. The bettors were in shock. And all the shills were happy as pie because they'd just made a score for themselves, not knowing how much Ty had made off the deal. "I told you I could beat all these sonnabitches," he bragged once again. "They just can't play as good as I can." And that's how, as an old man, he took them off for $10,000 right there at the World Series—just another one of Ty's deals that proved that any time you thought that you had the nuts on him, you actually were up against the nuts.

Ty used to play a lot of poker and golf in Corpus Christi. One day he was out on the course with Jesse Alto and a few other poker players and he beat the hell out of them. After the match they all went back to the Elks Club for some poker. "You're a good bunch of fellas," Ty told them. "But boy, I was really hot today at golf." They all just looked around at each other, agreeing that Ty was a helluva golfer. "Hell, I want to give you a chance to get even," Ty went on, "so I'll play you tomorrow left-handed if you'll give me about two a side. Of course, I don't have no left-handed clubs so somebody around here will have to round me up a set of them."

"You've got that one on," they agreed and proceeded to find Ty some clubs, not realizing that he could play scratch either left- or right-handed. Ty used to play with Lee Trevino when Lee was real young and I've heard that Ty taught him a lot about golf.

When they got out on the course the next day, Ty beat them again. They couldn't figure out how he could do that, so the third day he agreed to play them even. He took them off three days in a row, made them quit playing golf for a while. Playing poker with them, Ty threw off about twelve or fifteen hundred but that didn't make any difference to him—he had beaten them out of about $15,000 at the golf.

Ty was always figuring out a gimmick or two at golf, poker, any game. He showed me a gimmick that he used on the golf course, one that I later used a time or two. You take someone who is a scratch golfer and bet him that if he hits two balls, putts two times, chips two times and you pick the worse ball, he can't break 90. He has to hit them all, putt them all, and chip them all twice. A scratch golfer might think that you were crazy for making that kind of bet.

I played this deal for $2,000 against a scratch golfer about twenty years ago at a country club in Texas. When we came to the sixteenth hole, he had to make three holes in one to break 90. The eighteenth hole was five hundred yards. At that point, he just tore up the card and we went to the clubhouse. What happens is that they get out on the course, hit a good ball and then they hit a bad one. You pick the bad one and then they hit two more and you pick the worse one again. Then they might hit one up by the green and maybe they knock the second one into the sand trap. When they get up there on the green with, say, a twelve-foot putt, they might make it but then they have to putt it again and they usually miss it the second time. In other words, they get tired, frustrated, and they can't break 90, especially if the course has any water on it.

I never was a very good golfer, but Ty taught me another deal that I once used in Las Vegas. Austin Squatty, David Baxter, Gary Lumsford, Berry Johnston and I went to the country club to play some golf. Berry gave me one stroke a hole and we played for $1,000 a nine. He beat me the first nine but on the last nine, I got lucky and got even. So about five o'clock we all went into the clubhouse for some iced tea. While we were sitting around, I said, "I was real lucky to get even, but you know, I was just duffing that ball around out there to see how you all played, if you'd bet anything." They could tell that I wasn't much of a golfer. "But you know what I can do?" I went on. "Of course, I haven't told you all and nobody takes me to be a golfer, but I can take a driver and hit a ball farther than you can hit with a six and seven iron."

"Well, you've got that on!" they said in unison.

"Whatta you wanna bet?" I asked.

"I'll bet a thousand," Berry said.

"I'll bet $500," another one offered.

"I just want $50," Austin Squatty said and David Baxter also went for $50.

They practically ran over me getting up from the table to rush out to the first tee. They were ready to bet that I couldn't hit a driver farther than they could hit a six and seven iron—they just knew that they had the nuts. When we got to the tee, Berry said, "I'll bet another $1,500," and another guy placed an added bet. The total bets were over $6,000.

"You all go ahead and shoot," I said. They hit it right down the middle. I teed up and looked way down the fairway—and then I turned around and hit it in the opposite direction. Now they had to go down to where their balls were sitting and hit them back past mine, which was impossible to do. They turned white.

"It's a trick!" Berry said, kinda stuttering.

"Hell, it wasn't a trick when you all were trying to run over me in the clubhouse trying to get out on the tees and rob poor ole Cowboy," I said. "It ain't no trick, you all lose the money."

I never did get the money, but Austin and David paid me $50 apiece. "I was willing to pay $50 just to see what it was," David told me. That was just one of the golf propositions Ty taught me, but he had lots of others for almost any sport you can think of.

One time Ty was shooting pool at the Cotton Bowling Palace. A real mean fella named Charlie Boyd, a hijacker from Dallas, was standing around watching. After a while Ty looked over at Charlie, tipped his hat at him, and said, "Listen, Charlie, I know what you're thinking, you sonnabitch. But if you try to rob me, I'll shoot you right between your goddamned eyes." Ty carried a pistol at all times, a big ole long one. He could knock a bird off a wire, he was that good. Charlie left without another word.

Ty knew that Charlie had robbed Everett Goulsby and several other men right there in the Cotton Bowling Palace several months earlier. The day after the robbery, Charlie called Everett at the bowling alley saying, "Everett, I'm sorry I had to take your bankroll yesterday. You know I wouldn't intentionally take your money."

"Oh, I know you wouldn't, Charlie," Everett agreed.

"If you'll come on out here in the parking lot where I am, I'll give it all back to you," Charlie continued. "Just tell me how much I owe you."

Everett thought it was really something that Charlie wanted to return his money, so he went out to the parking lot to meet him. And Charlie robbed him again! I'll tell you how mean Charlie was: He once took a lawyer into a bank with a gun in his back and forced the guy to withdraw a lot of money and give it to him. Charlie finally went to the penitentiary and got killed there.

Years before I met Ty, he was playing golf at the country club in Tyler, playing real high with some of the wealthy oil barons from that neck of the woods. Two heisters, who had heard that Ty played golf for big stakes and carried a lot of money on him, shilled up as caddies for him and another man. Of course, Ty beat them all at golf and as soon as the match was over, the robbers drew their guns on him. But they didn't realize how fast a draw Ty was—he was the Matt Dillon of the golf links. Ty outdrew them, killed one of them right there on the golf course, and injured the second one. He wasn't prosecuted because he had shot in self-defense.

One year Ty got into a big poker game in New York with Rothstein, the guy who fixed the World Series of Baseball a long time ago, a big-time gangster-type from New York. In those days poker was played with cards made of paper and somehow or other, Ty could put a tiny bend on them that he could detect across the room when it came off the deck. He was so good at it that nobody else could see the mark. Ty and Rothstein began betting $1,000 or more on such things as the high card, low card and so on. Ty wound up beating the man out of $100,000. Of course, he had the best of it at all times.

Ty pulled off another of his card tricks on the corner of Irving Street in Dallas where the Red Men's Club was located on the top floor of a two-story building. He had noticed that every evening around five o'clock or so a breeze came up in front of the club causing quite an updraft. Ty discovered that he could pitch a playing card into the air and the wind would carry it to the top of the building. He practiced to the point that he could do it perfectly. Then one night while he was playing poker at the Red Men's Club, he bet the boys that he could throw a card all the way up to the top of the building. They went for that one to the tune of about $800. They got a deck of cards, went downstairs to the corner, picked a card, and watched as Ty pitched it to the rooftop. Doing it once wasn't enough proof, so they had him repeat the trick two or three times, lost about $2,000 to him on the deal.

★ Titanic Moves a Mountain ★

Ty was always looking for an angle. He could figure out more propositions that anyone alive. For example while he was in Wyoming playing poker, he and another guy drove together about twenty miles every day to the game, which was out in the desert somewhere. Every day they drove past a big rock that sat along the side of the road. "Boy, there's some big rocks in this country, ain't there?" Ty said. "Just look at all them rocks. That rock right there is a helluva rock, ain't it?"

"Yeah, yeah, there's a lot of rocks out here," the guy said, kinda bored.

The next day when they passed the boulder, Ty asked, "Wonder how much a rock like that weighs?"

"Hell, I don't know," the guy answered.

"Well, I was just wondering," Ty said.

The next morning Ty hired a man to take a truck out to the desert, load the rock on the flatbed, carry it back to town and weigh it, and then return it to its spot by the side of the road.

A few days later, after talking about the rocks on every trip, Ty said to his driving buddy, "You know what? I'd like to guess how much that rock weighs. In fact, I'd bet a thousand that I can come closer than you."

The guy had a little gamble in him, so he answered, "Well, we might get that on for $1,000."

"All right," Ty said, "tomorrow when we pass by here, we'll stop and go out there and guess at the weight of it," and they drove on to the poker game.

The next day they pulled the car off the side of the road and started looking at the rock. "You want me to guess first or you wanna guess first?" Ty asked.

"Don't make no difference," the guy answered. "I'll guess first if you want me to."

He guessed how much the rock weighed and they wrote his number on a slip of paper. Then Ty walked around the rock, studied it, kicked it with his boot, got off to the side a little distance and looked it over again, all that bull. Finally he made his guess and wrote it down next to the other guy's. "You know, I've always been a good guesser of weights, how much anybody weighs or their height or whatever," Ty said, putting down his story. "You know what? I bet I won't miss the weight of that rock within a hundred pounds."

"You're crazy," the guy said. "Ain't no way you can guess it that close, Ty."

"Well, I'll bet another two thousand that I can."

"I believe I'll just call that bet," the guy answered, figuring he had the nuts.

"How we gonna find out what that rock actually weighs?" Ty asked him.

"We can find somebody in town with a winch-truck to weigh it for us," the unsuspecting fella suggested and with that, they drove back to town. Ty had given the man with the truck $100 or so in advance not to say anything about it when they got there. When they drove into his filling station, Ty asked, "Who runs this place?"

"I do," the man answered.

"Well, we've got a bet on about the weight of a rock out in the desert," Ty said. "Is it possible for you to drive outside of town with your truck, load it with your winch, and bring it back here so that we can weigh it?"

"Yeah, I probably could, but it'll cost you about $100."

"That's all right, the winner will pay you."

So they went through the process of loading up the rock, bringing it back downtown, weighing it, and returning it to its resting place by the side of the road. Ty missed its weight by seventy-five pounds, won $3,000 on the bet. As always, any time it looked like you had the nuts on Ty, you didn't.

Ty and I kept our Red Men's Club open in Tyler for about a year and a half before we gave up our charter. He was ready to move on and I was tired of it myself so I returned to gambling on the road. The last time I saw him was at the World Series of Poker in 1973, the year before he died. That's when I took the photo of Ty, Benny Binion, and Marty Robbins sitting together in the Sombrero Room at the Horseshoe Club. Ty was a helluva guy and we had some good times together. I can only imagine the number of suckers that he parted from their money back in the '20s and '30s when there wasn't much income tax and some people were getting rich overnight and losing it the next day. Titanic was unique, one in a million.

It wasn't until 1972 that I opened my second joint, an AmVets club in Dallas. Later on I had dice and blackjack games in my townhouse in Dallas, so as you read the stories that I tell about road gamblers and poker players that I met during those years, keep in mind that some of the time I was traveling and other times I was running a game myself.

I got my second gambling joint the easy way. No, I didn't inherit it—I won it in a poker game.

TEXAS GAMBLERS

"A gambler lives like a millionaire whether he is or he isn't."
— *Johnny Moss*

I've played with more poker players in Texas than you can fit into the panhandle. After Titanic and I closed our joint in Tyler in 1963, I returned to my home base in Dallas and from there I took my game on the road fadin' the white line all across the Southern poker circuit. Then a funny thing happened in the early '70s that caused me to stick a little closer to home than I usually did.

I went to play poker one evening at the AmVets club on Greenville Avenue in Dallas near the downtown area. It was just a ratty looking place that was located upstairs above a carpet business, but it was big. The club hadn't been doing much business and was empty except for me and the owner, so we started playing heads-up no-limit poker. About the biggest thing I'd ever won in a poker game was my horse Ace, but by morning I had won something a little bit larger—I won the entire joint from him.

At that time I was on the road a lot between Dallas and Houston gambling, playing in good poker games and doing some hustling, making side trips to Brenham playing poker with Broomcorn and all those guys. I had just returned from Houston where I had won a whole lot of money playing craps. With all that craps money in my pocket, I paid "Big E," who owned both the downstairs carpet business and the building, to install cherry red carpet in my newly won club, had it painted, and built a big bar and a nice kitchen in it, spent about $30,000 fixing it up. I had some people in with me on the deal (a couple of them were Army veterans) who helped me run it. We worked in shifts because we were open twenty-four hours a day and I couldn't be there all the time. We installed an iron door with a buzzer on it and nobody ever bothered us. It wasn't long before we had a helluva no-limit hold'em game going. Everybody in the country came to play in it—Bob Brooks, Carl Biggs, Everett Goulsby, big Ken Smith. We also had two limit hold'em games going and boy, business was good!

AmVets is a veterans organization on the same order as the Red Men. The reason that people got Red Men and AmVets charters was because you could only take a drop legally if you had a fraternal charter. Your reason for taking the drop, you explained to the officials, was to support the fraternal organization, make charitable contributions, pay the rent, and so on. You didn't need to be a veteran to get an AmVets charter but we always got it in somebody's name who was a veteran because it looked better that way.

I never was in the service myself, because of a strange thing that happened while I was rodeoing. I had just come in from a rodeo in Memphis and was about a week late in registering for the draft. I was the perfect age, in perfect shape, and filled out all the forms and turned them in to the draft board. Seems that they had been in the process of moving the draft board office when I filed and I think they lost my papers during the move. They never contacted me and I never got in touch with them.

★ Mr. Robert A. Brooks ★

Anybody who ever played poker in Texas knew and respected Robert A. Brooks. For most of his life Mr. Brooks lived in Alaska where he owned all the gambling joints, including a craps game, blackjack game, some bars, and poker games. He also booked sports at 6 to 5. After he moved from Alaska to Texas in the late '70s, he played poker with us and later on, he and a partner opened up Barney's Casino in Lake Tahoe. He knew every angle in the gambling business and there wasn't a soul who could cheat him. Mr. Brooks was one of the smartest, wittiest men I've ever known and I loved and respected him.

He lived in Justin, Texas about forty miles from the club in Dallas, and used to drop by our house on his way to the game. He loved my wife Evelyn and me and told us some big stories about his days in Alaska. At one time or another he had been a brush pilot and a fisherman and knew everybody in the north country, including the Eskimos. An old miner once tried to sell him seventy pounds of gold for $15 an ounce, but Bob declined it for some unknown reason. The madam of the local cathouse used to play lowball in one of the games that he ran. "No telling how much money she lost," he said.

Nobody who played poker with him ever called him by his first name at the tables—we all addressed him as "Mr. Brooks" out of respect for his knowledge and character, knowing that his word was always good. Although he had more money than most people will ever see, he was not a pretentious man—he never dressed up and he drove an old car like he didn't have $20 to his name. One time I asked why he didn't buy himself a nicer car. "Hell, I don't need a new car," he answered. "This thing runs good, so why would I want a new one? Anyway, I'm a lucky driver." When he flew to Vegas for the World Series of Poker or just to gamble, Evelyn and I would offer to drive him anywhere he wanted to go. "Bob, you want us to run you out to the Strip?" we'd ask. "Hell no," he always answered. "I get a kick out of riding the bus and talking to the old people on it who are like myself. "

Once in a great while, he would have a drink or two and then he was really something—he wasn't mean, just tough. One time we were playing no-limit hold'em in Fort Worth and Bob had downed a couple of drinks. Everett Goulsby was in the game that night, winning a lot of money.

"Let's put $40 on it in the dark," Everett said.

"Hell, let's put $800 on it in the dark!" Mr. Brooks answered.

Everett shut his mouth.

Mr. Brooks had traveled all over the world and could always find a good poker game anywhere he was. We played in some pretty good poker games, Bob and I, the big games in Denton, Corpus Christi, Fort Worth, and Dallas. I never had to worry about having a bankroll when he was around. One time we played a pot-limit game with $5/$10 blinds for two days straight in Denton and I won $43,000. Mr. Brooks and I always split whatever we won.

I first met him in Fort Worth over twenty-five years ago when I was playing poker there. I had always had a poker or craps game going, so one day I suggested that he and I open up a poker game in Dallas. I had owned a Red Men's Club on Greenville Street, but I was out of it at that time. Because he trusted me, liked to play cards, and knew the poker business real well, Mr. Brooks agreed to the deal.

We opened our business on Park Lane Street in Dallas. I knew all the players around town, so we had some big players in our no-limit game. There usually was around $50,000 to $70,000 on the table, a bigger game that most of the ones in Vegas. About the second game that we ran, Dicky Carson came in to play and he's been laughing ever since about this next story.

Since Mr. Brooks had a good sum of money, we were giving out tab and he okayed everybody's slips. We could stand good for $20,000 or more and the players didn't have to worry about getting paid. We had this good game going that had lasted for about two days and we had around $40,000 out on credit. About nine o'clock in the morning, the game still was six-handed with a lot of chips on the table. We had to pay everybody two days later at the next game, so I suggested to Mr. Brooks that we straighten up with them at that time. "No, I want to pay them all today, " he said. "Go get your car and drive me to the bank and I'll get some money so that we can pay them before they leave." So we told everybody to just keep on playing while we went to the bank.

When we came to Greenville Avenue I asked, "Which way should I turn?"

"I don't know. Try turning left," Mr. Brooks answered.

"Well, where are we going?"

"To the bank, Byron."

"Which bank?"

"Hell, any bank's got $40,000 in it!" he snapped. "Just pull in to the next one you see." I was purely amazed, but I stopped at a bank about a block away. Dressed in coveralls and a straw hat, Bob went inside and twenty minutes later he came out with a paper bag full of money. I knew then that he must have a lot of money if he could get that much money from a bank he'd never been in before.

One time Mr. Brooks and a couple of friends had a Vegas-style craps game in Fort Worth with some big players in it. A guy who owned a Ford agency, another fella who had some nightclubs, Henry Bowen, and Curt Garrett all were betting high. Mr. Brooks was bankrolling it. During one session, he and his partners got off big losers. The game had a $500 limit but one shooter had beat them out of about $60,000 and another one had taken the game down for $20,000. His partners came to Brooks crying, "We're about $80,000 loser. We'd better lower the limit, what the hell else can we do? "

"Hell, *raise* the limit!" Brooks answered. "Let's wait till *I* get broke—then we'll figure out something." They had to laugh at that one. Of course they won the money back plus a couple hundred thousand. Mr. Brooks knew that they always had the percentages in their favor when they banked the craps. He used to say, "Anybody who ever got famous from shooting craps got famous for what they lost, not for how much they won." I know he was right about that—I wish that I had 20 percent of what I've lost at craps in my lifetime and 20 percent of what I've won banking games.

Whenever anything came up, Mr. Brooks knew the answer to it right away. I think he had read all the books in every library twice. Not only was he a smart man, he was a good man and I deeply respected him, and loved him like a daddy. He was always good to me, boy was he good to me, and we never had a quarrel. Any time I needed money to play on he wouldn't throw me $300, he'd throw me $20,000. He thought that I was a helluva player—of course, he was a good player himself—and he knew that he would get a good count with me. He was a tough ole sonnagun, too, so tough that nobody messed with him. I nicknamed Mr. Brooks "The Red Fox" and wrote a poem about him and some of his adventures in Alaska. Before he died in 1993 in Texas, he requested that someone read my poem at his funeral. I felt that he had paid me quite an honor. A lot of people who knew him still miss Mr. Brooks, especially me.

★ Everett Goulsby ★

Another man from Dallas who was a helluva poker player was Everett Goulsby. Everett was a player—played all the time. We used to play together in Dallas and he was about the best heads-up player ever—I'm telling you he was hard to beat head-up. His "hand" was Q-10. It seems like everybody used to have a poker hand named after them. "Fatman" Thompson from Corpus Christi played K-10 like it was two aces. In Houston, K-8 was "Kokomo" Slim's hand. And "Broomcorn" Herring played 6-3 like it was a pair of aces.

I used to be famous for playing 6-2, which we called "Aimsworth." I was in San Antone playing a big no-limit game with Jack Straus and Senator Red Berry and a bunch of the old-time players. Jack was on top of you all the time, but in full ring games he wasn't as tough as he was shorthanded or heads-up. He had two aces and I took the flop with a 6-2. A deuce came on the flop, he made a bet, and I called him. Off came another deuce on the turn, he bet, I called him. A third deuce came on the river and we got all in. When I showed him that 6-2, he said, "What the hell were you drawing at there, Cowboy?"

"Oh, I wasn't drawing at nothing," I answered. "Just aiming at another deuce. I guess I'm 'Aimsworth.'"

Another hand that I named is K-9, which is called "sawmill." Milton Butts and I were playing poker in Bryan, Texas, where they had a good game going on the weekends. We'd been playing for a couple of days when a hand came up in which I had a K-9. I made a pretty good hand with it, but I got broke to it. As I was driving back home to Houston with Milton, feeling kind of disgusted about getting broke with that K-9, we passed by a sawmill and saw a man sawing logs in the lumberyard. "As hard as that guy works for his money, I'll bet he would never get broke with a K-9," I told Milton. And that's how a K-9 got named "sawmill." Some of those names are still going around—Doyle Brunson mentioned the "sawmill" hand in his book, *Super/System*.

Everett was playing in a no-limit game with Benny Binion one time at the Horseshoe. Everett had two aces and Benny had two sevens. The flop came Q-7-something. Benny bet and Everett moved him all in. Benny thought about it for a few seconds and then threw away his three sevens! I couldn't believe that he would throw away the nuts. Later on Everett bragged to me, "I'll show you how to make one of them billionaires lay down a hand."

Everett was a good player and he was a lucky player along with it. One time we were playing in Arlington, Texas, where I had a Vegas-style craps game. Henry Bowen and Curtis "Iron Man" Skinner, who used to play golf with Doyle and them, were my partners. Curtis was nicknamed "Iron Man" because of the way he could hit a ball with those golf irons. I started playing heads-up poker with Everett and beat him out of $17,000 playing thirty minutes of lowball and thirty minutes of hold'em.

When the game broke up about three o'clock in the afternoon, Everett decided to shoot some dice. We had a $100 limit on the craps game and he got $30,000 loser. It seemed like there was no way that anybody could get out from that big a loss—at $100 limits, that's three hundred bets. But Everett hung in there until four o'clock the next afternoon. I might near had to put my stick men and dealers in the hospital because he had worn them all down. I put in so many new dice, I ran out of them—nothing was wrong with the dice, they were just on a streak. And Everett got out! Can you believe that? He got out $7,000 winner from being $30,000 loser. That's the biggest swing I've ever seen on a $100-limit craps game. You might not see another one like it in two hundred years.

★ Bobby Chapman ★

Bobby Chapman is another man who played with us in Dallas and we've played a lot of heads-up no-limit poker together. He was in the car business and was a helluva high player, high as anybody. One time when we were playing in Dallas, the joint closed up and we left to go partying around at the clubs in town. Bobby was a high roller—if there wasn't a table available in a place, he'd give the maitre d' $200 and he'd get a good table, don't worry about it. After this one place closed, Bobby hired the band and they kept the club open for us so that we could play some poker heads-up.

I'll never forget it—he was drinking Dubonnet wine and beat me just about every pot. Beat me out of about $20,000. I was sick. So after about four or five days, I bought a bottle of that Dubonnet wine and called Bobby. We met at the club and I got my money back plus some.

And boy would he gamble! One time we were playing no-limit six-card to high-low shuck, a poker game the old-time gamblers used to play, at another club. Bill Smith was in the game with us and together we lost $17,000. Bill got broke and went to the bar for a drink, but I stayed in the game with Bobby. I was pumping money all over town. Got $45,000 loser. Then I borrowed $5,000 more—a guy brought it to me at my house and then Evelyn took me back to the game. I'll never forget it because it was the night before O.U. and Texas played in the Cotton Bowl.

Bobby was still there when I walked back in. I just threw the $5,000 on the table and we started again. To make a long story short I started winning a few hands playing that lowball shuck—it's a helluva fast game—and it wasn't long before I got even. Won the $45,000 back plus about $10,000 more in around forty-five minutes. "Well, I guess you got broke again," Evelyn said when she came to pick me up.

"Hell no, I got even and won some!" I bragged. That's how high and how fast we played.

★ Harlan Dean ★

Harlan Dean was a real character. He had a poker game at Shreveport where I first met T.J. Cloutier. One time Blondie and Harlan and I had been playing poker at Harlan's joint for two days straight. A deck of cards cost about eight dollars and we'd been playing with the same deck for two days, so Blondie said, "Harlan, get us a new box of cards."

"What the hell you talkin' about, a new deck of cards?" Harlan protested. He was closer than one is to two. "You think you're gettin' cheated or somethin'? There ain't nothin' wrong with these cards. Deal 'em!" That's just the way he was, gruff at times.

Another time when we were playing in Harlan's game, we ran out of groceries. Dick Melvin was playing, along with T.J. Cloutier, Jeff Stewart, Homer Marcotte ("The Louisiana Man")—about seven or eight of us were in the game. Harlan asked Evelyn if she'd go out to get something for the players to eat. He ordered a pound of potato salad and just one chicken for seven players. Here seven of us had been playing for two days, paying to play, and he ordered some potato salad and a little bit of chicken for the cook to fix for us to eat. There wasn't any more than about half a chicken leg for each of us!

★ Lawrence "Broomcorn" Herring ★

Lawrence Herring was always called "Broomcorn," so a lot of people never knew his real name. He was a famous player in Texas back when Johnny Moss was in his heyday. Broomcorn used to play in the big game in Odessa at the Golden Rooster and usually ordered two beers at one time. His "hand" was 6-3—didn't make any difference to him what anybody else had, he was likely to go all the way to the river with it. Broomcorn used to play at my place in Tyler and was there the night Sarge broke all my players at Georgia skin.

My first encounter with him was at a lowball game in Brenham that I'd heard about—drove two hundred fifty miles to play in it with about $500 in my pocket. Martin Cramer ran the place, had a big Vegas-style dice game and the lowball game. Hubert Watson, Hugh Shoemaker, Broomcorn, and a bunch of others were there. I bought in for the $500 and about three or four hands into the game I was dealt something like two kings and two queens. Broomcorn was first to act and drew two cards. Hell, I wasn't gonna draw so I stood pat. Bet the rest of the money I had in front of me, about $300. He was pretty cagey, studied around and studied around. "I smell snow," he said and called me with two deuces. Broke me.

★ Hugh Briscoe and Some Others ★

Hugh Briscoe had a big poker game in Denton, Texas on the weekends. He wasn't that good a player but he had money. I remember the time that Bob Brooks and I won $40,000 at his place in two or three days. Sometimes Briscoe would come to Dallas and play in my game. One time when we had a big no-limit hold'em game going at the AmVets, Briscoe was in the game along with Speedy Meyers from Killeen, Texas who used to run around with Buck Buchanan. Hugh and Speedy were in a $20,000 pot together. Hugh flopped three jacks and Speedy flopped three fours. They made a bet on the flop and when no help came for either of them on the turn, they moved in. A lot of us were pulling for Hugh because he was a real good producer and that was a big pot.

We had a rule at the club that if you wanted to cut the cards, it would cost you five dollars. That way, people wouldn't be cutting the cards all the time and slowing down the game. Hugh threw five bucks into the pot and said, "Cut the cards." The dealer cut them, burned a card, and off came the case four! Speedy broke him with quad fours. That was one of the damnedest things I've ever seen. It sure broke Hugh of cutting the cards.

Bobby Baldwin, Bob Brooks, T.J. Cloutier, Ken "Whatta Player" Smith, "Catfish" Bullard, all the top players in that part of the country were playing with us in those days. Another man who played with us was my landlord, "Big E," who had a carpet business downstairs from my AmVets club in Dallas. Big E was a really big guy with a big bankroll, wore a size-19 ring. He wasn't that good a poker player, preferred betting the sports. One time while we had that $5 rule for cutting the cards, Big E said, "Cut the cards."

"It costs $5 to cut the cards," somebody piped up.

"Who's gonna make me pay it?" Big E answered. Nobody said a thing and the dealer cut the deck. Later on, two guys tried to hijack Big E, but they tried that trick on the wrong man. Big E didn't go for that hijacking deal—killed one of them, the other one got away.

Another fella I used to play with was Aubrey Day from Tuscaloosa, Alabama who used to come to the World Series every year for the tournaments. He was a high player in his day, used to play down South with Goody and all those guys. Deuce-to-seven was his main game and wherever they played really high, that's where you would find Aubrey.

Paul Harvey used to come out to the Horseshoe to play before they ever had a World Series. He was quite a character—had a big gambling joint in Odessa and played poker real high, used to play with Johnny Moss and all those guys in Odessa. He'd make a bet and put every dollar he had into the pot. They all liked to play with him because he played so loose and so high. Paul lost a lot of money, but then he had a lot of money so it didn't matter that much to him. I've played with him myself in Waco and Vegas and I know that most of the old-timers remember him.

Morris Shapiro used to play real high poker in Odessa with Johnny Moss and the others at the Golden Rooster, where I first met him. Morris probably is eighty-something now, but I remember when we used to play poker at the Red Men's Club in Dallas back in the '60s. A little biddy guy, Morris was really a top player in the '50s like Johnny Moss was.

Don Thrash and Donny Two are from Lubbock where they had some good poker games. Dale Suttle used to live there, but he's gone now. Dale is the man who entered Bill Smith in the World Series in 1985, the year that Bill flew to Vegas on a Lear jet and ended up winning the championship.

★ Blondie Forbes ★

Blondie was an old-timer from Monroe, Louisiana who went to Vegas when they first started playing hold'em there. I played a lot of poker with him down in Louisiana and in Vegas long before the World Series was invented. One time we were in Shreveport playing at Harlan Dean's place. We heard about a game in Leesville where Little Red and a lot of the guys were playing so we drove down there that night to play with them. I couldn't hold a hand and just about got flat broke. The next day while we were driving back to Shreveport to get some more money, Blondie and I started talking. "Man, I wish we'd got thrown in jail last night," I said.

"What're you talkin' about?" he asked.

"Well, we wouldn't have got broke if they'd raided the game and put us all in jail," I joked. He was pretty disgusted with our sorry state of affairs and didn't see the humor in it.

The next night we played at another place in Shreveport and were doing pretty good when sure enough, the police raided the game. Drove the paddy wagon out and arrested all of us.

"Well, we got a break tonight," I told Blondie on our way to the jail.

"What's that?" he asked.

"We didn't get broke—we got in jail," I joked.

"Man, I wish you'd be quiet," he said, kinda scared. Blondie was inducted into the Poker Hall of Fame in 1980.

★ Bobby "The Owl" Baldwin ★

Willie Struthers and a few guys from Oklahoma heard about the good game that I had going in Dallas at the AmVets and decided to come down to play in it. Bobby Baldwin came with them. He was just a young kid then and ended up moving to Dallas, I guess because the game was so good and nothing much was going on in Tulsa at the time. I also ran craps games and hired Bobby to help me with them.

He was a good hand and a good poker player, too, and just got better and better as he went along. Bobby and I played heads-up no-limit hold'em a lot of times right there in my joint, but although I played high stakes with Bobby Chapman and the others, I didn't play high with Bobby Baldwin.

Back then I was young enough to hang on and sometimes I would win, sometimes he would win, but we never played for any really big money. We were just trying to make a living. He didn't have much money, but he could always play poker because he was so good at it that anybody would stake him in a game. At first we called him "The Kid from Tulsa" and later we nicknamed him "The Owl" because it seemed like he could see in the dark—he could read a player better than anybody else in the world.

I don't know anybody who could play no-limit hold'em as well as Bobby could—or as fast as he did or could judge a hand as perfectly as he could. He wouldn't hesitate to put it in the center and sometimes he'd bet so much money that it wasn't poker to call. He'd make you look at your hole card, that's for sure. One night he was playing at my joint in Dallas with Bobby Chapman, who was a good friend of mine and a high-limit player. Chapman bet $20,000 at the end and Bobby called him with a king high, no pair—and won the pot! He had put Chapman on a flush draw and sure enough, that's what he had been drawing at. Can you imagine that? Calling a $20,000 bet with just a king high?

Chapman later went out to Vegas several times and one night during Amarillo Slim's Super Bowl of Poker, he and Bobby started playing heads-up. I heard that Bobby beat him out of $800,000. To the best of my knowledge, Chapman's never been to Las Vegas since then.

No-limit poker is the great equalizer. You can sit a monkey down at a poker table and teach him how to play limit poker and he's liable to beat you by catching a backdoor flush. But it's different when you play no-limit, when your whole bankroll is in the pot and you stand to lose your boots if you haven't read your opponent right. When Bobby was in his prime, he was the Tiger Woods of no-limit hold'em. He had a sharp mind and was right on top of you all the time. He was liable to grab a 6-2 offsuit, you'd show a little wiggle, and then he might say, "I'll bet you $10,000."

I'll never forget the time that I took Bobby with me to Corpus to play in a big poker game. We had about $20,000 with us and because it was no-limit, I let him play first. In two hours, he was broke, lost all our money. And I hadn't even gotten to look at a card yet—that's how fast he played. "What the hell are we gonna do now?" I wondered. I decided to fly to Dallas the next morning to get some more money. "I'll be back down here before sunset," I told Bobby. So I jumped on a plane headed for Dallas, got some money, and flew back to Corpus. When I walked into the joint, Bobby was sitting at the table with $30,000 stacked up in front of him! He had started playing with our last $200 and had gotten us winner off it, that's how great he was. Over the years, Bobby Baldwin has made a lot of players chill up playing poker.

★ The Gamblers Named Smith ★

Three of the big gamblers in Texas at that time were named Smith. Boston Smith was a big bookmaker in Fort Worth. He used to play some poker. Not a lot, but he knew a lot of poker players. One time in Hot Springs back when the town had wide open gambling, a poker player who got broke called Boston to borrow some money. "Boston, send me $500," he said. The phone line was sort of messed up and Boston could hardly hear him.

"I can't hear you," Boston said.

"This is so-and-so," the guy shouted. "Send me $500!"

"What did you say? I can't hear you," Boston shouted.

About that time the operator broke in on the conversation and told Boston, "So-and-so says to wire him $500. He's in Hot Springs."

"If you can hear him so good, why don't *you* send him the $500?" Boston suggested.

Kenny "Whatta Player" Smith was a great big guy who always wore a top hat like the one that Abe Lincoln had worn at the Ford Theater when he was assassinated. Kenny loved poker and was a helluva player, played with us around Dallas. We called him "Whatta Player" because when he won a hand, he'd stand up and yell, "Whatta Player, Smith! Whatta player!" I've been in big no-limit hold'em games with Kenny where he would just turn his cards face up and then draw out on you. He got a kick out of doing that.

Kenny also was an excellent chess player and wrote several books on the game. One time at my club he played chess against three people at the same time and beat them all. I think that he once played Bobby Fischer to a tie. Kenny used to come to all the World Series of Poker before he died in 1998.

"Smitty" Smith is another player who used to come to all the tournaments at the Horseshoe. He also roped calves as a hobby, so we used to call him "Cowboy Smitty." The last rodeo that I made with Smitty was at the Cow Palace in San Francisco. Smitty flew to the rodeo and he sent me, Eugene Johnson, and R.B. Carraway there in his brand new Buick hauling a two-horse trailer. When we got there, a big no-limit lowball game was going on in the tent with all the cowboys playing on the top of some bales of hay that they had covered with blankets. Smitty was a tough lowball player but he was running a little unlucky and was losing, so he called home and had some more money sent to him. Before the rodeo was over, he wound up winning about $70,000 off those California cowboys. They thought they had themselves a sucker, but Smitty took them off for some real money.

In the late '50s and early '60s, Smitty owned the Rainbow Inn in Monroe, Louisiana with open gambling just like Las Vegas. Smitty made so much money there it was unbelievable, but he got closed down soon after the former governor came out to his place to gamble. Smitty and the ex-governor had been good friends for a long time, but they got into a quarrel and ended up fighting. Being a rodeo man, Smitty was a pretty tough guy and I think that he got the best of it, but the ex-governor got on the radio, smeared Smitty's place, and was able to get the Rainbow Inn closed down. Cost Smitty millions, that one little ole squabble. Me, I'd rather have just blown it off and forgotten about the argument. Smitty's picture was in the first World Series brochure ever published by the Horseshoe.

This story is just one example of the kind of trouble that gamblers got into in the old days. Seemed like there was always some sort of danger hiding around the corner waiting to jump out from the shadows and drag you down. And along with everybody else fadin' the white line, I had my share of it.

TROUBLE IN RIVER CITY

"Ah like ya son, but ah'll put a rattlesnake in
your pocketand ask you for a match."
— *Amarillo Slim Preston*

Unlike the casinos today, we weren't always safe in our poker games in Texas. We had a lot of things to worry about—hijackers, cheats, police raids. We always took every precaution we could to protect ourselves, but it seemed like no matter what we did, it wasn't enough.

Even opening a club with a Red Men or AmVets charter didn't always keep the police and Texas Rangers off our backs. You see, gambling is legal in Texas if the folks running the game aren't making a profit on it for themselves. It's okay to run a chartered club game like the Elks, Red Men and AmVets because the rake is taken to support the club's charitable activities and to cover expenses. Of course when my business partners and I ran chartered clubs in the old days, we interpreted the word "expenses" very broadly. And it's okay to have a poker game in your home if you aren't taking a percentage of the action; otherwise it is illegal. But I never knew of any home games in the old days in Texas where the landlord didn't rake the game. How else was he gonna make a profit from it?

I've owned several poker places that the police have raided and then thrown me and everybody else in jail. Curt Garrett and I owned a Red Men's Club in Fort Worth years ago and we had a helluva business. In Tyler it was costing players 5 percent to buy chips, but in Fort Worth I was able to charge 7.5 percent—and nobody cared, they just wanted to play. For a little while we had the damnedest game I've ever seen. Then one day, the doors came tumbling down. At first I thought it was a heist, but it was the police swooping down on us with their guns drawn. They tore up my entire joint and then started loading everybody in a paddy wagon that was waiting out in front. A Texas Ranger packing two pearl-handled pistols was standing there by the wagon, the same Ranger who had shot a man six weeks before with a high-powered rifle after the guy had taken a hostage. Those Texas Rangers used to be brutal. As I started to get in the paddy wagon, this Ranger said to the cops, "Leave Wolford here to the last."

"Uh oh, it's goodbye Wolford," I was thinking. After they had loaded everybody else in the wagon, I was left behind with this Texas Ranger and another policeman. "Get in the back seat of the car," they told me. I figured I was going for a "ride." They drove me out to the highway but instead of turning left toward the countryside, they crossed it and drove toward town. Boy was I relieved! That's one of the few times I was happy to be going to jail.

When I got into the cell around midnight, Sam Benson was there along with Carl Biggs and Curt Garrett and the rest of the poker players. Sam was a bookmaker that we called "Lightning" and he was hollering at the top of his lungs, "Let me out of this sonnabitch! I've gotta open up my book at ten o'clock in the morning. A lot of my customers are depending on me—I've gotta take care of business!" We were all laughing at him, knowing that we'd be out first thing in the morning as soon as we'd made bail.

★ Hi-ho, Hi-ho, It's Off to Jail We Go ★

That was just one of the times that my butt landed in jail. The year that Joe Namath won the Super Bowl when his team was a 17-point underdog, I drove to Albuquerque with my girlfriend Donna where I had a friend named Marvin Rourke. Marvin was a wholesale used car buyer and seller who had told me that there were some good poker games in Albuquerque. Donna and I rented a nice apartment in a high-rise building and settled in for some good poker, and Marvin introduced me to some of the guys who played poker there. They had some good games and I played might near every night. I was doing pretty good, making a little money and living pretty high, when something happened that I really didn't like much at all—my gal ran off with another man. Never did find out who. Donna was a sweetheart, a real cutie, and she was smarter than a huntin' dog. Of course I've always said that if a woman will leave her mother, she'll leave anybody. Sounds funny now, but it wasn't funny at the time.

The games were so good in Albuquerque that I stayed on. A man named Gong (or something like that) who owned a restaurant in town played with us and he lost every time he played. One day Joe Tappett and I were eating in Gong's Chinese restaurant and he asked whether we wanted to go out to his house for some poker. We weren't about to turn down an invitation like that. "Hell yeah," we answered knowing that he couldn't play a lick.

Gong left his restaurant about six thirty that evening and we met him at his house and started playing poker on his kitchen table. We were winning pretty good when he got up from the game and called his wife, who was running things at the restaurant while he was gone. Speaking in Chinese, he told her that we were cheating him out of all his money. That was a bunch of bullshit because we weren't doing anything except just playing for ourselves. In about forty minutes the police showed up at his house, arrested us and took us to jail. Took all our money, went to my apartment and searched it top to bottom, tore it up real good. Guess they thought that I had some more money hidden there.

"Were you cheatin' that Chinaman?" the police captain asked.

"Hell no," I declared. "He can't play a lick, loses everywhere he plays, just ask around town. He just invited us out to his house to play poker and nobody was cheatin' nobody. The only dealings that I've ever had with this guy was when he asked me if I wanted to join the Communist party and I told him no, I hear it ain't worth a damn, and moved on to something else." The captain knew right then that I wasn't going to tell him shit.

"Take Wolford in the back and lock him up," he said with a smirk on his face. So there I was, sitting in jail in Albuquerque. The police had taken all my money, about $6,000, ransacked my apartment, and my gal had run off. How much better shape can a sonnabitch get in than that? If you can figure it out, tell me sometime—I'd like to hear your story.

Jerry Forrest, a Texan who was living in Albuquerque at the time, made my bond so I could get out of jail. He took me out to his girlfriend's house. A friend of hers was there with her, a real good looking lady about my age named Pat Lemmon. We all got to talking and I was thanking Jerry for getting me out of jail. "I'm real grateful," I said, "but I don't know what I'm gonna do now."

"I know where there's a helluva lowball game in Texas," Jerry told me. "Let's go on down there and I'll stake you in it." Sounded good to me.

The next day a story came out on the front page of the Albuquerque newspaper, something like "Wolford Beats Gong out of $40,000 in Poker Game." All those older folks who lived in my high-rise apartment building really liked me but when they read that story, they thought I was another John Dillinger. I packed up all the stuff that I had left to my name and got it out of there, and Jerry and I headed for North Texas together.

When we showed up at the house where the game was going on, there wasn't anybody around except three housemen who were propping the game. Of course I knew that they were all playing the same money, but I also knew that they couldn't play as well as me. Wound up breaking them all, won about $10,000 off them. After that score Jerry and I went on back to Albuquerque. Now that I had a little bankroll of about $5,000, I was fixin' to leave town when Jerry's girlfriend and Pat came by to see us. Pat owned a company in Albuquerque that manufactured big water culverts.

"You all come on and let's go to Houston," I suggested. "We can put together a bankroll there and buy some of those Volkswagens that have been damaged by the salt water on those ships. We can make us a lot of money that way." When the ships came into port in Houston, some of them might have been caught in a storm and sometimes the cars that they were carrying would get salt water on them and were totaled. I figured that you could buy them cheap, refurbish them, and make a lot of money reselling them. I was wheelin' and dealin' in those days.

Pat already had money, of course, but she thought that was a good business deal, so we all flew to Houston. I wasn't with Pat or anything like that—she had her own room and I had mine—but that deal didn't go through, so I figured it was time to get back to a poker table somewhere.

"I know some folks in East Texas who have a good poker game," I proposed. "Why don't we go up there and play some?" Jerry and his girlfriend wanted to go back home to Albuquerque, but Miss Lemmon liked the idea so she bought a brand new Lincoln off the showroom floor and together we drove to Tyler where my friend Johnny Wheeler had a game going. We stayed there a few days and I played in Johnny's game, but the action wasn't all that great so I called Curt Garrett in Fort Worth to see what was going on there.

"Aw, things are pretty slow around here," he said, "but there's a guy here who's in the real estate business who likes to play poker. He won't play me anymore, but he might play you." So Pat and I drove to Fort Worth to see Curt and try to set up a game with the real estate man.

As soon as we got there Curt set up a meeting with him. The real estate agent came to our hotel to take Miss Lemmon around town and show her some land. She was interested in buying some property where she could set up a culvert business like the one she owned in Albuquerque. We drove around all afternoon and then landed back at the hotel bar for a few drinks. After we had talked for a while and downed a drink or two, I brought up the subject closest to my heart.

"Hell, all this real estate talk is boring," I said. "I'd rather play poker."

"Man, I'd like to play some poker, too," the real estate man answered.

"Well hell, let's play," I shot back.

"Suits me!" he said.

"Okay, go buy a deck of cards in the gift shop and we'll play upstairs in my room." So he bought some cards and I got a couple of bottles of booze (he liked to drink), threw a blanket over the little table in my room, poured the drinks, and unzipped the new deck of cards. The game was on.

Curt was right. The man might've been the world's best real estate salesman but he was one bad poker player, couldn't play a lick. Won $70,000 off him, accepted his check as payment. Went to the bank the next morning and cashed it, then dropped by Curt's place to give him a piece of it for making the contact for me. A few days later Pat flew back to Albuquerque and left the Lincoln with me, so I decided to call up this guy and see if he wanted to play a little more poker.

"You know, I work for Miss Lemmon and I've never had this kind of money before," I explained. "I don't know what the hell I'm gonna do with it all. I'd like to have a drink with you and maybe play some more poker and see if I can lose it back to you."

"Sure, we can have a drink together and play some more poker," he said. So I met him and his wife that night at the Western Hills Motel there in Fort Worth, a big place with a nice bar, a real classy joint back then. About that time Curt Garrett just happened to walk in and join us, so we sat a spell talking and drinking. After a while I said, "Hell, I'm ready to play poker. How 'bout you all?"

"Yeah, I am, too," the real estate whiz answered and sent his wife home telling her that he'd see her a little later after poker. So I rented a room and he bought some cards and we started the game. Beat him out of another $50,000. Took me about two days, but I got the money from him.

Later he told Curt, "That guy's some kind of damn nut, ain't he? He won that $70,000 off me and then said he wanted to play some more and lose it back to me. I really thought he was gonna lose it all back to me so he wouldn't get in trouble with his boss over having that much money on him, and I'll be damned if I didn't wind up losing another $50,000 to him!" Curt listened sympathetically, I'm sure.

That was a pretty good score that I made from just bullshitting a little bit, you know, playing somebody that I knew I could beat. Those kinds of wins don't come along very often; I've only run into two or three of them in my lifetime. But you never know what's gonna happen when you're in the right place at the right time.

While I was in Fort Worth, Johnny Wheeler introduced me to a gal from Beaumont, Texas named Carolyn. "She'll make you a good gal," he guaranteed. Turns out he was right. Carolyn and I started messing around together and liked each other, so we went to her home in Beaumont and got married. She had real nice parents and two kids around ten and twelve years old; I treated them just like I was their daddy. A little while after we were married we decided to move to Shreveport where I was planning to set up a Red Men's Club.

After we had set ourselves up in an apartment, I went over to the Silver Dollar Bar, which was owned by Clyde Hyde. Harlan Dean lived in Shreveport and he had given me a tip about Clyde.

"I'm tellin' you, Cowboy, that Clyde is a mean guy," he told me. "I'm not kiddin' you, he's one tough sonnabitch."

When I met with Clyde I explained, "I'm lookin' for a place to have a poker game and I hear that you have a real nice apartment upstairs over your bar. What would you think about runnin' a poker game up there a couple of days a week?"

"Yeah, we'll have a game here a few nights a week," he agreed and showed me the upstairs apartment. It was perfect. Clyde gave Carolyn a job in the Silver Dollar tending bar and he and I got things set up for the poker game.

"Before this thing starts," I told him, "let's understand that I don't want you playing. We're gonna get 5 percent on the chips and that'll probably make us between $1,000 to $1,500 a night. I'll play and you can have 50 percent of my action. And I'll probably beat them because I'm a good player." He agreed to my terms.

Everybody I had notified about the game showed up—Homer Marcotte, Harlan Dean, Jeff Stuart, the whole bunch—and we started a helluva poker game. Clyde was running around asking everybody, "You want a drink, you want a Coke, anything?" being a good host. And then he sat down and said the fatal words, "Give me a goddamned hand."

"Clyde, you know what we talked about," I reminded him.

"Why don't you just let me play here a while until we get the game going good, and then in a few days you can play some if you want to." In a roundabout way I was trying to talk him out of playing. Looking over at Harlan I saw him shaking his head.

"Hell, I've got money!" Clyde protested and threw out about $5,000. "Give me a hand!"

Clyde couldn't play a lick. We're playing no-limit hold'em and he and I are in a pot together, I'll never forget it. I've got the nut straight with one card to come. I bet about $2,000 and turned my cards face up, the nuts, thinking that he surely would throw his hand away. I was trying not to win the money off him; we were partners. But he didn't know the difference and called the bet anyway, drawing at a nine-high flush with one card to come. He missed it and I scooped in the pot. Clyde lost $20,000 cash that night.

The next morning I was talking with Harlan. "Damn, Cowboy, I don't know what to tell you," he said. "That guy's an outlaw, you know, a tough sonnabitch. You'd better be mighty careful."

"Well hell, you saw me do everything I could not to take his money, even showed him the nut hand."

"I know you did, but just remember that he's rough." But surprisingly Clyde never raised any hell over it, just laughed it off.

A little while later I was talking with Clyde and suggested that we open a Red Men's Club. "That's a good idea," he agreed. "I know just the place," so we went down the street to take a look at it. Wound up renting it, carpeted the whole joint, put a lodge room up front with an American flag hanging prominently on the wall, and set up the "recreation room" in the back. Phoned all the Red Men to come look it over, elected officers, paid for all their hotel bills and eats.

The first morning that we were open, they were lined up at the door—Homer, Harlan, Jeff, every poker player from that part of Texas. Everybody liked the way we had it set up with a nice little kitchen, good lighting, a place to put your chips, a podium, the whole deal. Hell, we had two full games the first day, both no-limit hold'em. Everything went along real smooth for the next two weeks when here came the police looking the joint over from top to bottom.

We showed them our charter and explained what the Red Men's Club was, and explained how we were fixing to donate to the Police Benevolent Fund, the crippled children's deal, and all those charities, and they seemed to like us just fine. Left without a word of concern. Looked to us like everything was all right. But it wasn't.

I had been working day and night to get the joint off to a good start, so one night around seven o'clock I took off work early and headed for Mike James' place in Bossier City to mess around a little bit, have a few drinks, and shoot the bull at Mike's bar. I'm sitting there drinking a beer when I look up at the TV and what's the big story they're broadcasting? The Red Men's Club in Shreveport had just been raided! The police had torn up the club and thrown every sonnabitch in the place in jail. I usually was the first one they put in jail but since I wasn't there when they raided the joint, I stayed out of the pokey that time. I figured it was time to leave Shreveport.

"Let's get our stuff together and move to Beaumont," I told Carolyn. "I hear there's a good poker game down there." So we packed up our things and headed for her hometown with not much more than change for a twenty-dollar bill in our pockets. She introduced me to Walter Sekaly, Jr., a lawyer whose daddy owned a bar there in Beaumont. Walter Jr. is a judge now. Then I met Sonny Cribbs, Fred Carver, and some other lawyers and they invited me to play in their poker game.

The poker in Beaumont was good to me—they couldn't play quite as well as I did—and I started making money, a whole lot of money. And I made a lot of friends. Walter and I still talk on the phone occasionally. Walter's daddy was a sharp ole gambler who used to have all the gaming around Beaumont before the Kefauver investigation shut him down. He's the only player that I've ever heard say, "All rooms rented!" when he made a full house and showed it down.

★ The Biggest Bluff I've Ever Made ★

Around 1976 I bought a real nice townhouse in Dallas with a ten-foot high, wrought iron picket fence around it where I ran poker, blackjack, and dice games. On the ground level was a big garage that we converted into the game room. Our living room, a half-bath, kitchen, and one bedroom were on the second floor. The top floor had two more bedrooms and two baths. I enclosed the garage, had it soundproofed, and put nice carpeting on the floor. Then my wife Evelyn and I decorated the place to perfection.

We put in a beautiful horseshoe bar backed by stained glass. Then we had a blackjack table custom-made to fit around the bar and placed an antique gasoline pump in a corner near our solid oak poker table. T.J. Cloutier told me that it was the prettiest poker room that he'd ever seen. Evelyn cooked for everybody and we served drinks. It was while we were living there and running the games that I pulled off the biggest bluff that I've ever made, a bluff that saved my hide.

I've been hijacked three or four times but I've only been in one shoot-out. I had been playing poker at another joint in Dallas and about three o'clock in the morning I left for home. When I arrived at the townhouse I parked my Cadillac in front of the iron fence about forty feet from my front door. Under the seat in my car I had an automatic .45 that Curtis "Iron Man" Skinner had sold me out of his hock shop. I stuck it in the vest of my three-piece suit before I got out of the car and had just started walking toward the house when two guys wearing ski masks jumped out at me. One of them put a pistol to my head saying, "Get over there where your car is." So, I gave him my keys, got in the back seat, and laid down.

One guy was driving and the other one was leaning over the front seat with his pistol aimed at me. "Give me all your money and your jewelry," he demanded. So I got out my money and took off my diamond rings and handed them over. He halfway frisked me and asked, "Man, do you carry a gun?"

"Hey, I don't even carry a nail file," I answered. They already had my money and I knew that they were gonna kill me. "Man, it's a cool score," I said to try to persuade them to let me go. "You've got everything in my car, just kick me out somewhere and go on."

"Don't look up here or I'm gonna shoot your head off," he answered.

As we're driving, I'm trying to figure out how I can get a hold of my pistol and shoot him without his shooting me first. He had the gun right on me—if we hit a bump I was afraid that the cocked hammer might go off accidentally. So, I figured I'd better wait till they got me out of the car to make my move. Sure enough, in about thirty minutes, they stopped out where a bunch of houses were being built. The gunman opened the door and said, "Pull off your boots." I was laying in the back seat of the Eldorado and the dome light came on and I was afraid that if I raised up to take off my boots, they'd see the pistol in my vest.

"I hurt my back rodeoing," I moaned. "I can't hardly move."

"Stick your feet out here," he said. He pulled my boots off and threw them on the ground. Getting out of the car, I acted like I could just barely raise up. With him right behind, I started walking down the road like my back was killing me. Suddenly, I kicked the safety on my .45, whipped around and said, "Now, you sonnabitch, you're on the other end!" and shot at him right there in the dark. He fell backward and shot one back at me. Then he ran over to my Eldorado and they took off in a hurry. I shot at the car three times, but I was shooting low so the bullets just went through my golf bags and out the side.

There I was with no shells, barefooted, cold—and here they came driving back again! I didn't realize that it was a dead end road and they'd have to turn around to get out of there, so I started running through the construction area where the houses were being built, afraid I'd cut my foot off on something, but still running like hell. But they didn't stop; guess they didn't know I was out of shells. Then I saw a light in a house way up on top of the hill. It was three o'clock in the morning and when the owner came to the door I told him, "I don't want to alarm you, but I've been robbed and they stole my car. Would you mind calling my home and seeing if everybody's all right? And call the police. And turn off that porch light!" Pretty soon the police arrived and took me home to Evelyn and our boy.

I got into another scrape that same year when I drove over to Tyler to play in a big poker game that George Lambert and Henry Bowen had going there. Harlan and T.J. were in the game, along with all the guys from Tyler. The law raided us, took everybody's money and every other thing they owned at gunpoint. But the police didn't take anything from the players who lived in Tyler; they only took from the ones of us who lived out of town. Harlan had $10,000 on him and I had $3,500 cash in my pocket and about $2,000 in chips that I hadn't had a chance to cash out.

I went to see a lawyer in Tyler about getting my money back, but he wanted such a price to handle it for me that I didn't go for the deal. Instead I called Bill Bratton in Dallas and he drove down to Tyler to help me out. Bill walked into the courthouse in Tyler and charged the police with armed robbery! "They took the money from you at gunpoint," Bill explained, "and that's armed robbery."

"I didn't want you to go that strong," I told him. "They're liable to shoot you or something." But he's the type who won't dog it, and he got all our money back. He told me later, though, that he kept his eye on the rearview mirror all the way home.

★ Scam Artists and Card Sharps ★

The police and hijackers weren't the only ones that we had to worry about in those days—we also had to protect ourselves against the cheats and scam artists. I've been a road gambler all my life and I can tell you that I've seen some big scams going down the road. A lot of these hotshot poker players in this day and time—the ones who've picked up those poker books and started playing in the casinos and think they're the greatest players in the world (they catch every card in the deck sometimes) and have an ego bigger than New York City—hell, they wouldn't have lasted three months back when I was fading the white line. Too many people were doing things that these modern guys wouldn't be able to understand.

In the old days, every player took his turn dealing. Modern casinos employ professional dealers, and like I've said, these young poker players today have other types of protection in the casinos—the surveillance cameras, the floormen, and so on. Some of them have big bankrolls that a backer probably put up for them, they've got a big ego—and they wouldn't have lasted three months on the roads that I used to travel. They would've been put to the test and probably would've had to find themselves some racket other than playing poker because there would have been no win to it for them.

Of course I've played in lots of poker games, including some real big games, that were on the square, games where nobody was doing anything. But if somebody could do something and he was playing in a big no-limit game, he'd only have to do it every once in a while in a $10,000-$15,000 pot. If he was a good player, he could just sit back and be patient until another big pot came up, even it took three hours of waiting for the right situation.

I've seen some of the best holdout men in the world. I used to play poker with a guy named Jess Pierce, one of the best road gamblers I've ever seen, a big Indian from Oklahoma who's dead now. Jess could hold out a card on anybody in the world and I'm here to tell you that if you didn't know the move, you couldn't catch him. The first time that I met him, we were playing in a big hold'em game in Corpus and I saw him go out with a card. A pot came up and after all the cards were out, I had the nut flush. Then I saw Jess switch a card. I made a bet and he moved in.

I didn't know what he had and I didn't care because I had the nuts and I broke him. I didn't say anything right then because I'm not one to blow the whistle on anybody—if I don't like the situation, I'll just get up and quit the game. After the game was over Jess suggested that we go down to the cafe for some breakfast.

"I think you seen me go out with that card," he said over some bacon and eggs.

"Yeah, I did," I answered, "but it didn't make no difference. I had the nuts and knew that nobody could beat me."

"Well, you were pretty nice about it," he said. And he never tried any tricks on me again.

Our paths crossed again a few months later when I had a poker game going in Dallas with $100/$200 limits, a big game twenty-five years ago. We played five nights a week and I worked all the time, so I took a few days off for a trip out of town. While I was gone, Jess came by and played in the game. He broke every one of those sonsaguns, won about $20,000 off them and they never knew what hit them. He had left town by the time that I got back, but two days later I found an envelope in my mailbox. Inside was a note from Jess and a cashier's check for $5,000. "I came by your joint," he wrote, "and boy, there were some real lulus in there!" That's the last time that I ever heard from him.

One of the damnedest holdout artists I've ever met was Danny Daniels, a rodeo cowboy who got killed in Albuquerque holding out on a guy playing gin rummy. After the last rodeo that I made at the Cow Palace in San Francisco, Danny and I drove to Dallas to play at the Red Men's Club, where we rented an apartment together. Danny just loved holding out cards and nothing or nobody could stop him from doing it, so I probably should've known that not even being roommates could keep him from doing it to me, too. One night he held out a card and broke me in a big pot. I motioned him to join me in the little kitchen at the back of the place.

"Danny, I want my money back," I told him. "I don't care what the hell you do, I ain't gonna blow the whistle on you. But I can't stand you holding out a card on me."

"I didn't do nothing," he answered, looking as innocent as a newborn child.

"Don't lie to me," I warned him. "I want the money back that I lost in that pot and I want it now." He gave it to me on the spot.

Danny stayed around the Red Men's for about three months and broke everybody by holding out cards. He had the damnedest move that I believe I've ever seen. Playing hold'em he could burn a card and make the flop and when he came back with the deck, he could take a card off and put it with his two cards. Then he would come back after the flop and cap the deck with the card, which would become the burn card on the turn.

He was one of the best, but he was bullheaded and one tough sonnagun. They finally caught him doing his stuff at the Red Men's, so what did he do? He whipped the floorman and the guy who owned the joint, saying "I know I'm never coming back here again, but I'm straightening you sonsabitches out for the next one that comes down the road." Later when he was playing gin in Albuquerque, a guy caught him doing something, they had a beef, and the guy killed Danny. But as far as whipping him physically, that would've been hard to do because Danny was really tough, a bulldogger in the rodeos. And a helluva scam artist.

I've seen people playing top-hand in poker games, I've seen them marking the cards, I've seen everything in the world. Playing top-hand means that two people who are playing the same bankroll bet up the pot for each other. The first one signals his partner when he has a big hand and the partner stays in to build the pot by raising and reraising. At the end, the raising partner throws away his hand and the first man wins all the money from the suckers. Or a couple of guys who are partners playing on the same bankroll will use signals to pass along other information. Maybe a man has an ace of diamonds and a nine of clubs and he throws the hand away. Then the flop comes with three diamonds and the man signals his partner that he threw away the ace of diamonds. If the partner has the king and four of diamonds, for example, he knows that his king-high flush is the nuts.

I've also seen cold decks being brought in where a deck of cards with rigged hands is substituted for the regular deck. If I ever thought that I might get cold-decked, which has happened to me in the past, I'll tell you what I used to do to protect myself. After I sat down in a game that maybe didn't look too good to me, I would take a card that was in my hand, like the three of diamonds for example, and I would put a secret mark on that card. I don't mean on the back of it, I mean on the face of it so that you could see it when you looked at it in your hand. Then if I had to visit the restroom, after I had come back and had played for a while, when the three of diamonds showed up I would take a close look at it. If the card that I had put a secret mark on was still in there, I would know that the same deck was in play. But if it wasn't there, I would know that they had switched decks or put in a cooler while I was away from the table.

Marking a secret card was something that I always did in the old days just to protect myself in games that I thought might be a little suspect. Then if I didn't like the situation, I would quit the game. But as bad as the cheaters usually played, I beat a lot of them anyway, even when they were doing something shady. For one thing, they play too many pots, and when they know that they have the nuts, they gamble too much. I've never blown the whistle on anybody or hollered if I got cheated—if I couldn't beat them with what they were doing, I would just leave the game—but like I said, I've beaten cheaters lots of times because they couldn't play very well.

The scam artists used a little trick in lowball games in which a guy would take the deck and put twelve cards, "baby" cards, on the bottom of it when it was his turn to deal. Then he would shuffle up and shuffle up and cut them out of the middle. When everybody got their hands, the dealer would know that the cards were coming off in a certain sequence. Suppose a guy in seat four opens the pot and the guy in seat six raises. The first guy draws one card and the other guy draws one card. Now say that the scam artist-dealer knows that it's coming an A-4-6 and he's holding a 5-3-2. Knowing that an ace and four are coming off, he draws two cards. He makes a wheel and busts the other two guys. I've seen this play many times.

Sometimes I've seen a hustler try to turn somebody's head who was pretty sharp about watching everything. When the hustler thought the time was right to make his move, he might reach over and say, "Give me change for this hundred." The mark starts making the change and bam! A few of his chips are gone if he takes his eye off things for a second and doesn't realize what's going on.

In the old days when we didn't have center dealers, I've seen a man who was smoking a cigarette while he was playing heads-up, lay his Zippo lighter down in front of his chips so that when he dealt the cards over that bright Zippo, he knew exactly what the other guy had. Another guy might have a "shiner," a small convex mirror, hidden in the palm of his hand just beneath his pinkie finger at the point where the cards fly over it as he deals them. Or be wearing a ring with a highly polished crown that reflects the cards.

About thirty-five years ago I knew a guy who could imitate anybody's voice. His partner would be playing at a gambling joint where the mark was also playing. The voice imitator would telephone the joint and ask for the mark, acting like Benny Binion or some big bookmaker who was well known in the area. "Ole so-and-so is gambling down there and he's short of money," he'd say. "Give him $15,000 and I'll get your money back to you the middle of tomorrow. Right now I'm fixin' to catch an airplane to St. Louis or I'd go down there myself. He's a pretty good guy and he has plenty of money, but he's running short right now." I mean he could imitate a man's voice to a tee and you wouldn't know that you weren't talking to the real thing. So the mark would give the partner the money and the partner would keep on playing for a while, maybe win or lose a couple of thousand, and then leave. That was a helluva scam. They'd go from poker joint to poker joint pulling the same trick. I don't know for sure how much these guys took people off for around the country, but I'd estimate $500,000. I didn't hear anything about them after a few years, so maybe they took the money and invested it and got rich. There were some great scams around, but this was one of the best telephone scams that I've ever heard of.

In another deal two guys would be traveling together and stop at a cafe for a bite to eat. They especially liked Greek cafes because they knew that you usually could find a good "barbut" game in the backroom or the kitchen of Greek restaurants. While the first guy was paying his check, he'd tell the owner, "This ole man with me, he can't play poker worth a damn and he's got millions. He hasn't been treating me right, so let's get him in a poker game. I'll sit behind him while you're playing and I'll sign you what he's holding." Then the restaurant owner and the scam artist would lay out their signs and get the game on. The partner sitting behind the "ole man" might sign "no pair" and the sucker would say, "I want to bet $2,000 in the dark." The confederate would call the bet. Then the sucker would draw and the "ole man" would draw three or four cards. Of course the "ole man" was holding out two cards and at the showdown, he would win the money. This scam was what they called "the tip." I once knew a team who ran this scam all the time; it was all they did.

I've run into some characters in my life, that's for sure. About thirty years ago I used to play poker with a guy who would do nothing but lose, lose, lose. "Where in the hell does he get all his money?" I wondered. Found out later that he got it from his wife—she was sharper than a tack. She would go into a big jewelry story and look at a five-carat diamond ring. She'd put the ring on her finger, carefully inspect the stone, take a close look at the mounting and then tell the jeweler she might come back later to take a second look. As soon as she had walked out the door, she would have a ring custom made to look exactly like the one in the expensive jewelry store except that instead of being a diamond, the stone would be a fake. She was an expert at deception.

In about four or five days, she'd visit the store again saying, "I'd like to see that ring again. My husband is thinking of buying it for me." And that's when she would pull the switch. "I'll make up my mind in a day or two," she'd say and leave the store. They say that she probably made a million dollars for her husband to throw off at poker. And I've heard that she never got caught, that's how smart she was.

Some of the biggest scams known to hustlers were on oil leases but sometimes, things backfired and the mark got rich instead of the crooks. I remember playing in a poker game in Tyler when I was still on the rodeo circuit. A Jewish fella was playing in the game and I reckon he was the worst poker player that I've ever seen. Hell, he didn't even know the rank of the hands! He'd be in a pot and somebody would have to tell him the winner, that's how dumb he was at cards. Some of the guys that he played poker with were in the oil business and they had a bunch of leases in West Texas, about four or five sections. So they took the ones that they figured weren't worth a plug nickel, put them together in a big package and sold them to this Jewish guy, who they figured for a dummy since he was such a dunce at poker, for about $100 an acre. A hundred bucks an acre ran into a lot of money back then. All the leases were on the square, it's just that there wasn't any oil on them. And hell, he bought them without even looking them over!

Well, about eight months later somebody drilled a well on some land adjacent to those leases, but instead of going down three or four thousand feet like they usually did, they drilled down to eight thousand feet. Hit a gusher. The "dummy" followed suit on his leases and wound up with nothing but oil wells flowing on them. Made millions. Here the scam artists thought that they'd really pulled a good one by dumping off those leases that they'd bought for about three dollars an acre to the mark for $100 an acre. Ended up costing them millions trying to cheat the guy out of a hundred thousand! They kicked themselves in the ass for years about that one. With as much money as "the mark" had, even if he turned his hand face up and played them, they could never break him. I think that two or three died off not long after that, it upset them so much.

Titanic Thompson was a helluva scam man. Before plastic cards were invented, Ty could put a bend on a paper card that he could see from here to across the street. Of course you couldn't see it because you didn't know what you were looking for. Ty had to have the best of it or he couldn't win because he was a bad player.

Of course this is the space age, the era of the computer when technology is far more advanced than when I was playing on the road. But still, if a guy doesn't have street smarts or a feel for things, he has no chance. You have to watch things and know how to protect yourself because new things come out every day. And some more new things will be coming out by the time you catch up with the old ones. Even though the surveillance cameras in casinos stop a lot of it, there still are some very smart people out there who can figure out how to get the best of it. And if they've got the best of it, especially if they're doing something that's over the heads of the other players, in the long run they're gonna win the money.

You see, although they're supposed to win over the long haul, the best players don't always win playing poker. If a good player runs up against something that he can't understand or a situation where he doesn't know what's happening to him, he'll think that he's the worst player in the world before it's all over with. But if you're streetwise and have been down the road for fifty years and have seen what I've seen, you're a little bit harder to cheat than the regular fella. Like the oldest profession in the world, things will never change in gambling. There's always going to be somebody trying to figure out some way to relieve a poor sucker of his money.

Knowing who you're playing with helps. I always know who I'm playing with and I can tell automatically if he's up to something. Like, when a guy first walks in a place and takes a seat, I can tell whether he's on the square or not. I can tell by his conversation, the way he looks, the way he acts, how he plays his hands, the way he looks at the cards. And I know whether he's a policeman. You have to be careful all the time because the scam artists are always looking for new things. There's big money in poker, especially if you have the best of it, and the higher they play, the more chance there is that something is going on. If nothing else, there are a couple of people in the game playing top-hand. Yes, when the money gets big, you can be certain that somebody's doing something. I know. I've been around a long time and I *know*.

★ Tipping My Way to Jail ★

I've always been a pretty good tipper, but have you ever heard of anybody else that tipped his way into jail? It happened back in 1979 while I was visiting Curt Garrett in Fort Worth—I was in the wrong place at the right time. Curt was one of the toughest men I've ever known, but he also was a good guy who would do anything for me. I had a poker game in Dallas and Curt had just bought a bar in Fort Worth, where he was a bookmaker. I hadn't talked to him in several months so when he telephoned saying that he wanted to see me, I drove to Fort Worth to meet with him. I didn't know exactly where his new bar was but when I finally found it, Curt was sitting with two guys wearing suits. Policemen. Right off the bat, I knew that something was wrong. Unlucky for me, I didn't realize how much was at stake.

"These guys are policemen," Curt told me, "and they're letting us run the books here. They want to ask you some questions."

I found out later that these cops had been making a case on ten bookmakers in Fort Worth. The bookmakers had trusted these guys because they had let a bookie get out of jail, telling him that they had fixed things so that he wouldn't be bothered again. He would be allowed to continue making book in exchange for a little payola on the side. For almost a year, Curt and the other bookmakers had been making their payments, not knowing that every one of their transactions was being audiotaped for the police sting operation.

"You wanna book in Dallas?" they asked me.

"No, I don't book, never did," I said. "I've got nothing against it, but I just play poker in Dallas and Vegas and anywhere there's a good game."

"Well, do you know anybody else in Dallas who wants to book?" they asked.

"No, I don't. I don't bet the sports, don't know nothing about it. I just play cards."

"The reason that I'm asking is because my wife is in the hospital and I need to make some money," one of them said. I could tell that what he was saying wasn't all right, but I made a fatal mistake anyway.

"Nice meeting you all, but I've gotta go," I said, getting up from the table. Then I pulled $500 out of my pocket and handed it to him. "Put this on the hospital bill," I said and left the joint.

Sure enough, the FBI got a hold of me in a few days. They came to my place, surrounded the joint and one of them got on the roof. "We're just having a Las Vegas night here," I told them, "so come on in."

"This is the FBI," I told everybody in the room. "They're looking for something, nothing to get excited about, don't worry 'bout it. Just keep on playing your Las Vegas night." Bill Smith was dealing the craps game for me and just kept doing his job. The government agents practically tore up my entire place searching through everything. Then they left.

About ten minutes later, one of them telephoned me. "Meet me at the swimming pool," he said. "I want to talk with you." We sat on lawn chairs while he rolled out a string of questions about Curt Garrett and the other bookmakers in Fort Worth. Then he named a guy who was on the FBI's "Ten Most Wanted" list and asked if I knew his whereabouts. The man they were looking for was an Indian who had some bars right across the Texas border in Oklahoma. One night two guys had ambushed him in his joint, shot him, and narrowly missed killing him. Knowing that the Indian would come looking for them, they hid out in the woods. Sure enough, he found them and killed them. Then he went on the lam and that's when the FBI put him on their list.

"I barely know him, let alone where he is," I said. "Hell, I don't even know what my ole lady does!"

"Well, ask around and see if you can find out where he's hiding," the fed told me.

The next day I had all the gaming equipment removed from my house and drove to Houston for a few days to try to figure out what to do. When I returned home, I hadn't been in the house for more than five minutes when the phone rang. It was the FBI agent.

"Did you find out where he is?" he asked.

"No, I didn't," I answered. "I asked around, but nobody knows where he's hiding out."

"You're a lying sonnabitch!" he accused me. "I'm gonna send you to the penitentiary."

"Well, do you get to tell everybody goodbye, or do you have a trial—or do you just get sent up?" I asked sarcastically. Boy, that pissed him off. Right then I knew that I had some bad heat with him over nothing, because I really didn't know where the guy was that the feds were looking for.

About two months later, three treasury agents showed up on a Sunday morning just as I was getting out of bed. They threatened to break down the iron gates outside my place with a battering ram and kept leaning on the buzzer. When they showed me their badges, I let them in, still wearing my pajamas. They instructed me to put on some clothes.

"Do you want me to handcuff you right here in front of your wife?" one of them asked.

"I don't care what the hell you do," I shot back. They locked the cuffs on me, put me in their car, and we drove away. I didn't know what the hell was happening, just that they were treasury agents. We got on the freeway and turned toward Fort Worth. The only thing that I could think of was that maybe I'd taken in some counterfeit money in my poker game and didn't know it. We pulled up in front of the federal courthouse in Fort Worth. Ten bookmakers already had been arraigned and were sitting on a long wooden bench in the hallway.

"What're you doing here, Cowboy?" one of them asked. "You've never taken a football bet in your life."

"Hell, I've never even made a bet," I answered. They filed bribery charges on me right along with Curt Garrett and the other Fort Worth bookmakers. And it all stemmed back to that $500 I had given the officer for his wife's hospital bills. I had tipped my way into jail!

They got on the stand and swore that I had given them that $500 to have craps games and poker games in hotels and motels. "Hell, that'd be the last place I'd have a poker or craps game," I testified. "I might check in next door to a Baptist preacher!"

My lawyer tried to get them to play the tape that they had recorded our conversation on at Curt's place because I knew that if they would play that tape, it would clear me. But they said that the apparatus had broken down that day. That clearly was a lie because they had tapes of stuff that had gone on just before and just after our conversation in the bar that they played in court. My lawyer moved to impeach the FBI witness for obviously lying and guess what? The judge overruled him! I even offered to take a lie detector test swearing that if I failed it, I would plead guilty, but they wouldn't go for that idea.

Doyle Brunson and Jack Binion flew to Dallas and took the stand in my favor. And big Ken Smith got on the stand and testified, "Hell, Cowboy's liable to give anybody $500, that's just the way he is." Jack agreed, saying, "Yeah, he's always tipped big around the Horseshoe and everybody likes him."

The jury was out on Curt's case for about forty minutes but they stayed out on mine for eleven hours. When the jury read its guilty verdict that night, the judge sentenced me to four years with three months in prison and the rest of the time on probation. If he had thought that I was guilty, he wouldn't have given me such a light sentence. Curt got two or three years in prison.

I did my time at the minimum security prison in Fort Worth. The day that I checked in, it was 116 degrees in the shade, but I hadn't been in the joint for an hour before I made a deal to get a fan with a five-dollar bill that I had hidden. Damn, it was hot in there! And it was boring. But they say there's a silver lining to every cloud, and I reckon I found it when I figured a way to break up the boredom—I had a lot of time to think about the good times I'd had with all my rodeo and poker friends, so I started writing poems about them. You'll find a lot of them at the back of this book. Guess I was ahead of the times in writing cowboy poetry—my publisher told me that it's an "in" thing these days.

In ninety days I was released on probation. That's when I found out that my probation officer was worse than the feds! He really didn't like me, and to this day I don't know why, because I can get along with just about anybody. He'd come out to my house at any hour of the day or night and ask, "You been gambling all night? I'd better not catch you playing no poker."

"Hell, I ain't been playing no poker at all," I vowed. Even with him looking over my shoulder night and day, I could still make a little bit of a living but I had to slip around to do it. I had called Benny Binion in Vegas and he arranged for Sam Angel to send me $20,000 worth of good jewelry—I mean *good* jewelry, back when Sam sold the good stuff. When I got the jewelry, I sold it all within about three weeks, doubled the money on it, and sent Benny his twenty grand. All the while this probation officer was watching me like a hawk trying to catch me doing something wrong.

About fifty miles out of Dallas in Kemp, they had a country club with a golf course—and a poker game. So, I went to Kemp and paid $200 to join the country club, something that the probation officer wouldn't think too much about. I'd play golf with the folks there during the day and a couple of nights a week, we'd play poker. By the time I left, there wasn't change for a twenty-dollar bill.

But this probation officer was still getting on my nerves something awful—I had more trouble with him than anything else—so I finally drove to Fort Worth to see Richard Keithley, a federal probation officer that I knew who had been a rodeo cowboy. When I was released from prison, Richard had given me a broad hint that a bunch of new probation officers had been hired for "white collar" criminals and that they treated people like the Nazis did. Remembering what he said, I paid him a visit.

"I'm afraid to turn around," I said. "He bugs me all the time."

"Yeah, that guy's something else," Richard agreed. "Somebody's gonna whip his ass someday."

"Well, it ain't gonna be me," I answered. "I'm gonna have to move to Fort Worth just to get away from him."

"Okay, move on over here and you'll be under me," he said. "Go ahead and play poker, just be careful."

So I rented an apartment in Fort Worth so that I'd have a home address there, but I continued to live in Dallas. While I was still on probation and my case was on appeal, I couldn't leave the state. It was during that period of time that the cops raided Henry Bowen's place in Tyler and took all our money at gunpoint. The FBI man who had told me that he was going to send me to the pen recognized me.

"Hell, I've got you now!" he bragged.

"I'm still on appeal," I told him, so he called and verified that my appeal was still open and he couldn't do anything.

"Where're you staying?" he asked.

"Over at the Holiday Inn," I lied.

"I'll drive you over there," he said.

"No, I believe I'll just walk."

"But it's four or five miles away."

"Hell, I don't care," I answered. "A sonnabitch comes down here and gets broke the way I got broke with all his money taken out of his pockets and all his chips taken off the table, I *want* to walk. When something this bad happens, you oughta have to walk."

That persuaded him to leave. I called my wife and she drove over to pick me up. Thanks to Evelyn, I got off probation in twenty-two months. She was reading some papers and found a loophole in the terms of my probation and called my attorney, who filed a petition that got me off early.

★ Back in Business ★

A couple of years later in 1983, I started a craps game in the house that I had rented on four acres with a ten-foot wooden fence around it and lots of parking right in the middle of Dallas, but this time it was dice only. When I had first set it up in 1979, we played poker there but I took out the poker and put in the dice and blackjack tables because there was a lot more money and a lot less hassle in dice and blackjack than there was in poker. And you didn't have to let out a bunch of tab like you had to do for poker players.

We opened at noon, cash and carry. I had a good business going with a lot of important people in Dallas playing in the game, plus celebrities who came to our joint to play blackjack or shoot the dice when they were performing in town. Of course the usual assortment of gamblers also played in our joint—they were our bread and butter.

One night Ricky Sanders came in with his cousin and another guy. Ricky was a player and the three of them started rolling the dice and drinking pretty heavy.

"You guys are gonna have to act right around here," I warned them. "I don't tolerate no nonsense." It fell on deaf ears—they kept on shooting the craps and hollering so loud you could've heard them all the way to Houston. They were ahead about $1,200 when I had had enough.

"Cash 'em out," I told the cashier.

"What're you talking 'bout, cash us out?" they protested.

"I'm gonna have to tell you to leave 'cause you're raising too much hell," I said. And I evicted them.

As they were driving out of the driveway, Ricky's cousin bumped into a car being driven by a lady. There wasn't much damage so I told her, "Ma'am, I'll give you $500 cash to fix your car and you can call me if it comes to any more than that," trying to avoid any more commotion. But Ricky's cousin didn't want to do that. He was so drunk that I couldn't talk him out of going on home without making any more trouble. He wound up getting hauled off to jail by the police.

About three days later Evelyn called me saying, "You know those two guys that you threw out of the craps game?"

"Yeah, what about them?" I asked.

"They're on television right now," she said. "They've just robbed a bank in a shopping center and have taken some hostages. The cops have them surrounded." The police later discovered $120,000 hidden in their garage and they were sentenced to the state penitentiary.

That was one of the few times that I ever had any trouble in my home game, unless you count the fact that I should've won a million off the dice game but really played unlucky and wound up losing $140,000 to it. I sold it to Johnny Wheeler in 1984, the same year that I won second place in the $10,000 championship tournament at the World Series of Poker.

★ On the Road Again ★

Gambling on the road hasn't gone entirely out of style. The names and the places might have changed but the game is still the same. I know that right now I could go play in a different game every day in Texas, New Mexico, Mississippi, California, or Nevada. Everybody knows who's playing where and who the best players are, the ones to beat, just like we did in the old days.

If you go to Houston you'll have Tommy Grimes, Hertzel Zalewski, and Bill O'Connor to beat. They're all excellent pot-limit poker players. And if you go to Albuquerque you'll find Ron Watts, Freddy Cook, David Matthews, and Mike Alsaadi. If you go to northern California to the Lucky Chances Casino to play the no-limit game, you might run into Carl McKelvey. In Los Angeles at the Hustler it's Gary Pollak and Scott Lundberg. In Oceanside there's Billy Duarte, Jeff Stoff, Rich St. Peter, and Jim Shapiro. So, if you want to follow the circuit, you can still do it today.

When the big action moved to the casinos in Las Vegas in the '60s where it was safer to play, a lot of the road gamblers moved there and didn't have to travel the Southern circuit any more to find a big game. In fact, when I first went to Vegas in 1968, I was playing with the same guys that I had played with for years in Texas. I went there because I wanted to play in a big no-limit game that was going on at the Horseshoe. The game lasted nine months without ever breaking up. And that's when I met a man who became my friend for life, a cowboy and a gambler like me. The only difference was that he owned the Horseshoe Club.

BENNY AND THE BOYS IN LAS VEGAS

"The only bad luck for a gambler is bad health.
The rest is just temporary aggravation."
— *Benny Binion*

Before he moved to Las Vegas, Benny Binion had been a bootlegger and ran craps games in Dallas. As far as craps games went, he ran everything in town. Benny told me that he once drove nine hundred miles in his Model-A Ford to ask a guy who had a lot of money to loan him some of it. Benny didn't know the millionaire personally, but he had heard of him. When he got to the man's office, he had to wait for about an hour before he could get in to see him. When he finally got in to meet the man, Benny introduced himself and asked him to loan him some money so that he could start up a big craps game in Dallas. The guy turned him down.

"Sure glad I've met you," Benny said, shaking the man's hand, "and I appreciate you seeing me." Then he turned around and started for the door.

"Wait a minute!" the money man said. "Anybody who acts like that after I've turned them down for money must be all right." And he gave Benny the loan.

"No telling how much money I made for him after that," Benny told me.

In 1946 Benny loaded up two Cadillacs with both trunks full of money and headed for Las Vegas with his family. With the money he'd made in Dallas, he was able to open the Horseshoe Club in 1951. He also brought along Gold Dollar, his bodyguard. Gold Dollar was a real giant of a black man who had had his teeth filled and trimmed in gold that came from a twenty-dollar gold piece, hence his nickname. Benny put Gold Dollar to work at the Horseshoe as a security guard. Whenever a new security guard was hired, Gold Dollar would bet the new man that he couldn't handcuff him. Gold Dollar always won the bet because his wrists were so large that no handcuffs in the world would fit around them.

I have a lot of fond memories of the time that I spent with Benny. Seems that he had a friend named Blondie Hall, a big oil man who lived in Dallas, that he used to let play dice over the telephone—Blondie would call the craps pit and lay his bets by phone! One night he won about $20,000, so Benny called him saying, "Come on out here and pick up your money, Blondie." When he got to the Horseshoe, Blondie had a few drinks, started playing craps, and wound up losing over $200,000. This type of thing happened over and over again, Benny told me.

One morning Benny and I were sitting in the Sombrero Room when an old gray-headed man wearing his nightgown and carrying a coffee pot came into the cafe raising hell. "They ain't brought me my coffee!" he was hollering. Benny had a waiter take care of him right away.

"How can you let that ole guy act like that right here in the restaurant?" I asked Benny.

"He can do whatever he wants to," he answered. "He's lost twelve million here in the last five years. Hell, he don't have to wear no clothes at all if he don't want to."

One night Benny and Willie Nelson and I were eating dinner when Bunker Hunt from Dallas came into the restaurant. "Say, Benny," he said, "I'm looking for some land to buy to try to find some gold on it. Do you know anybody?"

"No, I'm looking for somebody that's already got the gold, Bunker," Benny answered. Willie and I both laughed at that one.

One of Benny's favorite poker stories was one that I told him years ago. I was at a rodeo in Montana, the last one we made before going across the border for the 1954 Calgary Stampede. The rodeos in Montana were held in the afternoon and at night they roped off the streets of the downtown section for a street dance. All the bars had five-card stud games going, so I got into one of them and boy, I couldn't win a hand—I don't know how many times I got my ace in the hole beat. It wasn't long before I got broke, so I left the bar and went to the street dance looking for somebody to borrow some money from. I ran into an ole cowboy that I knew and asked him for a loan, saying "I need a coupla hundred, I can give it back to you tomorrow. I'm playing stud over there at that bar and I'm getting my ace in the hole beat every time. Hell, I ain't hit a single pot."

"Well," he said, "I don't mind letting you have the money, but why don't you come on over to this bar where I'm playing? They back you up with a pair!" Benny just loved this poker story.

★ Benny Plays Some Five-Card Stud ★

Benny didn't play much poker but sometimes he liked to join the gamblers in his poker room at the Horseshoe for a session. One night he was playing in a big no-limit five-card stud game and over in the corner of the room stood his tommy gun, the kind you see in the old gangster movies. Benny kept it with him for protection because the racial riots were going on at that time over black people not being able to stay in the casinos where they were entertaining and some buildings had been set afire in North Las Vegas. After the game his wife Teddy Jane would pick him up at the side entrance in their big Lincoln and Benny would put the gun in his lap on the way home. This night they—Freddy "Sarge" Ferris, Bill Boyd, Blondie Forbes, and some guys from Chicago—were playing real high five-card stud. The change-in was $5,000 and the low card had to bring it in for $100.

I was sitting behind Benny watching the game. He really wasn't that good a player but that didn't make any difference; he had a lot of money and liked to mess around with the poker players. When he got up to leave, I asked, "Benny, you wanna put in $500 with me in this poker game before you leave?"

"Sure, Cowboy," he answered, "go ahead and try it. Here's my $500." I knew that the change-in was ten times that much but who was gonna tell Benny Binion that he couldn't play partners with me on a short buy-in in his own joint? He never won at the game anyway and they all knew it.

Of course I knew that $1,000 was no kind of money to play with when the low card had to bring it in for $100. But to make a long story short, I got lucky and started winning. I'll never forget it—I had two pair showing and made jacks full over deuces and this guy from Chicago had triple eights. What a hand playing five-card stud! I won a real big pot off him, you know what I mean? And eventually I wound up about $10,000 winner. That was a lot of money back then, so I just got up and quit.

The next morning when Benny came into the Sombrero Room, I went over to his table to say good morning. "How'd you do last night?" he asked.

"I won $10,000," I bragged. "Here's your $500 back plus $5,000 profit."

"Man, I can't believe you won that much!" he said, surprised. Hell, neither could I. "Say now, you didn't cheat them, did you?" he teased me.

"No, but I wish to hell I could've!" I kidded.

Benny's friends couldn't do any wrong and his enemies couldn't do any right. He put a lot of money into the Reagan presidential campaign trying to get a pardon (he'd landed in prison years before in some kind of railroaded deal). I think Reagan promised Benny a pardon, but he never gave him one. Boy, was Benny mad—he didn't like Reagan anymore after that. Jack Binion used to have a sign hanging in his office that said: "Benny Binion Believes in Justice ... Just Us!"

★ Benny Plays a Trick on Cowboy ★

Another time at the Horseshoe I was all dressed up in a suit and vest with my cowboy hat on, wearing my diamond rings and gold jewelry, playing poker with the boys. Two tourists walked by and saw Benny standing on the rail watching the game.

"We'd like to meet this Benny Binion," one of them said to him. "Do you know where we can find him?"

"That's him," Benny answered, pointing at me. "You'd better not bother him while he's playing cards, but that's him sitting right over there."

After I finished playing poker, I joined Benny in the coffee shop. He hadn't shaved or anything for a couple of days and was looking a little bit raggedy.

"Cowboy, you know what I done?" he asked.

"What was that?"

"Well, a coupla guys came by the poker room a little while ago saying they'd like to meet Benny Binion. You was sitting there all dressed up and looking good so I just pointed at you and told them that you was Benny Binion. Hell, you was all dressed up real nice and they weren't gonna know the difference. That ain't gonna hurt nothing," he laughed.

The next morning I had breakfast with Benny and R.D. Matthews, who was working at the Horseshoe at the time. I had made up a little story to tell Benny.

"You know, the damnedest thing I've ever seen happened to me last night," I started.

"What happened?" Benny asked.

"You know them two guys you told that I was Benny Binion? Well, I ran into them last night late and I think I really messed up." I was acting real serious.

"What'd you do?"

"Well, they asked me if I really was Benny Binion and since you'd already told them I was, I said, 'Yes, I am.' Then they told me that they wanted to put up some money with me but they didn't want to put it in the cage. They just wanted to put it up with me, Benny, as a bank to gamble against.

'All right,' I said. 'How much do you want to put up?'

'$25,000.'

'Okay, just let me have it,' I said, and they handed me the money and left. Then I drank a coupla beers and started shooting them craps—and I lost every goddamned nickel! I don't know what I'm gonna do if they come back down here."

"Oh, my god! We've gotta find 'em, we've gotta find 'em!" Benny was really upset. "I've gotta pay those guys that money this very minute. When they come around, holler at me and I'll give them their money." He thought I was really serious about taking the $25,000 off of them and shooting craps with it. Later on, I told him the truth and he got a laugh out of it.

One time after I'd gotten broke gambling at the Horseshoe, R.D. Matthews and I were sitting in the Sombrero Room talking about it when Benny came walking by. "Benny, I need some more money," I told him.

"Cowboy, I'm gonna tell you something," he answered. "I've just paid my income tax and I went on a guy's note for $20,000 and he didn't pay it. I just don't believe I can do it."

"Well, I'll be damned," I said, kidding him a little bit. "I guess if I had won, I couldn't have got paid my damned money. Thank you anyway, I won't bother you no more today."

"Wait a minute, Cowboy!" he said, pulling on my sleeve. "R.D., go down to the cage and get him that money! We don't want that goddamned story getting around."

★ The Benny Binion Dolls ★

In 1987 Evelyn and I presented the famous Benny Binion dolls to Mr. and Mrs. Binion at the Horseshoe. Evelyn is an excellent seamstress. She's been sewing and cooking since she was a young girl living on a sheep ranch with her folks in Wyoming. Evelyn can take a glimpse of something and then sew a copy of it, she's that good.

Down to the smallest detail, the two dolls were miniature replicas of Benny and Teddy Jane Binion. It took Evelyn four months to make the pair of dolls, which she made from scratch. I found a company in Fort Worth, the Coker Hat Company, to made an authentic cowboy hat for the Benny Binion doll. Coker had a size-4 hat block that the company had used to fill a special order for a baby's cowboy hat and they used it to make Benny's hat for me. Cost $300, but I felt lucky to find it. Then Evelyn found some fake buffalo hide to make an exact copy of the famous buffalo coat that Benny liked to wear during press conferences.

She even sewed tiny gold buttons on his shirt. She dressed the Teddy Jane doll in a white mink coat just like the one that Mrs. Binion liked to wear and placed a little pair of glasses on its face. When they were finished, the pair of dolls looked as though they were Mr. and Mrs. Binion standing in front of you.

Benny was as proud of those dolls as he was of anything in his life. When we gave them to him, he set up a special presentation deal in the steak house at the Horseshoe. Then he had them mounted in a glass case that hung at the entrance to the Sombrero Room for years. I estimate that while the dolls were there, twelve million people looked at them while they were standing in line to get into the restaurant. Lots of folks who came to the Horseshoe had never seen Benny and Teddy Jane, so the dolls were quite a treat for them.

After Benny died and the casino was remodeled, the dolls were removed from their place of honor and stored in a basement room. That kind of hurt my feelings, you know what I mean? I knew that Mrs. Binion never threw away anything, no matter what it was—she would even pick up rubber bands off the floor, bind them together and keep them—so I called the Horseshoe, found out where the dolls were stored, and brought them home with me. Today Evelyn and I have them in a display case in our den.

They became two of the most famous dolls in the world; they're priceless. I remember when we first unpacked them in our room at the Horseshoe before we presented them to the Binions. A maid was straightening up our room and when she saw the dolls, she cried, "Lordy, lordy, that's them, that's them!" Then Chip Reese and Doyle Brunson came up to see them and couldn't believe how realistic they were. Blackie Blackburn was helping to form an association of poker players at that time, and before we presented the dolls to the Binions he offered us $15,000 for them. He wanted to give them to Benny himself as a gift from the players association. I suppose we might sell them someday—I'm sure that the owners of some big casino would love having them as historic mementoes for their customers to see. After all, there's nothing else like them in the world.

The next year Evelyn made another one-of-a-kind, the "World Series Quilt." She sewed a picture of every World

Series of Poker champion from 1970 through 1986 onto it with the year that he won. In the center of the quilt are pictures of Benny Binion and his sons, Jack and Teddy. It's hard to give a multimillionaire something when he already has everything he needs or wants. What do you give a man who had Benny's kind of money? The dolls and the quilt were the kinds of things that he liked. Benny loved Evelyn, he loved our dog Rebel, he loved the dolls, and he loved the quilt. Benny's daughter, Becky Binion Behnen, owns the quilt today.

Evelyn also designs and sews my clothes, the "designer label" overalls and suspenders that I've become famous for wearing. Folks can't help but notice how distinctive I look in them and when they comment on them, I have a little joke ready. For instance, while Dana Smith and I were working on this book together, we were waiting for the elevator at Binion's when one of those gushy tourist ladies came up to me all starry eyed saying, "Those overalls are terrific! Wherever did you get them?" Looking her square in the eye, I drawled my stock answer: "Well, ma'am, I used to pick cotton for Liberace and when he died, this pair of overalls is the only thing he left me in his will." Dana cracked up over that one. I might've been wearing the pair with the playing cards on them, but it also could've been the ones decorated with tapestry like you'd find in a good whorehouse. Or the pair with the lucky dice rolling over the bib, or the ones that Evelyn sewed with leather and the logo of Ocean's Eleven Casino on them that I wore when I came in third in the pot-limit hold'em tournament at the World Series of Poker in 2000.

Benny was absolutely crazy about Evelyn and our dog, Rebel. He liked me, too, but after Evelyn made those dolls and that quilt for him, I think she became his favorite. It seems that when Evelyn gave Benny the dolls, he became a doll "expert," and even told her that John Wayne had been one of the biggest doll collectors in the United States. Benny was always at "his" table in the steak house and to most people, he seemed unapproachable. But after the dolls arrived, folks

had something to say to him as a conversation starter and
Benny really liked that. He loved talking to the average tourist.
One day he said to Evelyn, "Look at that woman sitting over
there—I was talking to her and she has the cutest Texas accent
I ever heard. Wouldn't have got to talk with her except for
them dolls."

Later Evelyn worked as a slot host at the Horseshoe for
a while and turned out to be one of the best hands they'd
ever had. One time a woman from California who had just
lost $70,000 playing the slots told Evelyn that the hotel was
getting ready to throw her out of her room. Evelyn knew that
wasn't right, so she raised so much hell with the sucker who
was the head of the slot department that he complained to Jack
Binion about it. Jack just laughed at him. He appreciated the
good way that Evelyn had with customers. She's a good poker
player, too—she was trained by an expert, you know—and in
1993 she won the ladies hold'em championship at the Queens
Classic against 125 players.

★ Benny's Boy, Jack ★

I've known all the Binions for years: Jack, Teddy, Becky
and her husband Nick Behnen, and Barbara, but I didn't know
Brenda very well. Before the Binions bought the Mint in 1988
and made it part of the Horseshoe, Teddy and I used to slip out
every once in a while and walk over to the Mint to shoot some
dice. Teddy would take $300 and try to beat the Mint out of a
thousand or two.

Over the past thirty years I've probably brought the
Horseshoe more business than anybody else—just ask Jack
Binion. When Jack was running the Horseshoe, I could get a
room and food, anything I wanted, and I got comps for the
chip players and craps players that I brought to the casino,
whether they were big or small gamblers.

Jack is the workingest man I've ever seen, works eighteen hours a day like he hasn't got a nickel to his name, but about once a year he takes off for a couple of weeks to go skiing. The government once tried to take the Horseshoe away from the family and if it hadn't been for Jack's persistence, they might've done it. Today he has casinos in Tunica, Mississippi and Bossier City, Louisiana.

Jack and Doyle Brunson flew to Texas to testify for me in federal court when I was charged with bribery and wouldn't even charge the plane tickets to me. Doyle told the judge that if he'd had a pistol the time when we got broke and I tipped off our last $50 to that waitress in Waco, he would've shot me and I wouldn't even have been in court that day.

Benny used to say, "Jack has a couple of weaknesses, but nobody knows what they are." Jack is pretty close with his money, although there's no telling how much he'll do to help somebody that he likes and trusts. There used to be a story that went around about the time when some guy asked Jack for a cough drop and Jack answered, "Let me hear you cough."

★ Craps Players ★

Howard McCormack, who owned a big trucking company in Oklahoma City, used to be the biggest craps player that Benny had at the Horseshoe. One time he was $400,000 winner and wanted to bet the whole wad on the hardway eight. Benny wasn't in town at the time and the pitman wouldn't take the bet. When Benny returned, he was hotter than a pistol. "Why didn't you take the bet?" he asked. "If he had won, it would've been the best advertising we've ever had!"

I knew Howard very well; he was quite a wheeler and dealer. In fact, Benny said that Howard was the smartest trader that he'd ever seen and told me this story about him: Seems that Howard went up to Detroit one time to buy out a big trucking company and Benny went with him since the two of them were good friends. As I recall, the owners were asking $2.5 million for this trucking outfit and Howard made a deal to buy it. After he had closed the deal, he and Benny went back to the hotel.

"Now I'm gonna show you something," Howard told Benny, and he picked up the telephone. He dialed the company that he had just bought and said, "You know what? I can't take the trucking company. I'm sorry, but there's just no way that I can buy it."

"But you've already made the deal," they said. "What are you talking about?"

"Well, it's gonna cost me a million dollars to register all those trucks and I just can't afford it."

Benny said that Howard kept talking it over with them on the phone, and the company ended up giving him the million to register the trucks! That's how good a trader he was. And boy, Howard was a big craps player back then, too. Of course he wasn't as big a dice player as Archie Karas, who won about $25 million off the Horseshoe. Nevertheless Howard was a big player.

Ricky Sanders, a little guy who used to shoot craps at my place in Dallas, also played big at the Horseshoe. Liked to drink, have a big time and raise some hell. Several years ago while I was playing poker at the Commerce Casino in California, Ricky was at the Horseshoe playing blackjack. When I came back to Vegas, Jack Binion asked me, "Do you know this Ricky Sanders from Dallas? He was looking for you. Did you hear about what he did?"

"Yeah, I know him and no, I don't know what he done."

"He won a million dollars off me at blackjack."

"A million? I can't believe it!" Of course, Ricky was the kind of player who would get a break and then just move the money in. It seems that he had brought about $20,000 with him to Vegas, won the million, and then left town with the money. From Vegas he flew to Florida, where he owned a furniture business like the one he had in Dallas. I wrote him a letter congratulating him on his win.

The next time Ricky flew to Dallas, he and I went down to Johnny Wheeler's joint to play some blackjack and he lost over $100,000. Later, he went back to the Horseshoe and starting playing some more blackjack. This time, I just watched him play. Sometimes he would bet $10,000 and stand pat with a nine—and the dealer would bust! It was the damnedest thing I've ever seen in all the years I've been around gamblers. Making a long story short, Ricky got $250,000 winner—and then gave it all back before he left town.

I stayed at the Horseshoe one time for about six months shooting craps and gambling. I realize that craps is hard to beat, and I also know that you can run out of patience and discipline at craps just like you do at poker—and boy, when that happens, you're a gone goose if you don't quit. I usually had done pretty well at craps, but this time I owed the Horseshoe $20,000. I was really getting worried about it so I went to see Benny.

"Benny," I said, "I owe a bunch of money at the cage. Some people down there okayed it and I ain't got a quarter."

"How much do you owe?" he asked, looking at me kinda funny.

"About $20,000."

Benny picked up the phone and called the cage. "Get Cowboy Wolford's markers out of the drawer and add 'em up," he said. "How much are they?"

"$20,250," the voice on the phone answered.

"Tear 'em up!" he ordered. "Tear every one of 'em up right now." Then he turned to me and said, "I ain't gonna give you no more tab, but don't be worrying so goddamned much." That's the kind of guy he was. Like I've said before, his friends could do no wrong and his enemies could do no right, it was that simple.

And nobody messed with Benny Binion. Some of the joints in those days were run by the mob, but they never messed with Benny, just an ole cowboy from Texas, because he wouldn't stand for it. He was a real good friend of mine, I'm glad to say.

REBEL AND MR. LUCKY

"Brothers and sisters, I bid you beware
Of giving your heart to a dog to tear."
— *Rudyard Kipling, The Power of the Dog*

Rebel, our nine-pound gray poodle, was one of the smartest dogs I've ever seen. When we had our pot-limit and no-limit poker game in Dallas, all the poker players there knew Rebel very well because he was always at the game. In fact, Rebel knew more poker players than any other dog in the world.

The first poker tournament that he attended was hosted by Jack "Tree Top" Straus at the Marina Hotel and Casino in Las Vegas in 1979. Evelyn and I didn't want to leave him home alone so we took him with us and while we were there, an artist painted a portrait of Rebel with Evelyn. He loved to travel—while we were loading our van for a road trip, he would be jumping up and down and running back and forth to the door trying to hurry us along.

Rebel was a ham. He loved to wear the custom-made clothes that Evelyn designed for him, including five cowboy hats and six pairs of sunglasses. He didn't seem to feel right unless he was all dressed up. We made a place for Rebel to sit between the two front seats in our van and when we traveled, he would look out at the world from his special roost. Sometimes when we stopped at a red light, people in the car next to us would gape at Rebel all dressed up in his sunglasses, cowboy hat, and vest.

He attended the World Series of Poker five or six times. Benny Binion loved Rebel—he's the only dog in the history of the Horseshoe that Benny ever gave a private hotel room. Evelyn made an outfit for Rebel with a buffalo hide jacket and cowboy hat that looked exactly like the clothes that Benny wore when the press photographed him. One time during the Series, Benny, Evelyn and I were eating dinner at the steak house. Benny had heard about Rebel's "Benny Binion Outfit," as we called it, but he hadn't seen it.

"Evelyn, go get that dog and put them Benny Binion clothes on him. I wanna see it," he said.

"Benny, you can't bring a dog into the steak house," I kidded.

"The hell I can't!" he said. "I own this sonnabitch."

When Evelyn brought Rebel to the restaurant all decked out in his Benny Binion getup, Benny insisted that he sit next to us in his own separate chair. Rebel liked the limelight and sat there through dinner like a perfect little gentleman. As people wandered over to look at him, Rebel wouldn't even glance their way—he thought he was a movie star and remained aloof, enjoying every minute of it. Benny really got a kick out of that. When we finished dinner, Benny and Rebel and I had our picture taken together in front of the million-dollar display just inside the side entrance of the Horseshoe.

During the Series Evelyn always walked Rebel in the mornings, then she would order a soda pop at the Horseshoe's antique mahogany bar. Dressed in one of his costumes, Rebel always sat on the barstool next to her. People would stop and stare—some of them thought he was a toy dog. One morning, a lady saw Rebel sitting there like a statue and said to her husband, "Look at that little toy dog over there." Wanting to prove that he wasn't a fake, Rebel turned his head to look at her through his sunglasses and she almost fainted.

★ Rebel, the Canine Gambler ★

One time when I was shooting craps at the Horseshoe with Rebel beside me giving me a helping paw, the Horseshoe's photographer snapped a photograph of us that used to hang on the wall near the pit. Everybody got a kick out of seeing Rebel in his cowboy hat shooting craps and once again, my little canine ham drew a big crowd. That same year the National Enquirer magazine was doing a shoot at the Horseshoe and took a picture of Rebel playing poker. The photographer told me that of all the movie stars and other celebrities he'd taken pictures of, Rebel was the most perfect subject he'd ever photographed because he was such a ham. You see, Rebel knew exactly what they wanted and he really enjoyed posing.

Rebel was born on November 11, Armistice Day, and we always baked a cake and threw a birthday party for him in Dallas. I'm glad that we videotaped some of those parties because they bring back some of the best memories of our lives. In 1995, just before his eighteenth birthday, we had to put Rebel to sleep. Evelyn and I were so sick about it that we tried to make a deal with the vet to put all three of us to sleep at the same time.

And that's the story of Rebel, the celebrity dog who knew more poker players than any dog that ever lived. Rebel had a great life and Evelyn and I have had better lives because of him. When Rebel died, we felt so low that we decided that we never wanted to own another pet—until something strange happened a short time later that changed our minds.

★ Mr. Lucky Makes His Entrance ★

Ever since the time when a cat saved my life during my rodeo days, I've been partial to cats the color of midnight black. Back then you might do a rodeo and then have to drive a few hundred miles that same night to make another rodeo the next day. Being on the road all the time made it a tough life and we were often dead tired. One year I finished a rodeo in Kansas around midnight and, with my horse and trailer hitched up behind my truck, I headed for a rodeo that was being held the next afternoon three hundred miles away in Nebraska. There were a lot of rough, gravel roads in those days, so traveling wasn't as easy as it is now.

I drove all night long and just before daylight I was about to go to sleep at the wheel, when a black cat jumped out of nowhere and ran across the road right in front of me, snapping me out of it enough to wake me up. I slammed on the brakes to be sure that I wouldn't hit it and found that I had stopped about ninety feet short of a railroad crossing. As I looked up I saw a freight train barreling down the tracks at one hundred miles per hour. I had stopped just in time to miss running into its path. That cat had saved my life—that's why I don't believe in the superstition that black cats are unlucky. Still shaking, I got out of the truck to try to find my feline friend so that I could take him with me and care for him, but he had run away. I think the good Lord had sent that midnight-black cat across the road to save me and when his work was done, the cat disappeared.

Many years later in Nevada I met another black cat that ended up saving me in another way. It happened just after

Rebel died and we had moved to Las Vegas. One morning Evelyn went to the Gold Coast Casino to play in the ten o'clock poker tournament and for some unknown reason, the patio door was left open, though we literally never left it open. I'd been out all night long playing poker and was dead tired, so I was still in bed when she left. That afternoon when she returned home, Evelyn looked in on me.

"What's this?" she yelled. "There's a cat in bed with you!"

"What?" I asked in disbelief. I looked down by my side and saw a little black kitten with white stocking feet, white whiskers, and a white tuxedo—the prettiest cat I'd ever seen. What is so strange about this story is that, just before Evelyn left that morning, I had said to her, "You know, honey, today is November 11, Rebel's birthday, bless his heart."

I decided to name the kitten "Mr. Lucky," because he was lucky to find the patio door open. We figure that he had been born in a dumpster and had been living off what he could scrounge before he found us. When he came to us that day as a kitten, he weighed four pounds; today he weighs in at fifteen pounds and change. He's sitting beside me now as I'm writing this book. In fact, he's always right here helping me in everything that I do.

Sometimes I think that Mr. Lucky is Rebel reincarnated— that Rebel has come back to us in a cat's suit—because Mr. Lucky has almost every trait that Rebel had. He's never met a stranger, he's a show-off, and he follows us everywhere we go. Mr. Lucky likes to lie under a china cabinet in our home, the same place where Rebel used to lie. "Come here, Mr. Lucky," I'll say and he'll walk across the room and sit down at my feet, just like a dog would do. He knows a hundred words and will do anything that Evelyn asks of him. When she is sewing, Mr. Lucky always sits by her side in case she needs some help from him. After she finishes a project, he walks around it inspecting it carefully, and tells her that he approves of her handiwork. We telephone my sister Pat every Sunday in Houston and each time, Mr. Lucky seems to recognize her voice on the phone and comes over to talk with her. She'll say hello and he'll meow just like they were carrying on a regular conversation.

Mr. Lucky doesn't like to travel nearly as much as Rebel did—he puts his head between his paws while we're on the road. We took him to the Commerce Casino where I was playing a poker tournament and when we checked in to the hotel I said, "This is the cleanest cat in the world and he's gotta stay with us here or we can't check in." I showed them a picture of me wearing a fur coat and Mr. Lucky in his "tuxedo" and they liked it so much, they asked for a copy of it to hang in the hotel office. You know, cats don't like to get dressed up in clothes, so the good Lord dressed Mr. Lucky in that tuxedo so that he would look like a movie star without having to wear anything man-made.

And Mr. Lucky has an extra sense. Whenever I've been out of town for several days, he goes to get Evelyn about twenty minutes before I arrive at our door, waking her up if it's nighttime. When he starts running back and forth through the house like he does when he's happy, she knows that I'll be pulling in the driveway within the next few minutes. Somehow he senses that I'm close but we don't understand how he knows it.

Sometimes I wonder whether folks from outer space brought cats to the earth when the pyramids were being built in Egypt. The Egyptians worshiped cats, you know, and they were the first people who had cats for pets. I never believed in reincarnation until Mr. Lucky wandered through that patio door to help fill Rebel's place in our hearts. I'll bet Mr. Lucky thinks that he hit the cat lotto when he found us, graduating from the dumpster to being the main man like he did, but Evelyn and I know that we're the ones who got lucky on that deal.

VINTAGE
LAS VEGAS

*"The stakes have to be high enough that it really hurts you if you lose—
the amount could be $100 for some people and $100,000
for others—that's what makes the game interesting."*
— *Doyle Brunson*

The first time that I came to Las Vegas in 1968, the big action was downtown at the Golden Nugget and the Horseshoe. Bill Boyd was running the Nugget poker room but the games were smaller than they were at the Horseshoe, and the Fremont had a little cheap game going. Poker action on the Strip was pretty thin, except for the Dunes (where Johnny Moss ran the room several years later). The Flamingo and Stardust were the other big gambling places for tourists.

In those days the Horseshoe was a small joint with only eighty hotel rooms. The poker room had four or five tables and was located in the older side of the hotel in the alcove where the high-limit baccarat room is situated today. That little alcove is where the World Series was first held and where we once played a no-limit game that didn't break up for nine months. Just down from there was the hotel check-in desk. The coffee shop was not downstairs then, it was on the casino floor.

Some of the gamblers that I knew in the old days used to come to Vegas to play five-card stud real high at the Horseshoe. The best stud players back then were Sarge Ferris, Little Red Ashey, Bill Boyd, George Barnes, Blondie Forbes, Sam McFarland, and Slim Etheridge, an older man who ran a big no-limit five-card stud game in Hot Springs, Arkansas. George Barnes, who used to run games in Oklahoma, flew to Las Vegas just to play high stud with them. In the long run, I think that Sarge wound up beating all the big stud games in Vegas pretty good. He was the best five-card stud player in the world—put the money in front of him and he'd make it interesting for you.

Of course Bill Boyd also was one of the finest five-card stud players in the world. I once saw him playing in a big game in Vegas with a mountain of money in the pot. When the last card was dealt, Bill bet all the money he had left, around $40,000. His opponent started studying hard, trying to decide whether to call the bet. So Bill just got up from his seat, put something over his cards to protect them and said, "Whatever you're gonna do, just go ahead and do it because I've gotta go to the restroom. If you pass, just throw my cards in the muck and push me the pot. If you call, just turn them up." Bill later said that he did that because he was bluffing and he didn't want the guy to get a tell on him. When he got back from the restroom, the other guy had folded and the dealer had pushed the pot to Bill.

After Mac McCorquodale introduced hold'em in Las Vegas at the California Club in 1963, a lot of the road gamblers that I was playing with on the circuit migrated to Vegas to play in those first, juicy hold'em games. Then when the World Series began to really take off in the late 1970s, most of them would go to it mainly to play in the side games as well as enter a few of the tournaments. That's why you see the names of so many old road gamblers on the winner's list at the early World Series events. It wasn't until around 1983 when somebody invented poker satellites that you started seeing players win events at the Series who hadn't been road gamblers or who hadn't played in the big games in Texas and Louisiana.

I knew most of the early World Series players, and played with them from Dallas to Waco to Corpus to Shreveport. Men like Johnny Moss, Bobby Baldwin, Doyle Brunson, Bobby Hoff, and Amarillo Slim were friends of mine that I had played poker with for years before they started coming to Vegas. These men and the others that I talk about in this section were what I call "vintage" Vegas poker players. They all were top hands who knew the ropes. Of course they were a lot younger back then, but you'll still see most of them today playing high poker in Vegas, their stompin' grounds. A lot of them have been inducted into the Horseshoe's Poker Hall of Fame. I'm starting off talking about a man that I played with on the circuit for years to give you some background to the story about the famous bluff that I put on him at the World Series of Poker in 1984.

★ Jesse Alto ★

Jesse Also used to live in Corpus Christi where he ran the poker at the Elks Club and owned a car business on the side. Jesse was quite a player. He played high and he played fast. He'd get hot and win a lot of money and then he'd run cold and get mad—Jesse had a pretty bad temper. He and I didn't get off to a very good start but we wound up being pretty good friends. Jesse came in second to Doyle Brunson at the World Series of Poker in 1976 when Doyle drew out on him with a 10-2, which became known as Doyle's hand.

At the final table of the $10,000 no-limit championship event at the World Series of Poker in 1984, Jesse and Jack Keller and I got down to three-way action trying to win the money and the title. In the key hand at the final table, I bluffed Jesse from start to finish.

Bobby Baldwin wrote an article about the bluff (with the help of Tex Sheahan, the main poker reporter back then) for a popular magazine and reprinted it in his book, "Tales Out of Tulsa." Here's how he described it: "It started when the A-9 of clubs and a diamond king flopped. When Wolford bet $15,000 at Jesse he was committed to the right-down-to-the-river bluff. When the king of hearts showed up on the fourth board card, he sent $40,000 more into the pot. Jesse called. The deuce of spades was the final card and Cowboy showed what he was made of, pushing his last $110,000 toward the center of the table. After a long consideration Alto slid his cards toward the dealer. The cowboy had won the money but the hand was so important to Keller's game when Wolford exercised a psychological option in choosing to show his nothing-but-nerve cards. In effect, that was the end of the tournament. And in retrospect, the real winner of that key hand was Jack Keller, but the bluff took Cowboy to an eventual second-place finish and $264,000. And maybe he'll get a new Stetson from Jack Keller."

When I pushed my last $110,000 into the center at the river, Jesse must've studied what to do for five minutes, with the cameras and lights on us and Evelyn and my son sitting on the rail watching. While Jesse was pondering, I looked over at them and winked and smiled. Finally he threw his hand away. Then I showed him my cards, a 5-3! When Jesse saw them, he got on tilt and went nuts, bluffed off all his money, every bit of it, to Jack Keller on the next two deals. Somebody said that I won the World Series for Jack. Jack and I had made a $50,000 save at the end, so I won a little more than $300,000 for second place. Some people say that it was the greatest bluff ever made at the World Series.

"It's always high drama time when the world's greatest poker aces get together at the Horseshoe," Bobby wrote. "A well-executed bluff is the most electric play in any poker game, but when it is pulled off in a four-bet sequence from the start to the river, coolly and deliberately with staggering sums of money at stake between the last three players, with wagers for over a million in cash and the world championship—that's electric. In the years to come it will be the stats that count when they publish the winners and the dollar amounts, but I can guarantee you that the players will never forget Cowboy Wolford and one of the supreme bluffs of all time."

Pulling off that bluff wasn't my first run-in with Jesse. One night years earlier when we were playing in Corpus, he'd been drinking and he was losing—and boy, did he get hot when he was loser. When he lost, he'd lose $30,000 to $50,000. Something came up, I don't remember exactly what, and I said something. It wasn't even directed at Jesse. Hell, I was friendly and wasn't even drinking. All of a sudden Jesse reached across the table and slapped me. Damn, I didn't know what to think! I got up and we squared off, fought each other right there in the joint with all the poker players standing around watching. He was supposed to be pretty tough, but don't worry 'bout it, I whipped him pretty good. I mighta had a little blood on me, so I just cashed out my chips and left. That was one of the only fights that I ever had around a poker room.

But after the fighting and all, Jesse and I became pretty good friends. He was a helluva good high-stakes poker player, but he sometimes let his temper get out of control. Just like he did when he went crazy after I bluffed him at the World Series and he threw off all his money.

★ Bobby Baldwin ★

One night years ago when Bobby Baldwin and I were playing together in Dallas, I asked him, "Bobby, you ever been to the World Series of Poker? It's coming up real soon." When he said no, I suggested that he and I make the trip to Las Vegas to play in it. He agreed and we took off for Vegas, getting there two or three days before the Series started.

The first night that we were in town, Amarillo Slim came up to me and pointed toward Bobby, asking, "What does he play?"

"Oh, just about anything," I told him.

"Well, he's come to the right place!" Slim said.

Slim set up a game and he and Bobby started playing heads-up. Well, Bobby ran right over him. Slim thought that he had cornered a rabbit, but instead he was cornered by a grizzly bear. Everybody around the Horseshoe noticed it. "You shouldn't have beat him the first night you played him," I teased Bobby. "No telling who else you could beat out here."

Later I introduced him to the Binions and Steve Wynn and they all liked him right from the start because he was such a sharp kid. Meeting the Binions was what you call being in the right place at the right time. Although we didn't know it then, it was perfect timing for Bobby.

In 1980 Bobby and I both played the deuce-to-seven tournament at the World Series, the one in which I had placed second to Billy Baxter the year before. It got down to me and Bobby and we each had about the same amount of chips, so we made a deal to split the money because at that time, it was quite a bit of money to both of us. We made a $2,500 side bet on who would win it and played for the bracelet, so Bobby got the bracelet plus the $2,500 side bet. I was a helluva deuce-to-seven player in those days and might have been a slight favorite over Bobby. After we had made the deal, I got him down to $15,000. Then he gave me a poker lesson—he started catching cards and it wasn't long before he broke me. After all the picture taking with Jack Binion giving us the money was over with, I was worn out and poured myself a beer. When I started to hand the $2,500 bet to Bobby, he already had forgotten about it.

Bobby has always treated me with respect—whenever he sees me in a poker game, he'll walk all the way across the room just to shake my hand and ask how I'm doing. In a way, I think of Bobby as a part of the family because I've known him since he was a kid. I can hardly believe that he now has grandchildren. After Bobby started working for Steve Wynn, he started going up, up, up in the corporate ranks. Today he's the main man at the Bellagio. Mirage Resorts couldn't have a better hand working for them than Bobby Baldwin because he knows the business and his record proves it.

You still hear stories going around about Bobby saying, "I used to make a hundred dollars a day working for Cowboy down in Dallas." So, the next time I run into him at the Bellagio, I think I'll tell him, "Say, Bobby, I used to pay you a hundred a day. I'm kind of an old worn out cowboy poker player now, so do you think you could put me on at one of your joints in Vegas for $100 a day?" I know he'd get a kick out of that! To go all the way from my joint at the AmVets club in Dallas to being a top man in Las Vegas is quite a feat for anyone to accomplish. I'm proud for Bobby and I'm proud of him.

★ Puggy Pearson ★

Puggy Pearson is another vintage player who is still around the poker scene—still kickin', like me—and he's quite a character. Some people really like him and some folks don't much care for him. He's been known to get on the dealers' backs a time or two, but I have nothing to say about that one way or the other because he treats me all right and that's what is important to me. Back in 1973 he won the World Series and has played in it every year since then. That's one reason why everyone knows him. Another reason is because he dresses in some outlandish costumes from time to time—one year he came to the Series dressed as a sultan with a big turban sitting on his head and his body draped in a flowing silk robe.

Puggy is a good poker player, no doubt about that, and he plays a lot of other games, too. He's a magnificent golfer—I've heard players say that he can teach you as much about golf as anybody in the world. Puggy drives around in a custom motor home with his favorite saying painted on it: "I'll play any man from any land any game that he can name for any amount that he can count ... if I like it." And he's probably not kidding about that.

I've known him for a lot of years going back to before the World Series started. Puggy, Sid Wyman, Sarge Ferris, Blondie Forbes, Little Red Ashey, Bill Smith, Sailor Roberts—a whole bunch of us used to play no-limit poker at the Horseshoe together. Mr. Binion would play with us every once a while, too. We had one game that lasted nine months without ever breaking up, about the longest I've known a game to keep going. When your name came up on the list, they'd call you in your room so you could come down and get your seat. Because we've been friends for so long, I wrote a poem for Puggy that he got a kick out of. In 1987 Puggy was inducted into the Poker Hall of Fame.

★ Johnny Moss ★

Johnny Moss was the world champion of poker three times at the Horseshoe. Stu Ungar, who won back-to-back championships in 1980 and '81, won his third championship in 1997 to become the only player to tie Johnny's record. In the old days Johnny was one of the best card players in the world. I guess he liked me because I was a cowboy and he had roped a few times himself just for fun. He and Benny Binion were real good friends and Benny even made a bet years ago that Johnny could rope and tie a calf in such-and-such a time.

I met Johnny Moss in Odessa, Texas in 1954 at the Golden Rooster, a club that was owned by Pinky Rhoden, who also owned all the liquor stores in the area. Doc Ramsey played in the game, along with Broomcorn, Morris Shapiro, Paul Harvey, and Johnny. What a game! I'd never seen a no-limit poker game that big. I was still rodeoing then and was staying in Snyder for a couple of months during the winter practicing roping and getting my horse ready for the rodeo in Denver that January. Johnny Mayfield and I took a break from practice and went to Odessa to play in this big game.

Later on I played with Johnny in a big no-limit game at the Elks Club in Waco and came to know him quite well. Broomcorn, Mac McCorquodale, Blondie Forbes, Buck Buchanan, Amarillo Slim, and a lot of other big-time players played in that game. I had met those guys in Odessa and they knew me, so when I heard about the game they had in Waco, I decided to go there to play. It was the wintertime and I caught the Greyhound bus, leaving the old car that I had rodeoed with at home. I was short of money, only had about $400 in my jeans.

After I checked into the hotel, I put on a clean pair of jeans, grabbed my cowboy hat, and caught a cab to the Elks Club. It was an old place upstairs with a bar and pool table in the front—Amarillo Slim was there playing one-pocket with Georgia Slim—and a big poker room in the back. The windows in the poker room had been boarded up for years but no one seemed to mind. It was a big game with thousands of dollars on the table. I bought in for my case $400, won a few hands, and quit when I was a couple of thousand winner. Hell, I was in pretty good shape for a country boy who had come to town on the Greyhound and needed a new car.

About sixty miles from Waco in Caldwell, Hugh Shoemaker had a joint with a Vegas-style craps game and a big poker game. I caught a ride from Waco to Caldwell with Johnny Mayfield. "It's gonna be a big game in Caldwell. You wanna put in with me down there?" I asked him.

"Aw hell," he said, "they've got too much money. You wouldn't have a chance." Martin Cramer from Houston was in the game along with Broomcorn and Carl Biggs, a big bookmaker from Dallas—all the same guys who played poker on the circuit just like we did rodeoing. They might stay in one game four or five days and then hit the road for the next game on down the line.

As soon as we got there, I put my name on the list for the game. Pretty soon a seat came up and I bought in for $1,000 of the money that I'd won in Waco, playing with the best players in the world. They say that you hold more hands when you're young, but I don't know for sure. Anyway, I won a few pots and then a few more, and it wasn't too long before I was $12,000 winner, half of what I could make in a whole year of rodeoing.

"Aw hell, Byron, come on and keep a playing," Johnny Mayfield said when I got up from the game. I guess he wanted to see me get broke since he wouldn't put in with me; he was kind of a funny guy that way.

"Hell no, I'm goin' back to Waco," I told him.

"Well, I'm not leaving for two days," he said. "I'm gonna stay here and play."

"I don't care, I'll catch a cab," I said. Having money in his jeans can make a man feel pretty independent. The sixty-five-mile taxi ride cost me $20. The very next morning I went down to the Oldsmobile dealer and bought myself a brand new Olds right off the showroom floor, a green and yellow bomb that was pretty as a picture. I was tickled to death. Here I'd come to Waco on the bus with $400 and had won me a brand new car with close to $9,000 left over. Knowing that Johnny Mayfield was coming back to Waco the next day, I parked that beauty right in front of the hotel where he'd be sure to see it. When Johnny arrived the next afternoon I could tell that he was pissed off.

"Well, how'd you do in Caldwell?" I asked.

"I didn't do no good," he said. "Got broke. Hell, I ain't got no sense, wouldn't put in with you. I must be nuts," he answered, bad-rapping himself.

"You see that new Oldsmobile out in front of the hotel?"

"Yeah, helluva car. Brand new, isn't it?"

"That sonnabitch is mine!" I bragged. "Bought it yesterday." He was really pissed off then. And there I sat with a new car and a bankroll. The cake was all dough and it was downhill and shady.

And that's the story of the first time that I went to Waco in the '50s and played poker with Johnny Moss and the circuit players. That's how I got in with the big boys and got to know all of them real well. I once was sort of a big boy myself, or so I thought. Johnny Mayfield and I opened a club at the Elks Club in Tyler several years later and I invited all the guys that I had met in Waco and Caldwell to come play at our joint—Johnny Moss, Sam McFarland, Doc Ramsey, Mac McCorquodale, Morris Shapiro, all the top players. Nobody in the world could beat that bunch back then because nobody had as much experience as they had.

Johnny Moss would come into a game and look around the table before he bought in. If somebody had $3,000 in front of him and another player had $4,000, Johnny would buy in for $10,000. No matter how much money anybody had on the table, he would double it. You might beat him in a pot or two, but every time Johnny beat you in a pot he broke you if you weren't real careful. He would have so much money in front of him when he beat you that you were a goner. Sarge Ferris, an ole guy named Carlo, Martin Cramer—some real characters— played with Johnny. They were all legends in their own time, but Moss was the best of them all. Nobody could beat him.

After Benny Binion bought the Horseshoe in Las Vegas, Moss moved there to play. That's when Benny got him to play Nick the Greek in the famous game that went on for months before Nick finally said, "Mr. Moss, I'm gonna have to turn you loose." Nobody knows where Nick got his money, but everybody knows that Johnny beat him out of a lot of it.

Benny told me that he and Jack once went to Los Angeles to pick up some money that Nick owed Johnny. The money was wrapped in a newspaper. Benny was one of the sharpest ole guys around so he looked at the date on the newspaper to try to figure out where and when Nick had gotten the money, whether he had had it hidden for a while or what. Of course a lot of people staked Nick the Greek to play poker and shoot dice and every other thing. I've been staked a lot of times myself to shoot the dice and I've won a lot of money for some people, as high as $30,000 or $40,000. But it seems like every time I played for myself I didn't do much good. Johnny told me that he had lost over $6 million shooting dice in his younger days before he quit.

In 1979 at Amarillo Slim's Super Bowl at the Hilton, it got down to Johnny and me in the $10,000 deuce-to-seven tournament and I wound up winning it. In one hand during the game I was dealt three queens. Johnny drew one card. I stood pat. He bet and I moved in. He studied and studied, then turned over a 9-8 and threw it away. I didn't show him all those queens. After the match a reporter asked me, "What do you think about beating Johnny Moss, one of the best poker players in the world?"

"Well, all I can say is that I guess I got lucky on my teacher," I answered, trying to make Johnny feel good.

"Yeah, I *am* his teacher," he said, hugging me and taking it up from there.

A long time ago Johnny used to go down to Birmingham, Alabama to play high poker with "Little Man," a big bookmaker who had lots of money. Booking was so much the nuts back then that it was unbelievable—people couldn't get all the information that they get these days. The two of them played lowball. They were playing so high that they rubber-banded their money into $10,000 bundles so that they wouldn't have to count it when they bet. I don't know how much money Johnny beat Little Man out of, but it was a lot.

People like Johnny, Blondie, Sarge, McCorquodale, and even myself paved the way for the younger guys so that all they have do these days is walk into a casino, order some chips, and play poker without having to worry about anything—the police wouldn't raid them and they wouldn't get hijacked or cheated. We had to face a lot of traps on the road in the old days and I've been in all of them. In fact I don't know of anyone who played back then who was never involved in some of them. Poker is so different now, just like rodeos where the old cowboys laid down the cornerstones to make rodeoing the big-time sport it is today.

Johnny Moss was a friend of mine. We always liked each other and never exchanged a cross word. All of the old-timers and I miss him. I'll guarantee you one thing: If he's in that big game in the sky, he's the favorite. Johnny was immortalized here on earth in 1979 when he became one of the first three players inducted into the Poker Hall of Fame.

★ Amarillo Slim Preston ★

Amarillo Slim is a legendary Texas gambler and probably the best-known poker player in the world. After Johnny Moss was voted best player in the first World Series of Poker and went on to win it outright the next year, it was Slim's turn to take the title. He won the championship of poker in 1972 against seven other players. And then he did something that took poker out of the backrooms and alleyways—he got on television shows with Johnny Carson and some others, talked poker, told a few good stories, spiced things up with some Texas humor, and got people thinking about poker in a different way. Slim showed folks that even though we used to play poker in the back rooms of bars and pool halls, these days anybody can go into a casino and play poker with their friends without having to worry because the casino and its "eye in the sky" protects them against cheaters and hijackers.

I've played poker with Slim for forty-something years and I can tell you that he's quite a character. He used to shoot a mean game of pool and knew all the angles at pool and poker, his two favorite games. Like I said in my story about Johnny Moss, the first time I met Slim was at the Elks Club in Waco when he was playing one-pocket against Georgia Slim on the pool table by the bar and then played poker with us in the big no-limit game in the back room. Of course he doesn't play as much poker as he used to in the old days. Some people thought he might be washed up but he proved them wrong when he took second in the pot-limit Omaha tournament at the 2000 World Series against one of those new kids on the block. Folks probably thought that I was out of the running, too, but like Slim, I proved them wrong when I came in third in the pot-limit hold'em tournament the same year. Reckon some of us old-timers can still play poker.

After he got so famous from his television appearances, he went on to being the host of Amarillo Slim's Super Bowl of Poker, some of the biggest and best poker tournaments ever. In 1979 he ran the Super Bowl at the Hilton and I won the $10,000 deuce-to-seven championship at it. A lot of us still miss his tournaments because they were so big. In fact, they were second only to the World Series. When Slim was inducted into the Horseshoe's Poker Hall of Fame in 1992, I read a poem during the ceremonies that I had written for him, even got a standing ovation for it. Slim cried when I read it.

★ Jack "Treetop" Straus ★

Jack Straus loved to gamble. His nickname was "Tree Top" because he stood about six foot seven inches tall. I played poker with Jack for forty years in Fort Worth, San Antone, Dallas, and in Las Vegas at quite a few World Series of Poker tournaments.

He was one of the best shorthanded players in the world—heads-up or three- or four-handed, I didn't know anybody who could beat him although a lot of them tried. He wasn't as good in a full ring game because he had too much gamble in him, but I can tell you one thing—sometimes he'd bet so much, it wasn't poker to call.

Years ago he used to put on tournaments in Las Vegas. In 1979 I played in the one that he hosted one at the Marina. I hadn't seen him for several months, so when I got to the hotel I asked, "Jack, how you been doin'?"

"I'm putting on this tournament," he answered, "but I don't know what the hell I'm gonna do, Cowboy. I don't have any money."

I won the deuce-to-seven lowball event at his tournament and after the whole thing was over, I asked him once again, "How did you do, Jack?"

"I lost $90,000 to the tournament," he answered.

"But I thought you didn't have any money," I said.

"I can get all the money I need to gamble on," he answered, "but I have hell paying my rent."

Jack was a bettor, loved the sports and loved the horses. One time at the Horseshoe I saw him bet $30,000 on a ball game leaving him with only four dollars in his pocket. "Hell, this is enough to eat breakfast on," he told me. And he liked to play golf. He and Stuey Ungar once played against Doyle Brunson and his partner for one week straight. Sounds unbelievable but they lost might near $1 million at golf in those seven days. Neither Jack nor Stuey could hit the ball one hundred fifty yards, but they liked to play golf and they loved to gamble.

Outside of golf Jack was a smart operator, cool. One time while he was living in Houston, he had a pocketful of money and decided to go to New Orleans for the races. He asked Bob, a big bookmaker in Houston, to go with him. "If you go to the races with me," Jack told him, "you can book me down there. That way, the odds won't go down and I'll have a chance to win something, or you'll have a chance to win something." They were pretty good friends so Bob agreed.

They got to New Orleans about three hours before the races began and checked into the Roosevelt Hotel. Jack had a scheme in mind in which he could "past post" the bookie and make a big score, so he left Bob in the room and went downstairs to the taxi stand outside the hotel to see if he could make a deal with the dispatcher. Sure enough, the dispatcher agreed to plant a cab in front of the hotel that Jack could identify by the number painted on it. Then he instructed the cabby not to take any customers until he saw Jack and Bob come out of the hotel door. Meanwhile Jack arranged for a man at the track to run to the telephone as soon as the first race had finished and call the dispatcher with the results.

When Jack and Bob, who had been in the hotel room together ever since they had arrived in New Orleans, came downstairs together, cab number 37 was parked right in front of the hotel. They hailed the cabby and got in the back seat. "Can you take us to the track?" Jack asked, signaling that they were his "customers." The races began around 1:10 and it was quite a distance from the hotel to the track. As soon as they pulled away from the curb, Jack began looking over the race form.

"Man, I guess the races have already started," he said to Bob, "and that's too bad because there's a horse that I wanted to bet in the first race."

"Hell, go ahead and bet," Bob said.

About that time, the dispatcher's voice came over the cabby's microphone. "Where you going?" the voice asked the cabby.

"To the race track," he answered.

"Well, after you drop your customers off at the track," the dispatcher told him, "pick up a man at 2304 Villa Street."

The key number was the last one in the street address, the four. After hearing the message, Jack messed around another minute or two studying the race form and then told Bob that he wanted to bet the four horse.

"Well, go right ahead," Bob said. "How much you wanna bet?"

"I'll bet $3,000 on him to win," Jack answered.

"You've got it!" Bob agreed.

The minute they got to the track, they checked on the winner of the first race and miraculously, the four horse had won it. The horse paid about 8 to 1, so Jack got $20,000-something winner on his bet. Of course they stayed at the track the whole day and Jack bet all the rest of the races—wound up losing about $3,000 for the day! That's how much he loved to gamble.

Jack was a helluva poker player. In 1982 he won the World Series of Poker after getting down to a single $500 chip. He had bet what appeared to be all of his money and his opponent, who had more chips than Jack, called the bet and won the hand. Thinking that he was broke, Jack stood up to leave the table when he noticed a $500 chip from his stack partly hidden under the rail of the poker table. If Jack had been the caller of the other guy's bet, he would've had to give that chip to his opponent, but since he was the bettor the chip was still in play. And that was lucky for Jack—he took that chip and went on to win the championship.

I miss Jack. He was a great poker player with a friendly personality and everybody liked him. He was a good man to have around the joints, too, because he played high and was pleasant to play with. I've seen Jack win some big scores and I've seen him lose some big scores, but through it all he was quite a man, a friendly guy who was full of life. In 1988 he was inducted into the Poker Hall of Fame.

★ Doyle "Texas Dolly" Brunson ★

Doyle Brunson is a gambling man. I first met him about forty years ago when we were playing $10 limit poker in Dallas at the Red Men's Club on Irving Street. I got to know him real well over the years and I can tell you that he's one helluva poker player. Doyle won the World Series twice, both times with a 10-2 on the final hand. At the 1976 Series, he made a big drawout on Jesse Alto with that nothing hand.

Years ago Doyle and I had been playing no-limit poker at the Elks Club in Waco and we both got broke. Had a car full of gas and headed home to Dallas with just $50 between us. On our way home we stopped at a small cafe along the road and ordered some breakfast. This little gal came to take our order and I asked, "Honey, how long've you worked here?"

"Oh, 'bout two or three years," she answered.

"You married?"

"No."

"Got any kids?"

"Yeah, I've got three." She was real nice and a good waitress, so when we were through eating I gave her the $50 bill and told her to keep the change. When we got back in the car, Doyle was madder than a wet rooster because I'd tipped off our case money.

"What'd you do that for?" he demanded.

"Hell, she can put that money to better use on her kids than we can giving it to any damned poker players," I explained.

"If I had a gun, I'd shoot you," he cried. True story.

Doyle eventually moved from Dallas to Las Vegas when McCorquodale took hold'em to the California Club. None of the poker players in Vegas could play a lick of hold'em. If Sid Wyman and the other guys had two fours in the hole, it didn't make any difference what came on the flop, an A-K-2 or whatever, they'd put all their money in the pot because they were used to playing stud and had never heard of hold'em. I wish I'd gone with Mac when he asked me, but I had just quit rodeoing and was too busy doing nothing, I guess. I'd probably have gotten rich if I'd gone.

Sailor Roberts, Doyle's good friend, went to Vegas with him. I first met Sailor in 1954 in Snyder, Texas at the Roadrich Drive-In. At that time I was living in Snyder with my wife and went there during the wintertime to practice my roping for a couple of months before I took off for the Denver rodeo in January. Sailor lived in Abilene and was a real good poker player. I used to play poker with him in Abilene and at a hotel in San Angelo where a lot of the old-timers used to play. One time while I was still rodeoing, I went there with Johnny Mayfield. I didn't have enough money to play in the big game, so I would just hang around and watch Sailor and the others play, or I might play in one of the smaller games. This particular time I decided to walk across the street to the beer joint and have one or two.

Still young and in good shape, I walked into the bar wearing my cowboy duds and hat and took a stool at the bar. The bartender, Blackie, asked what I wanted. "Gimme a Budweiser," I answered. When he brought me the beer, I gave him a fifty-dollar bill, the only money I had on me. He gave me change for a five-dollar bill. "Sir, you've made a mistake," I protested. "I know you didn't mean to, but I gave you a fifty and you only gave me change for a five."

"Oh hell, they try that here all the time," he said.

"Well, that's all the money I've got. Punch your cash register and I'll show you that I gave you a fifty."

"Don't try that old stuff on me," he answered, and came around the bar looking to throw me out. We got into a helluva fight right there in the joint. That sonnabitch must've weighed two hundred-something pounds, but I was a pretty good fighter. I'd been throwing those three hundred-pound Brahma calves, you know. I whipped him pretty good. Then I went over to the cash register and got my fifty out of it. Counting the change for the $5 that I'd gotten from the bartender, I made about four dollars on the fight. I was kind of skinned up and bloody so I went back to the hotel where Sailor and the other guys were playing poker to get myself cleaned up.

"Run into some barbed wire?" they asked.

When I explained what had happened, Sailor said, "Boy, that Blackie's a mean sonnabitch, you better not mess with him."

"I didn't mess with him, I just whipped his ass pretty good. He was laying on the floor when I left," I bragged. "Made four bucks on the deal, too."

Sailor's gone now but Doyle is still a big name on the poker scene. He is among the highest players and has become rich in the gambling business, partly because he's smart and partly because he was in the right spot at the right time when he went to Vegas with McCorquodale. His son Todd also is a top player and Doyle's wife Louise is a wonderful lady.

He didn't get rich from it, that's for sure, but one of the things that made Doyle so famous is his book *Super/System*. By his own account it took him close to twenty years just to break even on it, but the players who bought the book and used it made money off it right away. A lot of poker players owe Doyle for teaching them how to play no-limit hold'em, but not a one of them that I know of has ever learned to play it as well as he can. And there aren't many who can afford to play poker for the highest stakes in the world like he does.

Doyle is a golfer, too, and bets high at it. In 1998 Doyle and Mike Sexton won a big bet against a couple of young poker-playing golfers when he made a miracle putt on the sixteenth hole. When you're putting, the hole looks about the size of a dime, but pressure doesn't bother Doyle, not in golf and not in poker. He was put in the Hall of Fame in 1988. About twenty years ago while I was on vacation in the federal penitentiary at Fort Worth on that framed-up charge, I wrote a poem about Doyle that he got a kick out of. Here's the way I ended the poem. His son asks, "Did Daddy play tight or loose?" And the poem answers, "Figure it out for yourself: Daddy won a million dollars on a ten and a deuce!" And he's won a whole lot more than that in the years since then.

★ Chip, Blackie, Buck, and a Lot of Others ★

Chip Reese is a close friend of Doyle's who plays the highest limits, and he's one nice fella—might near anywhere I'm playing, he'll walk clear across the room and say, "Good to see ya, Cowboy, how ya doing?" Some folks believe that Chip is the best all-around poker player in the world and I wouldn't doubt they're right. Chip made the biggest win at the Horseshoe several years ago that I've ever seen when he played Archie Karas, a high roller who was a $30-million winner in the pits at the time. They played heads-up with $15,000/$30,000 limits. Chip was inducted into the Poker Hall of Fame in 1991.

Another poker player that I've known for a long time is Blackie Blackburn, who used to run around with Buck Buchanan and Speedy Meyers. We played in a big game one time at Austin, Texas in a house out in the countryside. Duck Mallard (a bookmaker), Doc Ramsey, Broomcorn, Blackie, Buck, and Speedy all were in the game. Johnny Joseph, who played deuce-to-seven really high, and Carl Biggs and Blondie Forbes, who all were playing on the circuit at that time, were there, too. Before he died, Buchanan always came to the World Series and everybody knew him. Blackie plays his poker in California these days, mostly Omaha high-low.

Several of my old-time friends are from San Antonio, where I used to play a lot of poker. Slim Lambert owned a nice place in San Antone where he had a big-limit poker game. Frank Butler, a gentleman and a player who usually comes to the World Series, used to play in it. When I was a host at the Maxim, Frank came to Vegas and played in my game there. To make me look good, he got a $200,000 line of credit. Frank started off as a bricklayer and wound up getting rich as a big builder, doing projects as far away as Japan, but I hear that all he's doing today is fishing for trout in Argentina.

George Collins was a quiet guy who played poker around Las Vegas for years and he was a top pot-limit player. One time Evelyn was playing in a cheap $1/$2 pot-limit hold'em game with him and she raised with aces full when the board paired kings. "You may not have the best hand," George said. Then he turned four kings face up and just called her bet. He could've broken her, but that's the kind of gentleman he was. George used to come down to Ocean's Eleven to play with us before he died of a heart attack a few years back. A lot of my old friends are gone now and I miss them all.

Crandall Addington, who got rich in the oil business, was another friend of mine from San Antonio. He's the man who came in second to Bobby Baldwin at the 1978 World Series of Poker. Crandall always dressed just as sharp as he played poker. I was playing in San Antone one time in a game that Crandall and a guy named Joe were running. Nobody showed up for it except me, so we waited around for a while and then started playing three-handed. None of us had a lot of money (this happened before Crandall became a millionaire). We hadn't been playing long when a hand came up that I'll never forget. I had an 8-4 and Crandall and Joe each had pocket queens. All three of us took the flop and it came 8-4-2. We got all-in and I broke both of them in that one hand. We named 8-4 the "San Antone" hand.

Joe Bernstein was one of the first really high gamblers to come to Vegas and boy, was he a stylish dresser! He used to come around the hold'em games when he wasn't playing himself and, after everybody had gotten all their money in, he would lay insurance, give them a short price. One time some players set up a hand especially for him, a long-price hand. Joe walked over to the table, laid some insurance on it, and lost about $14,000. After that, he quit the insurance business.

Sailor Roberts and I met in 1954 in Snyder, Texas, where he was a bookmaker (a good racket back then because people didn't get the information that they get now), and we played poker in San Angelo and Abilene. At one time, he and Doyle Brunson were road partners. And boy, could Sailor play poker.

If he had stayed straight and not gotten hooked up with drugs, there wasn't anybody who could beat him at no-limit hold'em.

For a long time Sailor ran with my good friend, Bobby Hoff, one of the best no-limit players in the world. In 1979 Bobby won second place in the championship event at the World Series against Hal Fowler, an unknown. It was a miracle of sports that Hal beat Bobby. Nobody's heard from him since. But Bobby has endured and today he plays at the Commerce Casino in Los Angeles. When he lived in Dallas and was on the road, Bobby and I used to play in Texarkana and a lot of other spots. His friend Carl McKelvey and I go back a long way before the World Series. A few years ago I got Carl to play golf telling him that hitting the greens every day would add ten years to his life, and now he's quite a golfer. In 1983 Carl took fourth in the Big One at the Horseshoe. In the $1,500 no-limit hold'em event at the 1995 World Series, three of us split top money for about $100,000 each. Carl took third place, but he won the most money because he had the most chips when we made the deal.

Ferris Greer used to run a game in Seguin, Texas near San Antone. It was a strange type of game, a big game. All you could bet before the flop was $5 but after the flop it was no-limit. I liked that structure because you could see the flop on almost any two cards. If you hit the flop just right, you could make a lot of money against somebody who had a big overpair. Buck and Crandall and I all played in the game.

One time when I was playing there, Joe Davis was in the game. Joe was quite a character and he was a legitimate poker player, too, but he got broke in the game. Hocked his false teeth to Ferris for $100! The next day Joe called Ferris to tell him to be sure to put his teeth in a glass of water overnight so that they wouldn't crack. Tony Salinas was there, too.

In the early '50s I rodeoed with his daddy, Juan, who was a calf roper. Tony rodeoed, too, but not professionally like his daddy did. Tony eventually moved to Vegas and became an oddsmaker at sports. Juan later became a sheriff in Texas.

Junior Whited from Austin, Texas was a good player who won Amarillo Slim's Super Bowl of Poker one year. Junior and I played poker together in Corpus, San Antone, Austin, Dallas, everywhere. He was quite a guy, Junior was—he could remember any kind of number but he couldn't remember names. When he thought about somebody, he remembered their phone number, not their name. Strange, but it worked for him.

Darrin Walters from Kentucky used to play at the World Series and plays pot-limit Omaha in Tunica these days. Al Karson played at the Series for years. He's a good pot-limit player and a good guy, too, the kind of fella that you could leave in a town with your bankroll and not worry about him taking a nickel of it.

Among the other players that I played with in the old days was George Huber, who won the big one at Amarillo Slim's tournament one year and won a hold'em tournament at the World Series in 1979, the year that I won the deuce-to-seven title against Johnny Moss. Bud Brown, who used to run the Elks Club in Waco, also was quite a player. He always dressed up in silk shirts and matching ties. Davey Baxter from Corpus also is a good friend of mine who won the big tournament at the Nugget one year and is always at the World Series.

I've know Steve Wynn for a long time, ever since he played at the Nugget before he bought it. Benny Binion put Las Vegas on the United States map and Steve carried it a step further by putting Vegas on the worldwide map. He's a very intelligent businessman who knows the business as well or better than anybody in the world.

★ The Times, They are a Changin' ★

Poker in Las Vegas has changed a lot since the old days. Today the big corporations run the casinos and the players run to the casinos to do their gambling. I liked things the way they used to be, but I'm living in a different world today. I've learned to adjust to the changes in the game, just like all good gamblers have to do to be winners. Today I live in Southern California on the edge of a golf course where the weather's always perfect and the action in the cardroom where I'm a host is always good. But that doesn't keep me from going back to Las Vegas several times a year to play some poker and talk about the old days with my friends. And tell all the new players my stories about how it was back then.

When Byron "Cowboy" Wolford retired from the rodeo circuit to begin his adventures as a road gambler in 1960, he was 30 years old.
This family photograph is the way he looked in the early days of his
professional poker career when he traveled the Southern circuit to
match wits with the best poker players in the world. Most road gamblers dressed nicely in the old days and Wolford was no exception,
always wearing a sportcoat, silk shirt, dress slacks and alligator
boots. In later years he began sporting his signature cardroom ap-
parel—bib overalls decorated with poker motifs, white dress shirt,
Stetson, gold jewelry and boots.

Cowboy and Evelyn usu-
ally brought Rebel with
them when they stayed
at Binion's Horseshoe
in Las Vegas. In this
photo, Rebel is stand-
ing on the registration
desk of the legendary
Downtown casino.

Celebrities have always enjoyed playing at the World Series of Poker. Gabe Kaplan of "Welcome Back, Kotter" fame, shown here in an early 1980s Horseshoe press release photo, has been playing in the Series since its early days. Kaplan also acted as commentator for several WSOP videos, most notably the 1997 event when Stu "The Kid" Ungar won his third championship.

Television and screen actor Telly "Kojak" Savalas playing at the World Series of Poker in the early 1980s. Savalas, whose Kojak character was known for sucking a lollipop, was no sucker at the poker table. Savalas was widely regarded as an accomplished player.

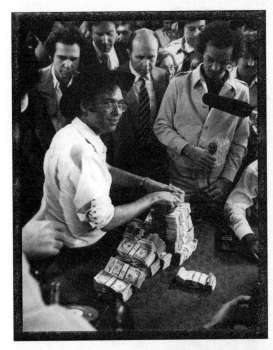

Left: Tom McEvoy (front) is flanked by Teddy Binion (L), Jack Binion (C), and WSOP champion turned commentator Bobby Baldwin (on the microphone) at the 1983 World Series of Poker when McEvoy won the World Championship. McEvoy made WSOP history as the first satellite winner to capture the title, and has since gone on to win three more bracelets and author a dozen popular poker books, incluing Championship Tournament Poker.

Perry Green, an Alaskan fur trader, in an early '80s Horseshoe press release photo. An entrant in many of the early WSOP events, Green won the gold bracelet for ace-to-five lowball in 1976, finished second to Stu Ungar in the 1981 championship event, and fifth to Brad Daugherty in 1991 (the first year the Series awarded $1 million for first place).

Stu "The Kid" Ungar, three-time World Champion of Poker (1980-81 and 1997). Arguably the best no-limit hold'em player of all time, Ungar cashed in his chips for the last time in 1998, the victim of his vices.

Jack Binion (C) divides the prize money for the deuce-to-seven tournament at the 1980 World Series of Poker between Cowboy Wolford and Bobby Baldwin. Baldwin won the tournament and was awarded the gold bracelet plus the $2,500 "save" that he and Wolford had agreed upon when they got to heads-up play at the final table. Wolford also placed second in the deuce-to-seven tournament in 1979 to noted lowball player Billy Baxter.

Right: O'Neill "Salt Lake" Longson in a vintage photo taken in the 1980s by Evelyn Wolford. A long-time entrant in the World Series of Poker, Longson was still winning bracelets in 2005 when he won the razz championship.

Left: Legendary road gambler Bobby Hoff— who traveled the Southern poker circuit with his close friend Sailor Roberts—playing poker in the 1980s at the Golden Nugget in Downtown Las Vegas. The unfortunate victim of a dramatic drawout at the final table of the 1979 WSOP, Hoff raised with pocket aces only to be called by Hal Fowler, who had 7-6 offsuit and made an inside straight on the turn to steal the championship from Hoff.

Jimmy "The Greek" Snyder at the Horseshoe's Sombrero Room in the 1980s in a photo taken by Evelyn Wolford. Snyder narrated the first WSOP video in 1973, after assisting Jack Binion in setting up the poker tables and laying out the chips for the thirteen men who entered the tournament. The video tape, possibly the most entertaining of the many to follow, showed the two finalists—champion Puggy Pearson and runner-up Johnny Moss—with their ladies seated alongside them at the poker table.

Blondie Forbes (L) with Benny Binion at the Horseshoe Club in the mid '70s. Cowboy Wolford played poker with the legendary road gambler in the '60s. Forbes was inducted into the Poker Hall of Fame in 1980.

World Series of Poker pioneers Terry Rogers (L) and Bill Boyd (R) at the WSOP in the early 1990s. Rogers, an Irishman and close friend of 1999 World Champion of Poker Noel Furlong, is credited with spreading the popularity of the World Series to Europeans. Boyd, who was inducted into the Poker Hall of Fame in 1981, was a master of five-card stud and was dealt the ceremonial first poker hands at both the Golden Nugget and Mirage card rooms.

T.J. Cloutier playing poker in Cowboy Wolford's home game in the '80s. The former football player turned road gambler later played poker in Wolford's card room in Dallas in the 2000s. Cloutier has appeared at the final table of four WSOP championship events, placing second to his close friend Bill Smith in 1985, fifth to Johnny Chan in 1988, third to Scotty Nguyen in 1998, and second to Chris Ferguson in 2000. Widely regarded as one of the world's premier no-limit hold'em players, Cloutier won his sixth WSOP bracelet in 2005 when he won the $5,000 no-limit hold'em event. The co-author with Tom McEvoy of four poker books, Cloutier's Championship No-Limit & Pot-Limit Hold'em is widely regarded as the definitive book in its field.

Sailor Roberts and Doyle Brunson in the early 1970s in Las Vegas during the World Series of Poker.

Cowboy and Evelyn Wolford displaying the World Series of Poker quilt on Fremont Street in front of the Horseshoe Club in 1987. Pictured in the center of the quilt are WSOP founder Benny Binion with his sons Teddy and Jack. The Binions are flanked by likenesses of the thirteen World Champions of Poker from 1970 through 1986.

THE LUCK
OF THE DRAW

If there had ever been a tournament in which you had to rope a calf and then play a poker hand—and take the best of the two against someone who had to do the same thing for the championship—there's no telling how many of them I would have won because I know that I was the best poker player of any cowboy in the world before or since my time. And I was one of the best calf ropers in the world when I was in my prime. I've never met a cowboy who played poker as good as me and I've never seen a poker player who could rope calves as good as I could. That would've been a *real* tournament. Sure wish I'd thought of it back then—I'd have a house full of trophies.

I've seen some strange things happen in poker tournaments and I've seen some unusual things happen in rodeos, too. But roping one of those wild calves, riding one of those mean bulls, throwing one of those big steers, or riding one of those bucking broncs is not the same as trying to catch a diamond or a spade or a running pair to win a poker tournament. Rodeo is where you get out of the storm and complete your ride or your roping with your own skill and knowledge and timing—it's all up to you.

Nobody can deal you a winner in a rodeo like they can deal you one off a deck of cards, that's for sure, and I can tell you that there's a lot of difference between the two. I guess I'm prouder of my rodeo career now than I ever was, maybe on account of my age. When I see all those cowboys at the National Finals, I remember when I used to rodeo with their daddies. A lot of them are gone now, but they were all good people and I miss them.

Rodeos in the old days were something like poker tournaments in that we all traveled from town to town entering the competitions, paying our own expenses, and not being guaranteed a quarter. The rodeos had five to seven events and today's big tournaments might have ten to twenty or more events, including two or three limit hold'em events with various entry fees. In both sports you can pick how many events you want to enter. And you can choose your own schedule, living wherever you want, working as much as you need, and traveling whenever you please.

Rodeo is still a comparably underpaid sport, but it's becoming more and more popular these days because of major sponsors and television coverage. If poker ever got on national television with big sponsors, it would do the sport a whole lot of good. However I don't believe that we'll ever get corporate sponsorship as long as poker players dress the way that most of them do—wearing shorts, faded T-shirts and baseball caps, and not shaving. If they all dressed up like gentlemen at the last table and told the audience some good poker stories, that would help the image of poker a lot. But as long as they're all sitting around looking like a shabby bunch of hustlers instead of clean-cut guys, I don't believe that the public will ever think that much of poker.

Let me tell you a story along this line: I once knew a cowboy named Wayne Dunnefin, a tall, slim, good looking guy who dressed to the teeth with a nice cowboy hat, shirt, and boots. One time when he was in New York City for the rodeo at Madison Square Garden, he was walking down Broadway when some advertising people from Marlboro stopped him on the sidewalk to ask if he wanted to become a "Marlboro Man." He had made such a positive impression with his dress and good grooming that he worked as a Marlboro Man for several years.

Making a stylish appearance in whatever you're competing at is a big plus, especially on television. All the golfers you see on TV in the big events dress up really nice. Doug Sanders used to dress exceptionally well, and the pool players even wear tuxedos for their televised matches. If poker players would do the same thing, I think we might take a giant step forward in getting corporate sponsors. Just as the best calf roper is supposed to win in the long run, so is the best poker player, but when somebody who is inexperienced draws out to beat you, you start to wonder about it. Sometimes the thickness of a card can make you rich and famous, or break you and send you to the rail. Suppose you have two kings in a poker tournament and another guy has two aces. You put all your money in the pot and the flop comes with rags—you have no chance of winning unless you can catch a king or a backdoor flush or straight. You can get frustrated and discouraged pretty fast.

That's when you have to say to yourself that what happened today is history—there'll be another tournament to play tomorrow—and keep playing your best until the cards start coming your way. When the cards finally come your way, it looks like magic—and when they don't, it looks like a fix. Like women, those cards do as they please. You have no control over luck, none whatsoever. During the bad times you just have to keep on plugging until Lady Luck smiles on you. You have to do the same thing in rodeoing.

Winning a major poker tournament is getting to be real hard to do, partly because there are so many more players now than there were in the old days. In 1984 when I came in second to Keller for the bracelet, there were one hundred eighty players in the tournament. In 1993 Bechtel beat a field of two hundred twenty to win the main event. In 2001 Carlos Mortensen had to make his way through 613 players to win it!

The satellite system is a major reason why tournament fields have increased so much. Many of the players who win seats in satellites are not experienced tournament players—they play for relaxation, fellowship, and just to say that they played the tournament. Naturally most of today's top players play in the major poker tournaments too, but they aren't always the ones who win.

Playing good poker and knowing when to get away from the second-best hand are a top player's edge when the cards break even, but that edge doesn't always work for you. Sometimes a novice gets lucky, catches the cards and wins the bracelet, or a weak player will take a bad hand and backdoor a flush or make a middle-buster straight or hit a bad kicker to beat you. When somebody draws out on you, it makes no difference if you're the best player in the world, you lose the pot—and sometimes you lose the whole tournament. It's hard to understand how a novice who hasn't played much tournament poker can beat you, but they're carefree, they've read all the poker books, they're willing to gamble, and sometimes they get the luck of the draw. If a diamond had come, you'd have been the world's champion—but it didn't and so you weren't.

That doesn't happen in rodeos. You don't see a cowboy who's never ridden a wild bronc or a bucking bull, or roped a fast calf or bulldogged a big steer, win a major rodeo. At the Houston Fat Stock Show, Madison Square Garden, the National Finals in Las Vegas, or the Calgary Stampede, no novice is going to beat you because it isn't luck that's in control, it is you. You are the only one who has control of what you do. It all gets down to skill and experience. Although you also need skill and experience to play good poker, it's different from rodeo. You might see a guy wearing a World Series bracelet who isn't really a top player, but you won't ever see a cowboy wearing a belt buckle from the Calgary Stampede who isn't a top hand, an experienced cowboy.

In my mind winning at Houston, New York, Las Vegas, or Calgary is like winning the Masters, the U.S. Open, the PGA, and the British Open at golf. No novice is going to win any of those big events on the golf circuit and no novice is going to win an event in rodeo competition. No new hand who has little experience on a horse is going to tie a calf in thirteen seconds, throw a steer in four seconds, or ride a two thousand-pound bull that jumps high and kicks back. But in a poker tournament somebody who is willing to put in all his money as a 10 to 1 dog with one card to come can win if his magic card pops out of the deck. And that is the difference between winning at poker and winning at rodeo.

Some sports have been dominated for years by certain players—Michael Jordan in basketball, Tiger Woods in golf, John Elway in football—but it's a different story in tournament poker. No one player ever totally dominates poker because of the luck factor. You can be holding two aces and raise the pot up high and still lose all your chips when a novice player with two fours calls your raise in a New York minute and flops a four to break you. Poker is a sport where the thickness of a card can make you rich and famous or send you to the rail whimpering and broke.

★ The Last Table at the World Series of Poker ★

Poker is a tough game in a lot of ways, but it's sure a lot of fun when you win. Getting to the last table at the World Series of Poker is like getting into the Super Bowl for a football player. The football player has a chance to win a Super Bowl ring and the poker player gets a chance at winning a World Series gold bracelet. After the football guy gets there, his team still has to win in order for him to get the ring, and after you get to the last table at the WSOP, you still have to win the championship to get the bracelet—and you don't have any teammates to help you out.

I've been lucky enough in my poker life to win a bracelet and I'm really proud of that. I've played at the last table in World Series events nine times and the worst that I've ever finished was third. The first year that I played the Series was in 1979 when I won second in deuce-to-seven lowball against Billy Baxter. The next year Bobby Baldwin and I split the deuce-to-seven tournament money, but he won the bracelet. I placed second to Jack Keller in the $10,000 championship event in 1984. At one point I had about twenty outs against Jack to win a big pot, which might have made all the difference in the world, but the cards didn't come and he won it. I also took second place in the World Series in a $1,000 no-limit hold'em event way back in the old days.

In 1991 I won the $5,000 limit hold'em tournament and that same year, I split the $2,500 limit hold'em event three ways. Then in 1995 three of us split the $1,500 no-limit hold'em tournament. I won third in the pot-limit hold'em event in 2001, but in the Big One that year, I ran into trouble when I had raised the pot $800 with two aces. The flop came with a queen and a four and I bet $1,800. Noel Furlong, the 1999 World Champion, called me. On the turn came a nothing card and I moved all in. Furlong called with a K-Q. There was $25,000 in the pot and only one card to come. Sure enough, a king came on the river and he broke me with two pair. When somebody takes so much the worst of it like that and beats you, it seems unbelievable but sometimes it's just the thickness of a card that makes the difference between victory and defeat.

I've taken second place at the WSOP seven times, so winning a bracelet in 1991 was quite a thrill. At the final table it got down to Erik Seidel and me. In the last pot that we played, Erik had two sevens and I had two black jacks that won the bracelet for me. Erik is a great player and since the blinds were so high, winning the title came down to who caught the best hand. Ole Cowboy lucked out.

In 1995 there were 366 players in the $1,500 no-limit hold'em event. When it got down to Carl McKelvey, Richard Klamian, and ole Cowboy, we split the money three ways. Richard outlasted us and won the bracelet. In the last hand that I played against him, Richard had two queens and I had the ace and 8 of hearts. The flop came with an 8 and we got all the money in the middle. Of course, his two queens beat my two eights. I shook the winner's hand and left with a lot of money in mine.

In the year 2000 when I finished third in the $2,000 pot-limit hold'em tournament at the Series, I was in sixth place with $42,000 in chips at the beginning of the final day, pretty low money to start with. I was able to double up once, but it didn't seem like I was catching very many good hands after that, so I decided to duck and dodge and let my opponents eliminate each other. When it got down to three of us—Jimmy Athanas from Missouri, Dave Colclough from England, and the ole Cowboy from California—I was in third place, which paid $44,000, but we struck a deal and my part of it added up to $65,000. Then we played for the bracelet.

The blinds were $6,000/$12,000 so I only had enough chips to post a few of them. That didn't worry me a whole lot because I knew that if you have the low chips in a pot-limit or no-limit tournament, all you have to do is double up a couple of times to become the leader. Unfortunately I wasn't able to do that. On my final hand, I raised all-in for my case $35,000 with a Q-9. Jimmy called with the ace and king of clubs and caught a king on the flop to send me home in third place. He went on to win it with Dave taking second. I was almost seventy years old at that time, which proves that you can play poker at any age. Actually I think that my mind is as good as it ever was, and I know that my patience and discipline are better than ever. When I'm playing poker, I don't feel old.

The fields at the World Series these days are so big that it takes a lot of endurance to get through them, but that doesn't bother me because I've always had plenty of stamina when I'm playing poker. If I have a chance to win a title or a lot of money, I can play eighteen hours straight if I have to. I don't worry about everybody else in the tournament, I just play the people at my table—I figure that all I have to do is beat 'em nine at a time. They'll be eliminating themselves all over the room anyway, so I just play my best poker like I do in a ring game. The only problem is that when you run out of chips in a regular game, you can reach into your pocket for more money, but when you run out of chips in a tournament, you're out of action—and that's a pretty sorry place to be. I try to avoid it as often as I can.

★ The Bet I Couldn't Lose ★

For several years I played most of my poker at Ocean's Eleven Casino in Oceanside, California where I worked as an executive host. I lived in a seniors mobile home park that had a golf course adjoining it in Carlsbad, just a few minutes from the club. The park is a beautiful place with lots of tall trees, a big clubhouse, an exercise room, and a swimming pool. A creek runs through the park and a big pond circles it. Wild mallard ducks swim in the pond and wait for food handouts from the residents; then at night they fly somewhere else to roost.

These ducks fascinated me, so I started calling them in to feed them. I buy cracked corn fifty pounds at a time and go to the pond with a gallon bucket full of it. There might be only four ducks floating on the pond when I get there, but as soon as I start with my quack-quack duck call, they come flying to me in droves, usually about two hundred of them, and land right at my feet knowing that they're safe with me. A few of them even come up and eat out of my hand.

I decided to use this "talent" of mine to have a little fun with Dick Davis, a golf buddy who is a retired basketball coach and plays poker at Ocean's Eleven. Dick used to give me a stroke a hole, but he quit doing that because he couldn't beat me giving up that much. One day I needed a ride home from the club and asked Dick for a lift. On the way back to the park I said, "You know, Dick, I've been practicing a duck call."

"What do you mean?" he asked.

"Quack-quack-quack," I gave him a sample. "Pretty soon I'm gonna get it down pat. Down there where I live, there's a bunch of wild ducks in that creek and pond. Betcha I could call two hundred ducks in within five minutes," I bragged, setting him up for a bet that I couldn't lose. Old habits die hard, they say.

"You've gotta be kidding!" he said in disbelief. "If that's true, you can damn sure bet me something on it."

"Well, what about $200? If I don't call two hundred ducks right to our feet within five minutes, you win."

"I've gotta see this," he answered. "You wanna bet more?"

"Nope, $200's good enough for me," I answered, letting him off easy.

We stopped by my garage and I picked up a gallon of cracked corn. When we got to the pond, there were seven or eight ducks and a few mud hens floating on it.

"Looks like I'm gonna lose this $200," I fibbed. "I don't see no ducks today."

"Yeah, I think I've got you this time, Cowboy," Dick said, trying to quit laughing at my outrageous proposition. "It's a good thing you didn't bet $500."

"I reckon so," I led him on, and started quacking in my best duck-call voice.

I'm telling you, it wasn't but two minutes before those big mallards started flying in by the droves! Some of them landed on the water and others landed right at our feet. Within three or four minutes, about two hundred fifty ducks surrounded us.

I threw that cracked corn out to them and they started gulping it down as fast as kids eat Jell-O.

"That's the damnedest thing I've ever seen!" Dick said, turning white as a sheet. "I'd have bet $1,000 that you couldn't call in that many ducks—hell, there weren't five ducks when we got here."

"Well, you'd have lost your thousand," I bragged. "I told you I've been practicing."

"It would've been worth it," he said.

"Dick, you're a good friend of mine so I'm not gonna charge you the $200," I recanted. "I'm giving it to you for driving me home—that's the highest cab fare I've ever paid!"

Dick still tells that story around the cardroom, laughing all the way through it. But it was like one of Titanic's bets, a bet that I couldn't lose. The next time you visit us at Ocean's Eleven, I'll be happy to lay you the same odds. And maybe I'll even rope four of them for you within three minutes—now that would be a good bet!

★ Cowboy's Closing Comments ★

The two trophies that I won at the Calgary Stampede sculpted by Charles Beil, Charlie Russell's friend and protégé, mean more to me than if I had won five World Series bracelets (which I might have done if the cards had come right). And the belt buckles that I won at the major rodeos—the Calgary Stampede back-to-back; Houston Fat Stock Show; Madison Square Garden; Phillipsburg, Kansas; Burwell, Nebraska; Mobridge, South Dakota—and many more that I could mention, about thirty in all, are things that no one can take away from me.

I was a champion calf roper and probably could have been the best that ever was if I had roped as much as I played poker. Whether I won a belt buckle or not was all up to me. And I knew that it was just me—me and my horse against a wild calf trying to do me in while I was trying to rope him a tenth of a second faster than the best hands in the world with fifty thousand people sitting in the grandstands hollering and the band playing loud. Those buckles mean more to me than any World Series bracelet that I ever could have won because I did it myself with my own skill, my own coordination, and my own thoughts. I didn't win them because a spade instead of a diamond came on the end.

I drove a million miles and roped my heart out to win those trophies and buckles. And I have a lot of memories, good memories, from the old rodeo days. Some of the best people that I've ever known were cowboys—down to earth, good family men, hard working guys. Rodeo was a tough life, but as I think back on it, I didn't realize until now how much fun I was having.

I'll always be a cowboy at heart.

THE COWBOY'S POETRY

★ Bronco Claude and Ole Midnight ★

The year was nineteen hundred and forty-eight
At the Fort Worth Rodeo and Fat Stock Show.
He was in back of the chutes gettin' things ready to go
Takin' up his stirrup and sharpening up his spurs
And lookin' under his bronco saddle for cuckleburrs.

It was the last night of the big rodeo and show—
No telling after this which way all the cowboys would go,
But it was gonna be quite a sight
'Cause Bronco Claude had drawed ole
"Five Minutes Till Midnight."

Claude had just come in from Denver,
The National Western Rodeo and Fat Stock Show—
Didn't win a dime but he drove his car through a lot of snow.
Tonight he'd be ridin' ole Midnight 'cause he needed the gold.

Sometimes I don't know 'bout this ole cowboy life,
Going from town to town and losing your wife,
Travelin' day and night, fightin' in bars,
Sleeping in a horse trailer under the stars.

Ole Midnight hadn't been rode in over two years,
He'd throwed every cowboy from Little Rock to Fort Pierre.
Claude looked at his watch, the time was gettin' near,
He started to get nervous—later would come the fear.

People are talking 'bout the ride that he'll take
Wondering how many of his bones ole Midnight will break.
Some are betting money, others are staying quiet,
If Claude can just ride him, he'll be famous overnight.

Claude sees him now coming into the chutes,
Big, black and shining, and meaner than a coot.
Ain't nothing new to ole Midnight—this is what he likes to do—
Throw off cowboys in front of a crowd and trample them till
they're blue.

Claude couldn't help it if he felt pretty scared,
He's not the first cowboy ole Midnight has put into fear.
But you still have to respect him, not because he's big and mean
But because he knows every trick 'round the rodeo scene.

Now they have ole Midnight's saddle on,
Looking like a grizzly bear standing there in the chutes.
While Bronco Claude straps his spurs to the heel of his boots.
Now his nerves are all right—he's gonna ride
That big black mean sonnabitch tonight.

The rodeo announcer says the time has came
Tonight Claude Kimberlin can make himself a name
So he crawls down and gets on ole Midnight's back,
Tightens his rein and then gives it some slack,
As ole Midnight quivers and tries to rear back.

Then the crowd gets quiet and rise to their feet
While Bronco Claude takes a little deeper seat.
Now it's just him and ole Midnight—
He'll either ride him or go down in defeat.

The gates fly open, looks like ole Midnight jumped eight foot high
You could see Bronco Claude spurring him against a blue sky.
One of them will be the winner,
There can't be a tie.

Mean ole Midnight twists back, he's kicking so high
Claude sees faces in the grandstands and lights in the sky.
Ole Midnight is snorting and bucking and rolling his hide
Trying to throw Bronco Claude off to one side.

Bronco Claude figures that six seconds are gone
And he can't imagine how four more can be so long.
But he's feeling like he's the one who's mean
And ole Midnight don't like it 'cause he's the top of the cream.

The whistle blows and the pickup man comes galloping by.
When Bronco gets off, he feels like he's still in the sky.
As he steps down and hits the ground
His knees kinda buckle and he hears a loud sound.

The crowd is going crazy
Throwing their hats into the ring
As they did in Rome when gladiators performed before kings.
Claude had become famous in only ten seconds it seems.

Cowboys rush out and take Claude in their arms.
They'd never seen a cowboy ride through that sort of storm
People are shouting, you can't hear a thing,
Pretty girls are screaming trying to get near.

Bronco Claude takes them all over to the bar
Orders everyone in the joint a cold Lone Star.
Cowboys are still shaking his hand
And new girls are asking him his name.
"Bronco Claude!" he shouts—now he's got the fame.

That's one night that he'll always remember well,
It's a rare experience for an old cowboy to tell.
Midnight was the best and Claude paid him the respect
he was due—
Claude was the last to ride him and this story is true.
Now that's the end of my tale 'bout Claude's rodeo days,
He had some hard ones and some good ones that paid.

And I guess ole Midnight's up in rodeo heaven
All saddled up in chute number seven
Waitin' for Bronco Claude to knock on St. Peter's door
So he'll have another chance to settle the score.
Counting all the angels, cowboys, gamblers, and whores
I'll bet the house is sold out—there just won't be any more.

★ Too Tall to Call ★

Cowboy wrote this poem to "commemorate" the ill-fated tip
he gave an undercover policeman in Fort Worth.

He had no respect for money
And not too much for the law.
He called all pretty women "Honey"
And tipped everybody he saw.

He was known the U.S. over
And by most was called a friend,
For whether broke or in the clover
He'd give anybody a ten.

Many said that none played higher
And that was the gospel truth.
He was a high-class dude, no crier,
Had a lot of early hoof.

But then came that black December,
It's hard to calculate the price,
But it's the tip he'll always remember—
That big fin he gave the vice.

But he's still in there a-grinning,
One battle is not the war.
And there's lots of time left for winning
And catching that shooting star.

And thus another gambling story,
The first to go beyond the pale,
But this feat brought him no glory—
The cowboy tipped his way to jail!

★ Nine Quarters and a Dream ★

It was a cold winter day 'round January the twelfth
WhenanoldraggedymanwalkedintotheHorseshoeallbyhimself.
He sat down at the snack bar to get a hot cup,
Reached into his pocket to see if he had a buck.

He had nine quarters and a dime, two nickels and three cents,
But he had no home so he didn't have to worry 'bout no rent.
The waitress came over and asked what it would be.
"One black coffee and three sugars, if you please."

The coffee tasted good, warmed him clean down to his shoes.
Road weary and tired, he was really feelin' the blues
When he looked over his should and seen a lighted-up machine:
"Video Poker, Five Quarters for a Dream."

He went over and sat down next to a beautiful young girl
Fixin' to play his last nine quarters on something open
to the world.
Puttin' four quarters in, it came A-3-4-5-and-6,
He drew and caught a jack—it looked like a fix.

Just five quarters left, not a home, a friend, or a dime,
Wonderin' if he should gamble—if he lost it would be a crime.
He put his last quarters in, that was playin' awful high,
And he had to get lucky. It was do or die.

It came a 10-J-Q of clubs, two fours on the end.
He erased the two fours and drew.
It came the ace and king of clubs!
Twenty-five grand—now he was in.

The lights came on, the bell began to ring,
Folks gathered 'round saying, "Look at that raggedy ole thing."
But now it's a different story, he's eating dinner in the sky,
A suite on the seventeenth floor, tipping waiters twenty bucks
for a piece of pie.

It just goes to show that a man's never really beat—
All you need is a little luck and a break now and then.
So let's all have a drink and tip our glass toward the sky
'Cause that raggedy old man was playing mighty high.

★ The Legend of Red Fox ★

Cowboy wrote this poem to honor his friend and mentor,
Mr. Robert A. Brooks

You talk about living legends—I know there's been lots—
But let me tell you the story of the legendary "Red Fox."
It would take a helluva author his biography to pen
But if I could tell his life's story and get it down just right,
I'll bet it would sell more copies than *Gone With the Wind*,
For the things he's done sound like fiction, they're so far
outta sight.

He started in Alaska over forty years ago
Where he showed them how to play wheel lowball.
He had three bars in Fairbanks with poker, craps, and all,
He didn't own the cathouse, but he won the madam's money
Each time she came to play some draw lowball
And gently told her as she left, "See ya next time, Honey!"

He's a man of many trades and master of them all
He's been a fur trapper, fisherman, and bush pilot,
And by the time I met him, he'd already lived four lives
With five wives and lots of good times.
It seems that with age he just gets better,
Not worse, like a fine vintage wine.

After twenty-five years in Alaska, he had beat them all,
So he went to Reno and opened up a gambling hall.
He called it Barney's and spread every gambling game.
Now he's a sure candidate for the Poker Hall of Fame.

He has read more books in his life, perhaps,
Than you could load into a boxcar on a train.
He's played more poker and faded more craps,
And run more gamblin' joints that anyone I can name.

He doesn't drive twenty-thousand-dollar cars
Or wear five-hundred-dollar suits,
But I've never seen him broke
So he must have won a lot of loot.

Travelin' across the country and hearing what folks have to say,
I think he has the highest respect of any gambler I know today.
His kids all look like movie stars—he must've been quite a stud—
I've heard he made Redford look like a truck driver stuck in
mud.

The Red Fox, the last of the great frontier gamblin' men,
Has done a lot for me and I'll always love and admire him.
But before I end this story, whether you like it or not,
Read the last stanzas carefully: They might keep you out of a spot.

If you're anywhere between Dallas and Fairbanks
And happen to drop by some friendly poker game
And if you happen to win a big pot off a gentleman

Who laughs and says, "Take it, ole pardner!"
Or if you lose one and he says, "Don't worry, hell, it's only
a game!"

It's eight to five you're playing with a living legend
Who's seen more hole cards than you'll ever have time to play—
And Robert A. Brooks will be his name.
They call Mr. Brooks the Red Fox because he's tricked many
a man
By acting like he has nothing and then showing the winning hand.
And when he slips the bonds of earth, I'll guarantee
He'll have a better hand than Hickok's aces 'n' eights, you wait
and see.

★ Respect ★

I rodeoed for twenty years roping calves and throwing steers
And I used to think that road was a little rough,
But according to the four hundred young poker players here,
Hell, that was easy stuff!
I've heard some of 'em say that I really played good,
And then they won four straight pots with the worst hands—
Like a tournament player should—
And sent me to the rail to join my fans.

Before there were tournaments, you were judged by your peers
And I've played with the best of 'em for fifty years.
All us ole road gamblers that went up and down the way
Ducking the police and the heisters just trying to play—
There's probably only a hundred of us left around
Who have been arrested for playing poker in most every town—
Hell, we made it easy for you young ones reading them books,
Studying them tapes and playing in them nice casinos every day.

All you young players with your smart thing to say,
If it wasn't for all the old-timers, you wouldn't be up there today.
So I'm telling you all that the next one I win,
If you say, "Man, he was awful lucky now and then,"
Remember that you're gonna have to face me tomorrow and again.
So when you win, do it with dignity and give credit to your brothers,
And when you lose, do it with class without blaming the others.

Son, you missed what I've been through with my ups and downs
On the back roads of Texas making the poker circuit rounds.
I'm seventy-plus now and I've looked at a few hole cards in my life,
Some that gave me wealth and a million more that brought me strife.
And when my poker playing's over and those pearly gate bells ring,
I'd rather hear a sucker holler than a pretty gal sing.

★ A Tribute to "The Kid" ★

*Cowboy Wolford read this poem at Stu Ungar's induction into
the Poker Hall of Fame in May, 2001, during the WSOP*

The first time I met him was many moons ago
At the World Series of Poker at the Shoe.
Benny Binion was standing there, too,
The man who started the world's greatest poker show.
He looked like a kid to Benny and me
About a hundred and twenty pounds so full of life
And I could tell by the glint in his eyes
He was ready to play some poker tonight.

I can't begin to tell you how good he played
No-limit poker and gin—
That would take me another week and
I still wouldn't know where to begin.
He won every major poker tournament
Where the entries were five-thousand dollars or more —

The World Series of Poker three times, the Super Bowl twice,
The Queens Classic—and three or four more.

He would bet you $200,000 at golf when he couldn't break
a hundred,
And $30,000 on a horse that ran slower than thunder.
There's nothin' wrong with that if you've got the heart,
But there's plenty of us who wouldn't know where to start.
There are some great ones who have passed on
Leaving the rest of us down here all alone—
Benny Binion, Jack Straus, Johnny Moss, Sarge and Bill Boyd.
And now one of the greatest—Stu "The Kid" Ungar—is gone.

I know there's a big game in the sky—the change-in is your life.
A no-limit game that'll last forever and probably never stop.
And if you ever get a seat in it, try to sit to the left of "The Kid"
Or you might never see a flop.
Someday I'll get lucky, the cards will come my way,
And another big tournament I will win.
I'm gonna dedicate it to Stu "The Kid" Ungar
Because he was one of my dearest friends.

★ A Poker Player's Woman ★

You must have looked dead when you came through the gate
After thirty hours of poker without a break,
Barely saying hello to your woman before you take a snooze,
Her not knowing whether you win or you lose.
It's been going on for ten years or more
And you couldn't blame her if she hadn't stayed four
Then you wake up midmorning or late afternoon
Dreaming of hands that you played too slow or too soon

Your clothes laid out, your dinner cooking slow
Her trying to help you get ready to go.
And when you sit down to eat some food
She's hoping you're in a good mood.
You ask about your kids you haven't seen in three days
It's not their fault, they don't call the plays.
She reminds you of Friday, the picnic this weekend.
"You all go on," you say. "I'm loser, I need to win."

I think it takes a special kind of girl
To put up with a gambler and his poker world.
You're good to her with money and diamond rings,
A shiny new car and lots of pretty things.
But the chances are good that her happiest days
Were when you started with nothing, before the big plays.
Don't you see? What she really wants is her man
While all you're thinking 'bout is catching a hand.

If a man ain't lucky, he'll go through women like hands
Trying to find a woman who understands.
Whether it's your first or ten of them you've had
When you get the right one, you'd better be glad—
Though there was never a horse that couldn't be rode
Or a cowboy that couldn't be throwed
Or a poker player with a good woman
Who could beat all the pros.

When you're a gamblin' man seems like all you do is play
A million or more hands with no night and no day.
It's hard to be a good daddy and make love between deals
But a good woman will do it for you cause she knows how you feel
It's something like being in prison with a lot of money
You have made her trustee because she is your honey.
And if you can fold the second-best hand and make your best play,
You don't worry, brother, if the cards ain't coming your way.

As poker players we are truly a rare breed—
It's the challenge and the ego, it isn't the greed.
So shuffle 'em up and deal 'em real slow
But don't lose that woman or you'll have a hard go.
Now let's stack up our chips and push back our chairs
Bow our heads and remember our women in prayers—
And hope they're home thanking their lucky stars for the hand
That dealt them a poker player instead of an ordinary man.

★ Those City Folks' Ways ★

*Cowboy wrote this poem right after he was released
from his "vacation" in the federal penitentiary in 1981.*

Evelyn pulled the car up on a dark winter's night
After eighty-nine nights and ninety long days
I wasn't used to them bright Dallas lights
And those city folks' ways.

We went into a restaurant to get a bite to eat
And there on the floor laid a long cigarette butt at my feet.
I looked all around to see if anyone else had seen
Then dropped to my knees and put it in my jeans.

"Your name, sir?" asked the host at the door.
"Would a candle-lit table by the window do?"
I gave him my prison number 40168-074
And asked, "Are you the new guard that comes on at two?"

As we sat down a man walked by in a dark blue suit
I thought he was the warden so I gave him a salute
Then I heard a guy saying, "Gimme another drink."
That's thirty days in the hole—next time I bet he'll think.

I was getting nervous so I excused myself to the men's room
The first thing I saw in the corner was a mop and a broom.
I grabbed the mop in my right hand and the broom in my left
Cleaned up the bathroom and wiped off the shelf.

Went back to the table but I'd been working so hard
Evelyn said, "Sit down, honey, you look kinda tired.
Would you like me to order some wine?"
"Hell," I said, "don't do that or we'll lose our good time."

Then a waitress come to our table saying the food was fine
So I grabbed a tray off a busboy and asked, "Where's the line?"
When I looked at the clock, it was a quarter till ten,
So I covered my head with the tablecloth for the count in the pen

Someone turned on the TV with the football score at six to nine
And I shouted, "I'll bet eight root beers if there's a halftime line!"
Then the jukebox started playing "I need a friend,"
So I pulled the plug from the wall 'cause I knew it was past ten.

When Evelyn drove us home and we stepped inside our door
I heard some dogs barking and I hit the floor.
"Honey, what's the matter?" she asked. "You okay?"
"They've called the bloodhounds," I said. "Can't you hear
them at bay?"

We went in our bedroom and jumped naked into bed;
Making love was fun and it cleared my head—
And then I knew that everything was gonna be all right.
I was ready for those city folks' ways and them bright Dallas lights.

★ Phantom Junket 727 ★

Claude Kimberlin was sitting in his Dallas office
At three o'clock in the afternoon
When he got a mysterious telephone call
From three thousand miles the other side of the moon.

The operator said to Claude,
"It's St. Peter calling, will you accept the charge?
Says he can't get no change up there
The other side of Mars."

Claude answered, "Operator, put him on the line."
In a second, St. Peter came on and asked,
"How you gettin' along, Claude?"
Claude says, "Oh, I'm doin' fine."

Then Claude asks, "St. Peter, how are you?"
"Well," St. Peter says, "I'm doing okay.
I'm calling you 'bout getting a junket together
For the Mirage in a coupla days."

"How many have you got?" Claude asks,
"And how high do they play?"
St. Peter answers, "I've got a hundred and ten,
And some of them play high but don't know how to win."

Claude says, "Wait a minute, let me figure out this deal."
St. Peter answers, "I'll have a coupla my angels fly us down.
We'll meet you tomorrow, twelve o'clock straight up at Love Field,
And then we'll go do the town."

"I'll call the Mirage right now and get everybody a good room,"
Claude tells him, "and I'll have my plane ready at twelve
o'clock noon."
St. Peter says, "I'll gather up the front money and we'll be on
our way.
These bastards are ready—it's been a long time since they've played.

"George Barnes and Corky McCorquodale
Want to know how high is the poker.
I told them that I don't know 'cause I've never played hold'em—
I just like to play with the joker.

"And there's a lot of old crap shooters, '21' players, and
Hustlin' gals from Dallas—you've known them all for years.
They'll be so glad to see you, Claude,
They'll all be cryin' tears.

"Now don't worry 'bout no tab, we'll stop at the Bank of Heaven
That just opened up on the moon
And I'll okay some checks for extra money. But if they lose it and
Want to come home early, they'll have to catch themselves
a balloon.

"Well, Claude, I'd better get off this telephone,
I know it's costing you a lot.
We'll see you tomorrow at Love Field
And we'll be there at twelve o'clock."

Claude had done it again!
He'd just put together the first junket from heaven—
A few old hole-card killers, some loose 21 players,
And a bunch who thought they could make the dice roll seven.

Well, the way the story ended is they all had a good ole time
It was the biggest losing junket ever at the Mirage, that's the
bottom line.

So when we're all gone, it don't mean that we're through playing—
That deal about you can't gamble after you're dead is just an old saying.

So while you're down here
Just act right and try to be good
So that St. Peter will let you into heaven
Just like he should.

And right before you die, be sure to run by Claude's office in Dallas
To put your up front money and he'll write your name on the list
For that Mirage junket that comes down from heaven—
Better known as Phantom Junket 727.

★ Jack Binion: One in a Million ★

The name "One in a Million" that I gave to Jack Binion
Isn't as funny as it seems. You'll see why when I explain a few things.
Let's start with the one who gave him his name, Benny the Boss,
Who taught Jack his trade and made him the number one hoss.

They say that in real estate he's as sharp as there is around
I figure that someday, he'll either win it or buy the rest of the town.
And you talk about hold'em—Jack might have invented the game.
I've never seen him lose and he never plays the same.

When he first started the Series I think that it was just an excuse
To bust all those Texans who play hold'em too loose.
I've heard that Jack's a great skier, but that's a game I don't know
Because I can't figure out how you can ante in the snow.

Jack is not a fair-weather friend, this I clearly understand.
He flew three thousand miles for me for just five minutes on
the stand.
I don't know how to repay him because money he doesn't need
It would be sorta like a farmer giving you all of his cotton seed.

Jack's probably seen more money won and lost than anyone
his age
I'd just like to have a dollar for every time he's gone to the cage.
Before he's done, he may become the only man ever to win a zillion,
And to me he will always be Jack Binion, "One in a Million."

★ St. Peter and Binion's Golden Horseshoe ★

*Cowboy Wolford wrote this poem in memory of Benny Binion,
who died December 25, 1989 at the age of 85.*

Christmas comes but once a year and it's a day of joy
When folks give thanks for what they have and kids all get a toy.
But on this day when people hand out gifts and pray,
The world's greatest gambler was taken away.
I know that if he had to set up a date, he'd have picked Christmas
The odds are far more than making three hardway eights.
Benny Binion went straight up to Saint Peter that day
And here's what Saint Peter had to say:

Binion, I've been waiting for you eighty-five years.
You made it thirty years later than most of your peers.
I see that your record's not absolutely clean,
But before you got here I done voted you in
Because the good you've done outweighs the bad,
So I forgive you for your sin.

Now let me tell you, Binion, this ain't Vegas in 1946
This is heaven and I got the fix.
I know you didn't bring no cash with you, you was kinda in a rush.
But don't you worry none, your tab is good with us.
Now Benny, if you got any questions, feel free to ask
'Cause up here there ain't gonna be no backlash.

Okay, Saint Peter, as a friend,
Did Bernstein and Sarge and Jack Straus get in?

As a matter of fact, they're all here in force.
I promised them that the first time they saw you,
You would be riding my Golden Horse.
Binion, the economy up here ain't all that good.
But we don't have no bills, so I think I'll let you open up a joint
'Cause I've got plenty of shills.

Okay, Sir, start off with two blackjack tables,
and eight slots in a small room,
And when Cowboy Wolford gets up here
Open up the craps 'cause then it'll start to boom.
Binion, the Cowboy laughs when he hears people say
That he shoots all his money off on craps every day.
But Cowboy says that some of his friends bet $200,000
On a football game and lay eleven to ten.
When he loses his last $500, it's all over town
But when they lose two million, they were gambling sound.
Now Benny, don't you worry 'bout the Horseshoe down there
'Cause you know that Jack will run it on the square.

Saint Peter, saddle up that Golden Horse.
I'd like to ride out and visit some of my friends
To find out all the outs and ins.
And by the way, it just come to my mind, here's what we'll do:
This joint you're gonna let me open,
We'll call it the Golden Horseshoe.

So get a hold of Steve Wynn and Bobby Baldwin, too,
And tell 'em that after they check in up here
To come on by and have dinner at the Golden Horseshoe.
Then send word to Henry and R.D. to tell them
That when they get here, there'll be plenty to do.
Tell Dicky Carson and Doyle Brunson that when they die
We'll have a World Series of Poker up here in the sky,
Hopefully before Johnny Moss gets on the fly.
And then tell Johnny Chan and Chip Reese
That before they can play up here, they'll have to be
deceased.

Well, that's almost all I've got to say except that we'll let
Blackie Blackburn and Pat Callihan run the Omaha every day.
And tell Jesse Alto down in Houston, if he's still on the loose,
That he can win it up here if he can beat a ten and a deuce.
Tell Jack Keller and Stuey Ungar to take their time
It'll be an easier game if they ain't raising it every time.
Maybe ole Cowboy and Bill Smith can be in the last numbers to go
'Cause them two need to make more money before they show.
I know they just can't wait to check in to the Golden Shoe
And Saint Peter, neither can me and you.

And for all of you down there, don't rush up your life
'Cause chances are when you get up here you'll run into
an ex-wife.
Just wait on the years because they will tell,
And when you all get to heaven, we'll be playing higher than
hell.

Time's running out and you don't have long
But ten million years up here is like singing a song.
So love and be good to your family, treat your fellow man right
'Cause you might not be in your bed tomorrow night.
If you knew how good it is up here, you wouldn't try to die so slow
It's downhill and shady and the cake's all dough.

Now this is the end of my story, give a little and take,
'Cept that they're paying twelve to one on the hardway eight.
Benny, we all love and miss you and we'll be seeing you soon
Just be sure to reserve all us good craps players a real nice
room.

THE CHAMPIONSHIP SERIES
POWERFUL BOOKS YOU MUST HAVE

CHAMPIONSHIP OMAHA (Omaha High-Low, Pot-limit Omaha, Limit High Omaha) by Tom McEvoy & T.J. Cloutier. Clearly-written strategies and powerful advice from Cloutier and McEvoy who have won four World Series of Poker titles in Omaha tournaments. Powerful advice shows you how to win at low-limit and high-stakes games, how to play against loose and tight opponents, and the differing strategies for rebuy and freezeout tournaments. Learn the best starting hands, when slowplaying a big hand is dangerous, what danglers are and why winners don't play them, why pot-limit Omaha is the only poker game where you sometimes fold the nuts on the flop and are correct in doing so and overall, and how you can win a lot of money at Omaha! 296 pages, photos, illustrations, New Edition! $29.95!

CHAMPIONSHIP STUD (Seven-Card Stud, Stud 8/or Better and Razz) by Dr. Max Stern, Linda Johnson, and Tom McEvoy. The authors, who have earned millions of dollars in major tournaments and cash games, eight World Series of Poker bracelets and hundreds of other titles in competition against the best players in the world show you the winning strategies for medium-limit side games as well as poker tournaments and a general tournament strategy that is applicable to any form of poker. Includes give-and-take conversations between the authors to give you more than one point of view on how to play poker. 200 pages, hand pictorials, photos. $39.95.

CHAMPIONSHIP HOLD'EM by Tom McEvoy & T.J. Cloutier. Hard-hitting hold'em the way it's played today in both limit cash games and tournaments. Get killer advice on how to win more money in rammin'-jammin' games, kill-pot, jackpot, shorthanded, and other types of cash games. You'll learn the thinking process before the flop, on the flop, on the turn, and at the river with specific suggestions for what to do when good or bad things happen plus 20 illustrated hands with play-by-play analyses. Specific advice for rocks in tight games, weaklings in loose games, experts in solid games, how hand values change in jackpot games, when you should fold, check, raise, reraise, check-raise, slowplay, bluff, and tournament strategies for small buy-in, big buy-in, rebuy, incremental add-on, satellite and big-field major tournaments. Wow! Easy-to-read and conversational, if you want to become a lifelong winner at limit hold'em, you need this book! 388 Pages, Illustrated, Photos. ~~$39.95~~. Now only $29.95!

CHAMPIONSHIP NO-LIMIT & POT-LIMIT HOLD'EM by T.J. Cloutier & Tom McEvoy. New Cardoza Edition! The definitive guide to winning at two of the world's most exciting poker games! Written by eight time World Champion players T.J. Cloutier (1998 and 2002 Player of the Year) and Tom McEvoy (the foremost author on tournament strategy) who have won millions of dollars each playing no-limit and pot-limit hold'em in cash games and major tournaments around the world. You'll get all the answers here—no holds barred—to your most important questions: How do you get inside your opponents' heads and learn how to beat them at their own game? How can you tell how much to bet, raise, and reraise in no-limit hold'em? When can you bluff? How do you set up your opponents in pot-limit hold'em so you can win a monster pot? What are the best strategies for winning no-limit and pot-limit tournaments, satellites, and supersatellites? You get rock-solid and inspired advice from two of the most recognizable figures in poker—advice that you can bank on. If you want to become a winning player, and a champion, you must have this book. 304 pages, paperback, illustrations, photos. $29.95

THE CHAMPIONSHIP SERIES
POWERFUL BOOKS YOU MUST HAVE

CHAMPIONSHIP TOURNAMENT POKER by Tom McEvoy. New Cardoza Edition! Rated by pros as best book on tournaments ever written and enthusiastically endorsed by more than five world champions, this is the definitive guide to winning tournaments and a must for every player's library. McEvoy lets you in on the secrets he has used to win millions of dollars in tournaments and the insights he has learned competing against the best players in the world. Packed solid with winning strategies for all 11 games in the World Series of Poker, with extensive discussions of 7-card stud, limit hold'em, pot and no-limit hold'em, Omaha high-low, re-buy, half-half tournaments, satellites, and strategies for each stage of tournaments. Tons of essential concepts and specific strategies jam-pack the book. Phil Hellmuth, 1989 WSOP champion says, "[this] is the world's most definitive guide to winning poker tournaments." 416 pages, paperback, $29.95.

CHAMPIONSHIP TABLE (at the World Series of Poker) by Dana Smith, Ralph Wheeler, and Tom McEvoy. New Cardoza Edition! From 1970 when the champion was presented a silver cup, to the present when the champion was awarded more than $2 million, *Championship Table* celebrates three decades of poker greats who have competed to win poker's most coveted title. This book gives you the names and photographs of all the players who made the final table, pictures of the last hand the champion played against the runner-up, how they played their cards, and how much they won. This book also features fascinating interviews and conversations with the champions and runners-up and interesting highlights from each Series. This is a fascinating and invaluable resource book for WSOP and gaming buffs. In some cases the champion himself wrote "how it happened," as did two-time champion Doyle Brunson when Stu Ungar caught a wheel in 1980 on the turn to deprive "Texas Dolly" of his third title. Includes tons of vintage photographs. 208 pages, paperback, $19.95.

CHAMPIONSHIP WIN YOUR WAY INTO BIG MONEY HOLD'EM TOURNAMENTS by Brad Daugherty & Tom McEvoy. In 2003 and 2004, satellite players won their way into the $10,000 WSOP buy-in and emerged as champions, winning more than $2 million each. You can too! You'll learn specific, proven strategies for winning almost any satellite. Learn the ten ways to win a seat at the WSOP and other big tournaments, how to win limit hold'em and no-limit hold'em satellites, one-table satellites for big tournaments, and online satellites, plus how to play the final table of super satellites. McEvoy and Daugherty sincerely believe that if you practice these strategies, you can win your way into any tournament for a fraction of the buy-in. You'll learn how much to bet, how hard to pressure opponents, how to tell when an opponent is bluffing, how to play deceptively, and how to use your chips as weapons of destruction. Includes a special chapter on no-limit hold'em satellites! 320 pages. Illustrated hands, photos, glossary. $29.95.

CHAMPIONSHIP HOLD'EM TOURNAMENT HANDS by T.J. Cloutier & Tom McEvoy. Two tournament legends show you how to become a winning tournament player. Get inside their heads as they think their way through the correct strategy at 57 limit and no-limit practice hands. Cloutier and McEvoy show you how to use your skill and intuition to play strategic hands for maximum profit in real tournament scenarios and how 45 key hands were played by champions in turnaround situations at the WSOP. By sharing their analysis on how the winners and losers played key hands, you'll gain tremendous insights into how tournament poker is played at the highest levels. Learn how champions think and how they play major hands in strategic tournament situations, Cloutier and McEvoy believe that you will be able to win your share of the profits in today's tournaments—and join them at the championship table far sooner than you ever imagined. 368 pages, illustrated with card pictures, $29.95